Street Kids

Street Kids

Homeless Youth, Outreach, and Policing New York's Streets

Kristina E. Gibson

NEW YORK UNIVERSITY PRESS
New York and London

NEW YORK UNIVERSITY PRESS
New York and London
www.nyupress.org

References to Internet websites (URLs) were accurate at the time of writing.
Neither the author nor New York University Press is responsible for URLs
that may have expired or changed since the manuscript was prepared.

An earlier version of chapter 3 was published in *Telling Young Lives:
Portraits of Global Youth*. Temple University Press. Philadelphia. 2007.
Reprinted with permission.

Library of Congress Cataloging-in-Publication Data

Gibson, Kristina E.
Street kids : homeless youth, outreach, and policing New York's streets /
Kristina E. Gibson.
p. cm.
Includes bibliographical references and index.
ISBN 978-0-8147-3227-4 (cl : alk. paper) — ISBN 978-0-8147-3228-1
(pb : alk. paper) — ISBN 978-0-8147-3289-2 (ebook)
1. Street youth—New York (State)—New York. 2. Homeless youth—
New York (State)—New York. 3. Social work with youth—New York (State)—
New York. 4. Social work with the homeless—New York (State)—New York.
5. Police services for the homeless—New York (State)—New York. I. Title.
HV1437.N5G53   2011
362.74—dc22   2010047475

New York University Press books are printed on acid-free paper,
and their binding materials are chosen for strength and durability.
We strive to use environmentally responsible suppliers and materials
to the greatest extent possible in publishing our books.

Manufactured in the United States of America

c   10 9 8 7 6 5 4 3 2 1
p   10 9 8 7 6 5 4 3 2 1

For street outreach counselors:
the work you do is critical.

Contents

Acknowledgments

When I arrived in New York City with a half-formed plan to study street kids, I never guessed the magnitude of what they and social workers were facing. Had I known, I would probably have been too intimidated even to begin the research. Early conversations with Jim Bolas, Adam Bucko, Kim Ya-Nan Lee, Lisha McCormack, Philip Paul, Rickke Manazala, Erik Christensen, Rick Koca, Carl Siciliano, Reed Christian, John Welch, and other dedicated individuals nonetheless convinced me to follow this path. I could not have done this work without the aid of my fellow outreach workers; in particular, Jonathan Bannet, Adam Grandt, Alanna Rosenberg, and Marshall Rose. My research was made possible through the boundless generosity of street youth organizations in New York City. In particular, StandUp for Kids—NYC, The Door, StreetWork, Reciprocity Foundation, Neutral Zone, FIERCE!, and Ali Forney gave me enormous support and assistance throughout my fieldwork. Street kids have more opportunities and a better chance of surviving the streets because of these groups' work. I would particularly like to thank the members of the Empire State Coalition of Youth and Family services for feedback on early ideas and for explaining to me the many acronyms of youth services.

I would like to thank my mentors for critical feedback and for giving me the freedom to find my own research paths. Lynn Staeheli, Tim Oakes, Sam Dennis, Anne Costain, and Lorraine Dowler all shaped my development as a geographer and scholar far beyond the scope of this one book. I would also like to thank the members of the Brooklyn Urban Geography Reading Group (BURG) for insights into what makes a great book (and, just as important, what does not). My editors at New York University Press were generous and thoughtful in their time and feedback.

This book would not have been possible without the continuing support of my family and friends. Molly and Sarah: you probably have read these chapters more times than I have, and a few of them survived only because of your care and attention. I cannot thank you both enough.

Finally, the heart of this book is the young people out on the streets, the toughest, nicest, bravest bunch of kids I've ever met.

Preface

Ali Forney, the Death and Life of a Street Kid

In the early morning hours of December 5, 1997, a young man was shot and killed on a sidewalk in East Harlem. His name was Ali Forney, and he was a street kid. In New York City and most urban areas across the United States, public violence involving street kids is not groundbreaking news. Nearly five thousand unaccompanied young people die each year in the United States, primarily from violence, illness, and suicide.[1] Even though public violence involving more affluent young people shocked the city in the late 1990s, Ali Forney's death did not merit even a paragraph in the next day's newspapers. According to Carl Siciliano, a social worker who knew Ali: "I remember when there were one or two murders of young people in the city . . . there was a white social work student who was murdered in Prospect Heights. It was on the cover of the paper for days and days. These kids would die and there'd be nothing. Nothing." Ali's was the third violent death of a street kid in six months.

Ali Forney's life story is sadly representative of the many young people growing up on our city streets today. Forney had been arrested several times for drug dealing and prostitution. Estranged from his family, he had been living on and off the streets since his early teens. Given his prior arrest record, city police assumed that his murder was another drug deal gone wrong. But people like Carl saw a more complex picture:

> I don't want to romanticize what it was like in those days. There was a lot of crack dealing and prostitution and drugs. But it was the street economy. There are an awful lot of young people who grow up in really ravaged environments, who don't get educated, who get traumatized, who don't get parented. . . . They live in the street economy. They survive in the street economy. Selling drugs, prostitution, pimping . . . I don't want to say any of it is any good, but they do it to survive.[2]

Ali had been surviving in and around Times Square for several years and had become involved with a drop-in center for street kids. Perhaps because of his own risky involvement in sex work—Ali was a cross-dressing African American youth who had frequently been exposed to violence and harassment during his life—he spent his free time volunteering as a peer outreach worker, giving out safe-sex information and condoms to other street kids on Friday nights. A few months before his death, he helped put on a talent show at a homeless youth shelter, singing a gospel song—"His Eyes on the Sparrow"—to a crowd of street kids and social workers. Carl, who founded a youth shelter and program in Ali's name, explained why Ali stood out to those who knew him:

> One of the common experiences you have when working with homeless youth is that you often work with young people who have been battered, hurt, abused . . . and through necessity, the kids build a kind of armor around themselves, to protect themselves. They can be distant and distrusting. There was something about Ali that was so naked in his desire to show his love and his gratitude. There was something really profound about his need for community. You really sensed how much he missed being with his family and how hard he tried to create a sense of family with the people that were around him.[3]

Typically, only a few friends and social workers mourn the death of a street kid, and their stories and fate fade quickly from the public's interest. At Ali's funeral, seventy people showed up to mourn a young man whose generosity and vivacity touched everyone around him. His death sparked the anger of social workers and friends, who wondered why more was not being done for kids like him. Why were kids like Ali ending up dead on street corners far from their friends and support networks?

According to social workers, Ali Forney and many like him were pushed out of the Times Square area in the late 1990s as part of a city-supported effort to revitalize the neighborhood. The city's growing neoliberal ethos had led to policies supporting the commercialization of public spaces and the criminalization of anything deemed to be "bad for business." Business improvement districts (BIDs), or private corporations established in several neighborhoods, including the areas around Grand Central Station, Penn Station, and Times Square, imposed a tax on local businesses to pay for private security and to clean up public spaces.[4] Street kids hanging out in Times Square thus were a prime target for private security guards, and the zero-tolerance policing measures by the New York City Police (NYPD) were intended to improve the "quality of life" for local business ventures and middle-class shoppers. "Quality-of-life" ordinances, a form of order maintenance policing, authorize police to ticket, stop, search, and arrest people for minor infractions such as blocking the sidewalks, making noise, panhandling aggressively, holding an open container (of alcohol), and littering, all to quell signs of disorder. So-called order maintenance policing is based on the "broken windows" theory, which links minor forms of public disorder to more serious criminal activity. Proponents of this theory believe that by targeting minor misdemeanors, communities can prevent urban blight and produce an environment more conducive to redevelopment, commerce, and tourism. These ordinances, however, are often enforced selectively against marginalized groups. In particular, quality-of-life ordinances have been used to move homeless people and youth out of tourist, commercial, and gentrifying neighborhoods.[5]

Social workers therefore watched with growing concern as street kids were pushed out of relatively safe public spaces and away from the established social service locations around Times Square. As Carl put it, "It started feeling like the youth were under siege. It started feeling like, 'Where are they going to go? What's going to happen to them?'"[6] Street kids in the city were experiencing a new wave of "revanchism"[7]—a literal banishment from the public spaces in which they were surviving—driven by the city's reordering for commercial tourism. At the time, social workers were concerned that the risk-filled street economies in which these youth participated would simply move further from sight, into more dangerous sections of the city. According to Carl, "When you remove it, when you sweep it away, when you clean it up . . . you still have all these people. So what happens to them?"

A few months after repeated police sweeps had forced many street youth to leave the Times Square neighborhood, Ali Forney and two of his close street friends were dead, all killed in separate incidents, all in neighborhoods far from Times Square. Street outreach workers, many of whom had known Ali and his friends for years, blamed the cleanup of Times Square and the actions of BIDs and police for pushing vulnerable, homeless, and street-involved youth into unsafe neighborhoods, away from contact with social service drop-in centers and street outreach workers. In their eyes, policing policies had swept the problem of street youth "out of sight." They believed that the privatization of some public spaces and zero-tolerance strategies drove these young people into more dangerous environments, far from the supportive networks that social workers were attempting to build around traditional hangout sites like Times Square.

The late 1990s were a particularly deadly time for street kids like Ali. The increasing availability of crack cocaine and the HIV/AIDS epidemic devastated youth attempting to survive street economies based on sex work and drug dealing in places like Times Square. They had few employment or housing options. When New York City's policing campaign to "clean up" Midtown Manhattan began systematically cracking down on illegal behavior in order to remove the major impediments to tourism and new development, the homeless youth who were pushed out had few options. The crackdown removed sex shops, prostitution, drug dealing, and panhandling. For kids like Ali, this meant removal from streets, sidewalks, and subway platforms. Excessively ticketing street kids for minor infractions like panhandling forced them to "move on," effectively squeezing them out of the city's prime public spaces. Although Times Square has been "cleaned up," what has been the cost?

In the year after Ali Forney's death, both the *New York Times* and the Associated Press featured his story as an example of the city's increasingly harsh treatment of homeless youth and the hopeless situation of the city's street kids.[8] Both pieces directly linked Ali's death to policing tactics and city ordinances targeting street youth in the cleanup of Times Square. Their coverage crystallized social workers' anger and resentment over New York City's increasingly harsh policies toward the homeless. There were few outlets for this frustration, however, as social work programs were suffering from the same revanchist processes as were those they served. Services for homeless youth were steadily being driven out of revitalized and gentrifying neighborhoods through community pressure, complaints, and rising rents. Even drop-in centers and street outreach were blamed for "attracting" street youth to newly affluent neighborhoods.

Due in part to the superficial success of the Times Square cleanup, similar policing tactics have been employed across New York City. When street youth using parks in Lower Manhattan began complaining to social workers that police and business owners were telling them to "move on" and to "go home" or be ticketed or arrested for loitering, solicitation, or panhandling, social workers and street outreach counselors feared that the Times Square process was being repeated.

The memory of Ali Forney shadows the current debates surrounding people's rights to the city's public spaces. His death and life speak to a broad set of social concerns, including our society's understanding of the rights of young people, how we shape and regulate public spaces, the social construction of youth homelessness, the structuring of opportunities for street kids to navigate homelessness and the street, the role of social service providers in street kids' lives, and the devastating effects of revanchism in urban spaces. Ali was more than a random victim of a drug deal gone wrong; he and all the young people like him are being systematically banished from the city's public spaces and from public view. When youth are pushed out of the way, what do they do, and where do they go? This book is about what happens to street kids when they are pushed out of public spaces and to the people who work with them.

Introduction

The Street Youth Dilemma

I first heard about Ali Forney at a community board meeting in Manhattan's affluent West Greenwich Village, a picturesque and historic New York City neighborhood of tree-lined streets shading meticulously preserved brownstones. An eclectic mix of art galleries, high-end restaurants, old taverns, and specialty shops make this neighborhood both a busy commercial center and a popular tourist attraction. Greenwich Village also was the site of the 1969 Stonewall riots that launched the gay civil rights movement, and it has been an epicenter for gay culture in New York City for more than one hundred years.[1] Gay youth have traditionally made their way to this neighborhood to explore and express their sexuality in an accepting environment. The neighborhood bustles with gay bars, alternative coffeehouses, avante-garde theaters, and adult-themed stores, dispersed among the high-end specialty-food stores and the lower-end chain stores like McDonalds and Starbucks. Today, the majority of kids hanging out in the West Village are gay youth of color from all five New York City boroughs and northern New Jersey. They flock to the main drag, Christopher Street, in search of friends, a community, and a safe place to be "out." In New York City, 30 to 40 percent of the homeless youth population is made up of gay youth, most of whom hang out in the West Village. A survey of young people in Hudson River Park, at the end of Christopher Street, found that nearly half those surveyed did not live with a parent or guardian; 90 percent were people of color; 88 percent self-identified as gay, lesbian, bisexual, transgender, or questioning (GLBTQ); and more than half were using social services for at-risk, street, and homeless youth.[2] On a typical summer evening, hundreds of young people traverse the West Village, converge along Christopher Street, and end up on the piers stretching out into the Hudson River along the West Side park. There they hang out, dance, chat, pick up dates, and create their own public community.

At the community board meeting I attended, a social worker stood up and told Ali Forney's story to a mixed crowd of white residents of the West Village and mostly African American and Hispanic gay youth who were at the meeting to discuss public-space policies and the behavior of young people. The influx of large numbers of teenagers, especially in the summer months and on the weekends, had led to tensions between adult residents and youth. In the meeting, the mostly white, middle-aged, and elderly residents sat in silence in the center of the room, while nearly forty youth of color stood around the perimeter, holding up large, hand-painted poster board signs that read "Safe space" and "It's our park too." The conflicts arising during this meeting and the many others that followed reflected the contentious position of street kids in the public sphere and public space. In the past, they have had only marginal voices in public debates over the right to use urban public spaces.

Advocacy groups worked with the young people on Christopher Street for several months in an effort to teach them how to represent themselves in public forums. These same advocates also collected harassment reports from young people in the West Village, detailing their interactions with the New York Police Department (NYPD), private park security agents, business owners, and residents.[3] Increasing tensions over the governance of public spaces, the public identity of the West Village neighborhood, the private control and commercialization of the area's public spaces, and the place of youth in this environment were rapidly coming to a head. Each group claimed a different form of "ownership" and "rights." These debates had their roots in prior struggles, particularly the nearly decade-old cleanup of Times Square, Ali Forney's old haunt.

Residents of the West Greenwich Village neighborhood in particular had formed a succession of committees and called many community board meetings to discuss the maintenance of order and the policing of their neighborhood. They already had requested and received more foot-police patrols, and Hudson River Park had a 1 a.m. curfew. Among other requests, the neighborhood had further restricted access to the park, citing noise, disorderly conduct, and safety issues, which they attributed to primarily young people. The West Side piers and newly established Hudson River Park are an ongoing development project, the latest segment of which (around pier 57) is predicted to cost $210 million.[4] The site stretches from Battery Park on Manhattan's southern tip five miles north to Fifty-ninth Street in Midtown. The park is intended to make the West Side of Manhattan an elite residential, shopping, and entertainment district linking Battery Park, Tribeca, the West Village, and the Meatpacking District. The piers and the park are an important gathering place for New York City's street youth. When Hudson River Park opened in 2003, a curfew was put in place and additional park security was employed to patrol the newly renovated piers along the waterfront. By late 2005, the 1 a.m. park curfew was drawing a flood of youth into the neighborhood every night, sparking complaints of noise and large, intimidating groups of young people blocking the sidewalks. In turn, the young people complained of harassment from the police, park police, and private residents.

At one community board meeting, a middle-aged resident stood up and, in a trembling voice, expressed the strong emotions of many West Village residents, that the young people hanging out in the park were "intolerable" and like an "army of occupation." She concluded by asking, "Why don't they party in their own neighborhoods?"[5] What was most troubling during these meetings was the wish of many residents that the young people would just "go home." This sentiment was voiced repeatedly, despite efforts by social workers and youth advocates to educate the community about youth homelessness (particularly gay youth homelessness), the dangers to abused young people of returning to their neighborhoods of origin, and the current lack of services for street youth, both in the West Village and citywide. At the end of one community board meeting attended by hundreds of residents and youth, a social worker stood up to speak. This was Carl Siciliano, the director of the Ali Forney Center. He had been a youth worker when Times Square was "cleaned up" and had seen at first hand what happened to young people pushed out of public spaces "back to where they came from." He had been the social worker called when Ali Forney was killed years earlier. The cleanup of Times Square and the deaths of Ali and several other youth had convinced him that street kids were in profound danger from both the street environment and the police. As he said years later:

> Every couple of months one of our kids was dying on the streets. It was just like a regular thing, that we had to have these memorial services at the church next door. We'd be trying to figure out how to bury the kid . . . and it was horrible. It was so clear to me that the condition of being out and alone and homeless on the streets put kids in danger of death, in a very stark way.[6]

What social workers tried to prove was not just that the young people being displaced had as much right to be in a public space as did any other member of society and, furthermore, had nowhere safe to "move on" to but also that many of the youth were on the streets because they had been abused and, more often than not, had been kicked out by their own families and communities.

The 1990s was about watching kids slowly become defeated. Because there wasn't a way to get them any alternative. We certainly don't have the capacity today to meet the needs of all the kids in the city. . . . If you're going to profoundly neglect a bunch of homeless kids and don't give them access to shelter and jobs and housing, then what are they supposed to do?[7]

Public-space regulations that pushed street youth out of the West Village were not helping them get off the streets, for they did not go home. Rather, constantly being moved around only narrowed their options. A spokesman for a national street outreach group for youth put it bluntly: "Children aren't living on the streets; they're dying."[8] When kids are pushed out of public spaces around the city, their plight not only is worsened, it also is made invisible. Far from becoming someone else's concern, they become no one's concern.

Social workers tried to convince neighborhood residents that by choosing the West Village, these kids had become *their* kids, part of *their* community, and deserved *their* (positive) attention. The West Village had historically been a refuge for gay youth, many of whom had grown up to be economically successful adult residents of the neighborhood. This generation of West Village youth, however, face more complicated intersections of race, class, sexuality, and homelessness, as well as greater stigmatization.

I wanted to understand how such marginalized young people experienced the spatial organization of their lives, especially in regard to public-space ordinances that apply to street kids. Youth homelessness is experienced through marginalization processes that are controlled in space, by governance, in the performance of "deviant" social behaviors, and by means of mobility and invisibility. Social theorists have critically addressed how social regimes are naturalized in spaces, bodies, practices, and performances.[9] More recently, social scientists have been grappling with the complicated intersection between social regimes and processes of physical and social mobility.[10] My theoretical focus is on the new regimes of public-space governance, which, through interlocking systems of mobility and invisibility, are shaping the lives of street youth. I decided to approach this problem through the role played by social service providers, such as street outreach workers.

The social workers who spoke at community board meetings told a powerful story of how changing social regimes were harming "their kids."

From the summer of 2004 to the summer of 2006 I conducted an ethnographic investigation in public spaces throughout New York City. I gathered additional information during return visits to the field from 2007 to 2010. I collected data primarily by practicing street outreach, particularly on the intersection of street youths' experiences, street outreach performances, and the regulation of public spaces in neighborhoods around Midtown and Lower Manhattan. Because the street is a dangerous environment for youth, my data are primarily my and other outreach workers' notes. Because a typical street conversation is distracted, fast, and interrupted by the myriad activities and demands of street life, it was recorded as accurately as possible into field notebooks immediately after each outreach. I did not tape-record any kids in public—drawing the attention of a pimp, drug dealer, or even the police can be harmful for them—but I did conduct some formal interviews in drop-in centers and other sites. Because these sites are institutional and under adult control, I cannot claim that these interviews are directly representative of or substitutable for the thousands of conversations I had on the streets, but these youth were better able to reflect comprehensively on some of their experiences in these sheltered environments. I also conducted formal interviews with most of the fewer than thirty street outreach workers in the city active during my tenure as a street counselor.

To understand how street outreach workers and street kids interrelate in a place called the "street," I have combined a number of different literatures, empirical data, and social theories and situated them in a framework of activist, ethical research. The study of street youth and street outreach sits at an intersection between ethical activism and the processes of marginalization. Feminist scholars have pointed to the need for a critical understanding of ethics, care, and activism in work with marginalized populations.[11] During my time as a street outreach counselor, I was able to spend six months conducting independent observations of street youth hangouts and public spaces, as well as in-depth interviews with twenty current and former street outreach counselors and hundreds of informal conversations with homeless youth. I also was fortunate enough to participate in a statewide coalition of homeless youth agencies and advocacy groups and attended two street outreach retreats. These meetings were invaluable opportunities to lay out early theories and receive informed, expert feedback.[12]

What I learned is that there are many kinds of street youth, many different experiences of being young and homeless, and many kinds of street outreach being carried out in public spaces. Although each street kid and outreach worker that I contacted had a different story to tell, certain widespread social forces colored all their experiences. In this book, I use a feminist sensibility, which seeks to uncover the unfolding of power in society. Seeing mobility as both an empowering and a disempowering sociospatial force framed by a public revanchism encouraged by neoliberal polices is central to understanding the street youth experience. This book reveals the social structures, social actors, practices, and places that shape street youths' abilities to navigate the roots and routes of homelessness. All too often, however, the stories of street kids remain untold; Ali Forney's is an exception.

This book begins with the presupposition that youth homelessness exists in the intersection of social discourses, social services, public spaces, and the everyday experiences of youth. But my study is not a traditional ethnography of youth. Previous ethnographies have situated the researcher as a caring visitor, albeit one attempting to lend power and authority to young peoples' experiences. Many studies of street youth make policy recommendations for public aid through the provision of social services, and calls for increased street outreach are common.[13] My goal instead is to understand the multitude of experiences and intersections that influence street kids' encounters with public aid in the form of street outreach. In addition to kids' experiences, I wanted to explore the experiences of people like Carl who work directly with youth in public-space environments. I wanted to know what happens when policing regimes fundamentally alter the sociospatial relationships built between outreach workers and street kids.

Street Kids and Youth Homelessness

> Where are you from?
> —Outreach counselor speaking to street kid
>
> I'm from here.
> —Street kid responding, pointing to a bench in a public park

Street youth have been saddled with a powerful societal image of what it means to be both young and homeless. The popular image of street youth found in movies and TV shows is both a romance and a morality tale. Usually this tale involves a teenaged white male from suburbia who leaves home to seek freedom and adventure. Eventually he drifts into the unforgiving city, with old army backpack and antiestablishment attitude in hand. Several months later, he is strung out on drugs and begging for coins. This image should not be surprising, as it speaks to social norms that construct street youth as socially deviant and out of place while simultaneously belying the complex experiences and situations that lead young people to the streets and structure their lives there.

In the context of this book, street youth[14] are young people, twelve to twenty-four years old, who are living without family support or a stable residence, both on and off the actual streets and in the public spaces of cities and towns. They may live intermittently in shelters, with friends or relatives (couch surfing), or on the streets. In order to survive, street kids typically participate in the street economies of theft, sex work, drug dealing, and panhandling.[15] In the United States, an estimated 1.6 million to 2 million kids leave home every year,[16] and of these, a quarter will not return.[17] Homeless youth are one of the fastest-growing segments of the homeless population in North America, making up an estimated 25 percent of all homeless people.[18] Nonetheless, despite the growing presence of homeless youth, national discussions about "ending homelessness" focus exclusively on adult homelessness and related issues such as poverty and affordable housing. The reasons that young people become homeless in the Western world have been well documented in both the academic and professional literature.[19] These studies have found that the most common routes to homelessness among youth are abuse and neglect, family breakdown, aging out of government (foster care) programs, and, last, poverty. The National Alliance to End Homelessness's 2006 report on youth homelessness was a compilation of recent studies concluding that nearly half of homeless youth had been abused and more than half had been told that they were no longer wanted by their families.[20] Another study found that more than 75 percent of female street youth had been abused. Children who are abused in the home early in life are more likely to suffer from depression and self-esteem issues, which become dangerously critical once these children are on the streets.[21] Depression and self-esteem issues are exacerbated by street life experiences, may lead to higher rates of suicide and death, and increase children's risk of further victimization.[22] In addition, a study of the foster care system in the United States has shown that 25 percent of young people aging out of foster care at age eighteen will become homeless before the age of twenty-two.[23]

The paths that lead kids to the street vary, but once homeless, their experiences are, sadly, uniform. Studies report that young people have few options for surviving on the streets,[24] with the majority engaging in high-risk activities such as survival sex[25] and the drug trade.[26] As many as one-third to one-half of all street youth in places like New York City engage in sex work in exchange for money, food, shelter, and clothing.[27] Young people who live on the margins of society, with few job skills and no identification, can rarely find and keep jobs in the formal economy. Those who try to make their way by means of less risky activities like panhandling are either ignored by the public or harassed by the police.[28] Homeless kids are often chronically tired and dependent on drugs (some use drugs to stay awake for long periods of time), and they are at high risk of contracting HIV and other diseases. A recent in-depth study of eighty homeless youth in New York City found that 75 percent were clinically depressed,[29] and another study of homeless youth in New York and Toronto found an attempted suicide rate of 46 percent. Most of these young people reported feeling trapped, lonely, and/or without any hope of leaving the streets.[30] In addition, studies have found that the mortality rate of street kids is two to twenty-eight times that of their peers, with the most frequent causes of death being suicide and drug overdoses.[31] Homeless youth are also six to twelve times more likely to become HIV positive, compared with the general youth population.[32] The common stereotype of street kids as criminals or "on an adventure" thus belies the realities that drive youth into life on the streets and the risks they encounter once there.[33]

Every year, New York is estimated to contain more than 10,000 homeless youth, with 3,800 seeking shelter or services on any given day.[34] Although these homeless kids can be found in all five boroughs, Manhattan acts as a magnet for street kids from across the city as well as the rest of the United States and Canada. According to the most recent social service counts, the population of street kids is evenly divided among African American, Hispanic, and Caucasian youth, two-thirds of whom are male.[35] Social work professionals estimate that 30 to 40 percent of the homeless youth in New York City are gay, lesbian, bisexual, transgender, or questioning (GLBTQ) and may be living on the streets because of conflicts over their sexual identities in their home communities.[36]

Only sixty emergency shelter beds were available to youth, despite their long history of homelessness, in New York City's shelter system in 2006. Today that number stands at only slightly more than one hundred emergency shelter beds, still a grossly inadequate number. In the summer of 2009, all the emergency youth shelters in the city were full by June, and that month, the two largest shelters—Covenant House and Safe Horizons—had to turn away almost ninety kids. With so few beds, shelters often give priority to younger street kids, thereby leaving those over the age of eighteen with few options. Despite empirical research showing a clear connection between access to social services and a reduction in homelessness, high-risk behavior, and street kid mortality,[37] programs for street kids continue to be underfunded and, increasingly, defunded, with the economic recession of 2008/2009 only making the situation worse. Social service programs are now seeing increasing numbers of older youth, who traditionally have found entry-level jobs and have relied on the support of their extended family for shelter, looking for emergency shelter and aid. Meanwhile, both city funding for and charitable donations to social services have gone down, resulting in shelters being forced to reduce the number of youth they can serve. Drop-in centers and outreach workers across the city now have no places to refer kids for shelter. A 2007 survey by the Empire State Coalition found that as many as 1,600 youth find shelter nightly in abandoned buildings, unlocked cars, and the city's public transportation system.[38] Many street kids ride subways at night, gaining some measure of warmth, camaraderie, and protection in these "moving hotels."[39]

Even those young people who do seek help have surprisingly few options. Because street youth are not a highly visible segment of the homeless population, services are sparse, overstressed, and underfunded, with long waiting lists. Gentrification and NIMBY (Not In My Backyard) land-use policies have forced many shelters and drop-in centers to move away from the tourist sites and commercial zones where street youth congregate. In recent years, government cutbacks also have pushed the work of youth services onto private, faith-based, and nonprofit groups. Ironically, several of the social service organizations that had advocated for street youth in the West Village and whose members had attended community board meetings had themselves been pushed out of the neighborhood several years earlier by rising rents, zoning changes, and community pressure. At these meetings, calls by local politicians for more social services for youth in the neighborhood were met with anger by social service providers, many of whom had seen their ability to stay and work in the neighborhood systematically blocked by residents, business owners, and the local government. Currently, street outreach teams are the only effective means of reaching kids hanging out in neighborhoods far from drop-in centers and shelters.

Street Outreach

Contemporary street outreach is based on a model of social service provision implemented in the 1950s to connect social workers with youth gangs on their own turf in an effort to reduce gang violence.[40] In this definition, *turf* is a physical, social, and metaphorical location, just as the process of *reaching out* is simultaneously a performance, a direction, and an end result. The goal of early models of detached youth work was to build a "bridge" from the increasingly institutionalized social service sector out to the streets where young people were being drawn into street activities and economies, including but not limited to gangs, violence, vandalism, drug dealing, sex work, and theft.[41]

Current street outreach with homeless youth relies on a similar model. Outreach workers from drop-in centers, shelters, and medical clinics either walk or drive out to where street youth spend most of their time, in both public and private locales. Even though street counselors go to where these kids physically are, the process of street outreach work is primarily meant to bring professional social workers into the social sphere of these young people's lives. Outreach might be on a street corner, in a park, a movie theater, a store, or a hallway. By physically approaching kids, outreach workers place themselves in the competitive social context of the street environment. As one outreach trainer explained, "A pimp can spot a new runaway in minutes. We need to be able to do that. That's our competition."[42] Successful outreach workers must be both "street smart" and almost preternaturally aware of street activities and social performances. A worker can get herself and the kids she is attempting to help in trouble very quickly if she blunders into a drug deal or a fight with a pimp or interferes with police activity.

Street outreach workers are often young, and sometimes they are former street youth themselves. They are trained to identify the various locations where street youth hang out and the activities in which young people engage as part of their participation in the street economy.[43] Outreach workers must be sensitive to the economic, racial, ethnic, gender, and social divisions that form street youths' lives. Once they make contact, street outreach counselors often struggle to create a kind of momentary safe space out of the chaotic, competitive environment in which the kids live. This "safe space" of outreach is socially and geographically contextual and constantly changing. For street kids, survival usually involves an exchange of goods or services with other members of the street economy: drug dealers, pimps, store owners, and social workers.

When street outreach workers approach young people, the kids usually assume that the workers want something from them. As one veteran outreach worker commented, "When working with homeless youth . . . you often work with young people who can be distant and distrusting." The outreach space is thus built around precarious lines of trust that are different for each encounter between the kid and the outreach worker. It is only within these fragile spaces that outreach workers can advise, sometimes console, often cajole, and, at best, help street youth. Despite the stresses of conducting outreach within the view of a sometimes hostile, sometimes indifferent public, street outreach is, nevertheless, perceived as an efficient way of linking youth living on the streets to the social service world housed in the private spaces of institutions.

A typical outreach ranges from being tedious and boring (looking for street youth) to being tense, fast, competitive, and potentially dangerous for everyone involved. Yet small gains can be made even in the briefest of interactions. Outreach workers distribute condoms and food, and their presence provides a form of surveillance against pimps. The most marginalized of street youth—those who have never been into a drop-in center, new runaways, and those too scared to seek help—receive information about resources, places to seek help, and, perhaps most important, the time and location of the next street outreach. For new runaways, street outreach counselors are often their first contact with youth-oriented social services. Because most of these kids have been abused, many are hesitant to go to adult-run social service agencies. But over time, consistent contact with an outreach worker can begin to put a name and a face on the apparently cold and indifferent world of social services. During outreach sessions, workers try to assess the risks to both themselves and the kids, keeping in mind the competition they face for the street youths' time and attention. A relationship of trust is critical to youth engaging with sited, institutional social services. Indeed, a study in Montreal found that when outreach services linked to medical and housing resources to street kids were increased, their mortality rates fell dramatically.[44]

In New York, social service providers began rejuvenating 1980s and 1990s street outreach programs aimed at homeless youth, mostly in centralized locations in Manhattan. By the 1990s, eight active street outreach programs nominally covered all five boroughs.[45] In the early 1990s, three of these groups, with fewer than a dozen outreach workers, were contacting more than 13,000 street youth annually,[46] or approximately 40 percent of the homeless youth population.[47] In 2003, street outreach programs across the country that received federal funds reported making 630,000 contacts with homeless youth on the streets of U.S. cities, which was nearly one-third of all homeless kids.[48] In New York City, three independent outreach groups reported giving out condoms, food, and information to more than 3,000 street youth in a single month.[49] By 2005, a single outreach team of three people was able to engage 3,000 young people over a six-month period.[50] But street outreach represents only a small portion of local and national funds allocated to social work with homeless youth. In 2006, the total federal budget for street outreach work was only $15 million of the $102 million set aside for homeless youth programs, and by 2009, the federal budget for street outreach to homeless and runaway youth had been reduced to $5 million.[51] Even though street outreach is a powerful model for helping hard-to-reach young people, social service agencies expect that funding for street outreach will continue to be cut over the next few years.

As funding for government programs declined, volunteer street outreach groups—primarily nonprofit and faith based—have tried to fill the gap. Labeled *neoliberalization*, this is a broader trend toward privatization in society grounded in a belief that certain social systems and goods are better regulated by a free market. In the case of social services, this means that the public aid once provided by government services is now often left to private organizations, with street outreach work at the leading edge of this trend. But charities have always offered services to disadvantaged youth. It was not until in the middle of the twentieth century that the United States began offering significant public social services to homeless youth. Then, the fiscal crisis of the 1970s and the 1990s led to a series of governmental pullbacks from these services. Although the federal government is currently funding street outreach through limited grants to private, nonprofit agencies, these groups must compete with one another for dwindling state funds and also must seek (unpredictable) private funding. In New York City, only one organization can receive the street outreach grant provided through the federal Runaway and Homeless Youth Act, so the remaining majority of street outreach is volunteer and charity based.

Even though street outreach operates on a simple model of finding and providing services to young people, it is complicated by their mobility and invisibility, as well as their instinctive distrust of adults. The intricate nature of outreach can lead to misidentifying housed youth for street youth. One volunteer outreach counselor expressed the frustration of identifying street kids:

> We asked a lot of kids who weren't homeless if they were on the streets. This is in part because it is fashionable to look grungy. Also, many of the homeless kids don't look homeless—they spend a lot of time and effort on their appearance to look stylish.[52]

Kids around the East Village and Union Square area may indeed be blending in with college and high school students who affect a "street aesthetic" in their clothing, book bags, and general fashion. Wearing ripped clothing and carrying a beat-up army duffel does not look out of place. In other parts of the city, street kids may be wearing the latest off-label sports or hip-hop clothing—all kept immaculately clean—in compliance with a different street aesthetic. Street kids are like other kids; they have their own subcultures and styles and do not think of themselves as "homeless." An experienced outreach worker described the more subtle ways of assessing kids' needs:

> When I was doing outreach, we had to learn how to ask all kinds of questions in order to identify who's homeless. Because if you ask a kid if they're homeless, they'll say "no." They don't think of themselves as homeless. And that's great! That's what I want to build upon. So what we had to say was, "How many places have you slept in the last six months?" All kinds of questions that helped us determine that the kid didn't have stable housing.[53]

Outreach workers have to be skilled not only at engaging with young people but also reading and interpreting the many social factors involved in conducting social services in public. Outreach workers' effectiveness begins with how well they intersect and engage with kids living on the streets. Their engagement with street youth is based on how young people experience and cope with their ever changing public-space environments. Even skilled outreach workers are often frustrated by the social dynamics of street youths' lives. Because outreach is only one player in a competitive system, where and how outreach workers interact with young people is crucial to effective interventions.[54]

To sum up, street outreach tries to find homeless kids on their own ground, to engage with them in a supportive and caring manner, and to create a momentarily safe space in which trusting relationships can form. The goal is to create trust and respect that will lead to further contact with social service institutions, such as drop-in centers, clinics, and shelters, that can provide more extensive and lasting counseling, treatment, and education. Recent policing tactics in New York City have focused on removing street youth from popular public spaces, which has dramatically altered the environment and social dynamic of street outreach.

In the past two decades, new waves of policing strategies have led to the profiling and systematic harassment of marginalized social groups in cities across the United States. Primarily because of public pressure to "clean up" urban public spaces and gentrifying neighborhoods, cities have enacted ordinances that allow the ticketing of minor offenses such as loitering and aggressive panhandling.[55] Outlawing the practices by which homeless people survive is part of the "antihomeless" movement that has swept most urban areas in the United States. Scholars argue that public-space laws that drive any perceived source of disorder from gentrifying or commercialized public spaces are "revanchist," that they punitively deny people a right to space.[56] In effect, these laws dismiss homeless people as legitimate social subjects with the right to exist in public.[57] Middle-class concerns with urban livability have created popular normative discourses of the ordered and "good" urban life that oppose the presence of the poor, the homeless, and minorities. In cities like New York, the implementation of quality-of-life ordinances are the tangible mobilizations of these discourses that falsely link social phenomena like urban blight to homeless people. Public-space ordinances are being used to spatially exclude marginalized groups while simultaneously constructing some groups as deviant, disorderly subjects with no right to an orderly, commercialized city.

The phenomenon of order maintenance policing has already spread to cities around the world. Research on homeless youth in countries as diverse as Indonesia, Ecuador, Australia, and Brazil have found that harassment, ticketing, curfews, and physical violence are being used to cleanse public spaces of the perceived polluting presence of homeless kids.[58] At best, these regulatory tactics create a type of spatial apartheid, separating youth from the rest of the public.[59] Thus authorities often force young people into "a geographical game of cat and mouse"[60] or push them to the margins of urban centers.[61] In their worst form, these laws reflect a global trend of urban revanchism that actively punishes street kids for their social position.

Homeless youth now report being frequently ticketed for minor infractions and threatened by police.[62] Studies show that many homeless youth are being driven into progressively less visible and more dangerous situations and activities,[63] because the police and public are telling them that they do not belong in public areas and must move on or risk arrest. A recent New York City study found that 76 percent of street youth had been arrested and a third had spent more than a year incarcerated.[64] Street outreach efforts and the street outreach model itself are being undermined by the increased mobility of New York City's street youth, the time they spend incarcerated because of unpaid tickets and misdemeanor warrants, and the disruption of traditional hangout sites such as Times Square and the West Village by police "sweeps."

Mobility of Street Youth and Street Outreach

The difficulties experienced in finding shelter often lead to a kind of nomadic roaming pattern: typically youth arrive on the street, stay outside for a few days—perhaps in parks, all-night restaurants or walking the street—find shelter with friends in someone's apartment or a squat, move to a hostel [shelter], migrate to another hostel, and then begin the sequence again.[65]

This kind of migration is a common pattern of mobility for many street youth. For most of them, being "on the streets" is not a fixed state: young people often run away or are repeatedly thrown out by their families. Instead, becoming homeless is often a progression in which kids run away and/or are kicked out, stay on a friend or a relative's couch, go home again, leave again, couch-surf until their welcome has worn out, stay at crisis shelters and drop-in centers, and, in some cases, live on the streets. Many homeless youth, however, manage to survive using their own social networks and never actually sleep on the streets. One young homeless woman described this shifting round of temporary residences:

My dad said, "You should go—you should do what you want to do. . . ." I was eighteen, which to a lot of people would just be like leaving home because you're eighteen . . . but I was not prepared at all to leave. I spent a couple of days before I left looking at shelters. And then my best friend said, "You need to come and live with me." But it wasn't better when I went to live with my best friend. . . . I was more depressed . . . it was a lot of things all happening at once. I wasn't taking my medication . . . so I left one morning. No one was home. I took all my stuff and moved in with another friend. She had a one-bedroom apartment and let me crash. But that got crazy there . . . so I moved again.[66]

This young woman managed to continue a pattern of couch surfing and temporary residences for four years. Even though she spent most of her days wandering around the city, she managed to avoid sleeping on the streets during her homeless years. But many young people run out of options. Summertime in North America causes a rapid increase in the number of kids living outside in northern cities like New York, whereas warm, southern cities like San Diego see winter influxes of street kids. The number of young people physically living on or off the streets varies daily, monthly, and yearly. Although each young person has a unique experience of these processes, in the end most spend some time on the street, wandering from place to place and becoming involved in some form of the street economy.[67] When kids are on the street, hanging out in known locations, street outreach workers are able to intercept their nomadic roaming pattern.

In New York City, workers report that while they are still finding large numbers of street kids, they are not able to find the same kids consistently. Anecdotal reports from street youth and social workers suggest that the spatial behavior of street youth may be changing in reaction to new policing tactics and public-space regulations. As I pointed out earlier, in the past fifteen years, the way that New York and other cities govern public spaces has changed dramatically. The police's targeting of sex work, panhandling, and other street youth survival activities has forced these young people into more dangerous private spaces that are out of the view of the public. Many homeless youth—clearly a highly mobile population to begin with—have become hypermobile both within urban neighborhoods and between cities. Some young people are moving into progressively less visible locations that are harder for outreach workers to reach, and others may be returning to abusive homes and relationships, further isolating themselves from the opportunity to seek or receive help. In other words, the police's tactics and the street kids' coping strategies to avoid ticketing and arrest may serve to break down the "bridges" that outreach workers build. In sum, young people are not just being driven out of the sight and minds of the public; they also are being run off the social service map.

Research with Street Kids

This book was a result of my desire to conduct an ethnographic study of youth in conflict over public space. To this end, I spent several weeks observing public spaces around New York City during the summer before I began my fieldwork. These initial forays convinced me of the great diversity of young people's activities taking place in public spaces. But simply walking up and questioning young people at random in public seemed like a dubious strategy for an ethnographic project. I wanted my research to be practical, ethical, and, above all, useful. Thus I needed more direction. During trips to New York over the next several months, I sought out professionals who worked with young people in a variety of settings, not just public spaces. I met with a youth advocacy group in the West Village, visited a drop-in center and an after-school program in Harlem, and spent time in community gardens with youth programs throughout the city. During these preliminary discussions with adults working with youth, I heard about street kids and their problems with the police, other kids, the public, and public-space regulations. Newspaper reports and community meetings concerning minority and gay street youth occupying the affluent, white, gay enclave of the West

Village particularly stood out. When I first began researching youth and public-space issues in 2003, before I began my fieldwork, I heard about meetings concerning unruly kids hanging out in a newly gentrified park on the West Side of Manhattan. Cool, I thought. I had wanted to do a qualitative study of a variety of young people hanging out in public spaces across New York City, and these meetings seemed like a good place to start. By the time I began my fieldwork in the summer of 2004, the heated debate over the use of Hudson River Park and the allegations that the city was totally ignoring the plight of street youth and the advice of social workers had convinced me to narrow my interest to the experiences of street kids, the effects of the new emphasis on maintaining order, and the role of street outreach workers. I was struck by stories of young people being told outright that they did not belong in a public park or on a public sidewalk. Despite the many injustices in the world (and the many ways in which young people are marginalized in our society), these injustices seemed particularly petty and mean.

Nevertheless, I was hesitant to take on a topic as daunting as youth homelessness, as many scholars have found it difficult to work with exploited and vulnerable youth populations.[68] Only after I began talking to street outreach workers did I decide I had to address the issue of street kids, because I could not stop thinking about the passion and intensity with which the outreach workers spoke. I liked their pragmatism, humor, and camaraderie as they talked about one another, outreach, and "their kids." Going out and finding kids felt more proactive than waiting around a drop-in center or shelter for the kids to come to me. As I explained my research project to the all-volunteer outreach group StandUp for Kids, outreach was practical in a way that appealed to me, and in the summer of 2004 I got permission to work with their New York chapter.

When I first began planning my research, the thought of walking up to kids on the street frightened me, and I decided that it might be easier if I filtered it through the legitimizing structure of street outreach. As a relatively affluent, white, female researcher, I felt I had very little in common with homeless teenagers, and so I would not be able to "connect" with them. By channeling the majority of my fieldwork through street outreach, I increased my access to street kids but altered my position as a researcher. What I learned (aside from the fact that there is no "easy" research with street kids) is that in every outreach, workers struggle with these same fears and difficulties. After more than two years of street outreach—in every extreme of weather and tracking hundreds of miles over the same city blocks—I now know that finding street kids and engaging with them for even a few moments is a herculean task.

Through my first months of outreach, I waited in trepidation for kids to begin telling me about the abuse, neglect, depression, and despair that follow a life on the streets. But what I heard more often were stories of humor, resilience, frustration, and survival. What I learned is that when young people tell adults anything about their lives, it is a gift. To form the bonds necessary to achieve lasting change in street youths' lives, outreach counselors must be on the streets for years. Those things that motivate street outreach workers to seek out street kids, to slowly build bonds with them, and to share their pain have also become part of this book. As in many ethnographic studies, the most important results may not have been posed as initial research questions and may spark future questions and projects.

Understanding how outreach workers interact daily with street kids and in the context of the governance of public spaces seemed like a tangible goal for an urban ethnographic project. I intended to conduct observation, participant observation, and interviews with street kids and outreach workers over an academic year (about nine months). Two years later, I was painfully extracting myself from my field site and from innumerable commitments to several outreach organizations. I had become a semiprofessional social worker training new outreach workers. I had boxes of jumbled field notes, photographs, and interviews, half of which I was uncertain that I could ethically use. In the end, I collected data for this study over nearly seven years in New York City through the direct observation of four public spaces frequented by street youth; through an intensive two-year participant observation of a case-study street outreach group, as well as time spent with two other outreach organizations; through interviews with street outreach workers across New York City; in meetings, workshops, and conferences; and, finally, through a wide variety of archival data that included websites, newspaper reports, flyers, and press releases. My later work as a consultant with two street youth surveys and as a trainer of peer outreach counselors was toward the end of my field study and added further depth to my data and insight into my field data and into critical ethnographic research.

Many practical and ethical hurdles caused me to question the nature of research on and with street youth. Two concepts now stand out from my early discussions with youth workers that influenced my research focus and ethnographic data collection process: invisibility and vulnerability. The first concerns the fact that street youth are largely ignored in the United States. Even though international studies of street youth are gaining recognition, questions about domestic youth homelessness seems to be disappearing from the national consciousness. I believe that our current social ordering is disciplining street youth into invisibility. Society normalizes social invisibility as proof of the absence of phenomena like youth homelessness. Social invisibility has had a far-reaching influence on social services, including street outreach. Because street youth are notoriously hard to count, programs are underfunded, social workers are overworked, and outreach counselors are frustrated. Invisibility especially determines which kids outreach workers approach, and therefore, the data I was able to collect for this study.

The fragility of the housed state for many youth was another theme that came up in several early conversations with social workers. When social workers describe a young person as being "off the streets," they may give the impression that finding housing is a permanent end state, that there is a linear trajectory from the street to the home. Having housing may also be assumed as the same as having a home or that these young people had conventional homes before hitting the streets. For many street youth, however, being housed and then homeless is an endless cycle of residential vulnerability and neglect in which they have been trapped throughout their lives. One conversation during the early stages of my fieldwork stands out because it illustrates the ambiguity of many young people's homeless state. I was doing outreach with a youth worker who also was working with high school students in several working-poor neighborhoods across the city. As we walked through the East Village, scouting for street kids, I asked him what he saw as the difference between his high school kids and the street kids we had encountered that day. I expected him to say something like "family support" or "caring adults." But he told me that there was very little difference. Any of the kids in his high school programs could be homeless tomorrow. Indeed, they already might be homeless and hiding it from him and other adults. A parent's lost job, a fight, an abusive relationship—any of these could result in a teenager's quickly becoming homeless. Deciding which kids are homeless (even abstractly) is a never ending struggle for outreach workers, although many workers feel it is a moot point. Seasoned street outreach workers try to help any young people who ask for aid, regardless of their current housing status. For them, every kid is a potential street kid.

A Road Map of This Book

This study uncovers the sociospatial processes that shape youth homelessness, the behavior of street kids, and the practice of street outreach in public spaces. My hope is that a better understanding of the intersections of street youth and social service provision will contribute vital information to ongoing debates about the regulation of public spaces, the rights of street youth, and the value of street outreach efforts. I explore four broad themes: (1) how social norms concerning young people are shaped by and, in turn, shape broader ideologies and public policies toward street kids; (2) how street outreach operates in relation to street youth and the current neoliberal and revanchist regulatory environment of public spaces; (3) how the implementation of order maintenance policing strategies have altered the physical and social regulation of public spaces and the behavior of street youth as socially illegitimate public subjects; and (4) how the interrelated phenomena of street kids' mobility and invisibility place both them and public social services out of the view of society. My research focuses on the changing patterns of spatial behavior among street youth and their effect on street outreach. In essence, how are experiences of mobility and immobility shaping street youths' access to social aid?

My hope is that by answering these fundamental questions, I can begin to address a broader set of conceptual issues: What is the role of the social regulation of public subjectivities in street kids' experiences and identity projects? That is, how are street kids "emplaced," or sociospatially constructed, as both on the street and of the street? How is the street constructed as a physical, social, and moral environment in discourses surrounding youth homelessness? Why has the street come to occupy such a central and powerful space in the social organization of youth homelessness? How well does the tangible geography of street kids align with the metaphorical geography of youth homelessness that society envisions? How complicit are social service models like street outreach in the location of street kids' identities? And finally, how might street outreach create spaces for other imaginings of street youth and the street? The possible mismatch of street outreach tactics with the highly mobilized spatial behaviors of street youth is a problem that has been exacerbated by the changes in the social regulation of public spaces and marginalized populations.

In chapter 2, I review how the history of youth homelessness in the United States has evolved in tandem with ideological conceptions of childhood, the place of youth, and public space. The history of street youth in New York City, and indeed the public perception of youth homelessness throughout the United States, is closely intertwined with the development of professional, ideologically driven social services. Traditionally, social workers, religious groups, social activists, and the state have decided what constitutes a homeless youth. Throughout history, society's changing conceptualization of street youth has also changed the social service models and aid to street youth.

Street youth today sit at the center of dual and competing social mythologies that construct homeless youth both *on* the street and *of* the street.

Chapter 3 is a profile of one homeless youth, "Blacc." Blacc is familiar with many of the shelters, drop-in centers, and public spaces common to street youth. He has been harassed by police and participated in the street economy. While his experiences are, of course, his own, it is useful to contextualize what Blacc has gone through since becoming homeless, especially in light of current trends in youth homelessness and social service provision.

As Blacc's story illustrates, street outreach is dependent on locating homeless youth on the "street." In chapters 4 and 5, I discuss the role of street outreach. Chapter 4 examines the development of street outreach as a situated social service practice based on the sociospatial construction of street youth and the moral geographies of public space. Street outreach is a performative practice that seeks out street kids "where they are," both physically and metaphorically. The ability of social service professionals to understand the spaces and identities of street youth have influenced the practices of street outreach workers, street outreach goals, and, most important, structures or limits possible alternatives to current outreach models. A neoliberalizing trend in social service provision has significantly shifted the landscape of service provision toward volunteer and faith-based services. In New York City, street kids are losing services and receiving conflicting messages about the availability and desirability of social aid. Inconsistent aid for street kids and increasingly "uneven spatialities of emergency services"[69] have led to confusion and frustration for street kids and outreach workers alike.

Chapter 5 describes the various sites where I did my research and how one street outreach organization works in each of these neighborhoods. Because my knowledge of different outreach areas (and thus how I describe them) is closely linked to my experiences learning to read the streets as an outreach counselor, I have created a descriptive, spatialized timeline of an outreach group learning to perform in its "turf." Learning a "turf" is critical to effective outreach, yet this process is complicated by myriad public-space regulations, rapidly changing mobility behaviors by street kids, and unpredictable responses by police and local business owners. The effectiveness of an outreach group can vary dramatically from week to week and across different neighborhoods. It is not uncommon for outreach workers to be informally banned from particular public spaces by police or even warned away by street kids. This chapter looks at the deceptively simple-looking, yet complex practice of providing public social aid.

Chapter 6 examines in more detail the evolution of order maintenance policing and the social regulation of public subjects. Current trends in public-space governance that focuses on minor public-space infractions first appeared in New York City and have since been adopted by cities around the world. It is important to understand how social norms of commercialized public spaces and normative public subjects determine how quality-of-life ordinances are conceived, perceived, and mobilized in relation to street youth, other marginalized populations, and broader communities. When cities implement quality-of-life regulations that organize urban space around idealized social imaginaries of middle-class entertainment and consumerism, street kids disrupt the picture. I believe that the neoliberalization of public-space governance has initiated a new wave of urban revanchism focused on street kids. When street kids are perceived as causes of disorder in an environment of increasing order, their expulsion thus is naturalized. Driving street kids out of the picture increases their mobility and invisibility while potentially exacerbating the larger problem of youth homelessness. Indeed, urban revanchism may be condemning street kids to a future as homeless adults as their opportunities to access social aid are cut off.

In chapter 7, I theorize that for street youth, two related strategies—mobility and invisibility—may be both empowering and disempowering. The way that young people experience mobility and discuss motility is tied to how our society historically has both penalized and romanticized nomadic populations. Mobilities (and, to some extent, immobilities) complicate current street outreach performances. When street outreach workers create momentarily safe spaces in public, they also are creating temporarily "still" spaces for street youth. There is no well-developed theory about how the spaces created through outreach function in public and are experienced by street kids and outreach workers. In this chapter, I also consider how practices of mobility are tied to processes that socially erase street youth and that may obscure the value of social services for homeless youth. Outreach workers often experience street youth as being present but absent during the outreach process while counselors seek out youth who may or may not be found. Indeed, it often feels as though street youth "haunt" the practice of outreach, as outreach itself becomes a mobile and strategically invisible practice.

In chapter 8 I consider the current state of youth homelessness and street outreach in New York City and conclude with recommendations for social work professionals, policymakers, and academics. Research on street youth has traditionally called for more street outreach. Uncritical recommendations are no longer sufficient in a changing economic climate of state withdrawal from social services, uncertain private-sector aid, and increasingly harsh public-space regulations. Street kids and street outreach are being pinched between the harsh realities of urban social change and the unexamined assessments of policymakers.

As is true for all research, the methods and methodology, my personal code of ethics, and my position as a researcher are present in various aspects of this study. Recognizing this, I include methodological content and commentary in each chapter. Nonetheless, the many methodological hurdles and ethical issues in studying street outreach with youth do warrant a separate treatment. In appendix A, I describe my methods of working with homeless youth and outreach counselors during my ethnographic fieldwork. As a proponent of critical ethnography, I believe that good analysis begins with an understanding of our own positions as researchers and participants in the social field. We all carry our own particular moral codes and ethics into our research, and work with homeless youth and relatively marginalized social service providers often presents ethically charged minefields to navigate. Over the course of this research, I rarely felt there were clear moral decisions and outcomes, as every situation presented its own arrangement of ethics and power. In this final section I examine more fully my position as a researcher/activist, the insider/outsider issues involving street outreach workers and street youth, and the ethics of conducting feminist research with marginalized populations.

While writing this now, I understand that before I began I had internalized many of the negative images and stereotypes of homeless youth that permeate our society: that street youth are chaotic, unpredictable, and damaged people (who probably smell bad). Today I consider street youth as a diverse and complex group that is underserved and overlooked. And the lives of street kids *are* disruptive, violent, fast, boring, fragile, ephemeral, and often fatal. Despite the daily struggles of an estimated 1.5 million street kids in public spaces in the United States, homeless youth are nearly invisible to the general public.[70] The processes by which street kids are erased from view are not fully understood by policymakers, nor have they been adequately addressed in the academic literature. Yet social invisibility ensures that young homeless people remain an all-but-forgotten population. In turn, their invisibility lessens their access to social services and denies them chances to survive and to "get off the streets."

The Space of the Streets

In 1995, independent filmmaker Larry Clark directed a documen-tary-like movie that chronicles twenty-four hours in the life of a group of New York City teenagers, starring several street kids. Clark already had attained notoriety for his stark photography of young male hustlers in the Times Square area in the early 1980s. Times Square traditionally was where young homeless men survived through sex work, and in the 1990s, Ali Forney and his friends were surviving there by similar means. Clark's *Kids* follows a group of young people as they fight, take drugs, steal, get high, hang out, and wan-der aimlessly from noisy streets to empty apartments and then back to the streets, actions typical of many disaffected urban youth with nowhere to go and no place to stay. The movie's plot entails an HIV-positive teenager sleep-ing with and possibly infecting a series of progressively younger and younger girls, even as a former girlfriend halfheartedly tries to find and stop him. One scene graphically depicts a group of white street youth brutally beating a black man with their skateboards in the center of Washington Square Park (the heart of New York's gentrified West Greenwich Village) in the middle of the afternoon, in front of horrified onlookers. Questions of adolescence, masculinity, violence, and sexuality form the heart of the film, which Clark depicts through the everyday actions of street youth in various spaces across the city, from abandoned apartments to crowded public spaces.

The movie strikes a particularly unsettling chord in its audiences, in part because of its themes of lost innocence and senseless violence perpetrated by teenagers. It also perpetuates the long-standing social stereotypes that urban youth are irrational, violent, and out of control. Perhaps most shocking is that for the film, Clark recruited kids hanging out on New York City streets. A *New York Times* article summed up the firestorm of debate in the national media:

> Drawing equal measures of praise and criticism due to its unflinching por-trayal of amoral urban teens, *Kids* sent the nation's parents into a frenzy of paranoia and became one of the first unrated films to receive wide release

and general critical acceptance. With its pseudo-documentary feel and startlingly frank dialogue, *Kids* proved an effective wake-up call to both teens and parents alike regarding such topics as drugs, sexually transmitted diseases, and violence among disaffected youth.[1]

Kids was marketed by its producers as

a deeply affecting, no-holds-barred landscape of words and images, depicting with raw honesty the experiences, attitudes and uncertainties of innocence lost. . . . The kids at the core of the story are just that: teenagers living in the urban melee of modern-day America. But while these kids dwell in the big city, their story could, quite possibly, happen anywhere.[2]

In June 2006, more than ten years after *Kids* was released, *Entertainment Weekly* ranked it as one of the twenty-five most controversial films of all time.[3] What exactly did its audiences and critics mean by a "wake-up call"? How are phrases like "innocence lost" and "urban melee" used to convey how we think of young people and the street in Western society? Where is the "anywhere" associated with the problems with urban street youth? What does the absence of street youth in one locale tell us about their presence somewhere else? The answers to these questions frame how society—and social aid—has evolved in tandem with social constructions of childhood and public space. Moral geographies are entwined throughout our understanding of children and their "place" in society. By constructing particular sociospatial knowledges of the "street" and "youth," children are physically placed on the streets or socially associated with public spaces, and their social identities are "emplaced" in paradoxical constructions of marginalization in urban centers.

Human geographers contend that social subjects are also spatial subjects, that as social beings, people understand the world through grounded and contextual categories. Moreover, places help naturalize social structures and hierarchies by their seemingly stable existence. In the popular lexicon, there is a place for everything, and everything has a place.[4] Places are always both physical and social locations organized through powerful social ideologies. This sociospatial construction is a process of "emplacement." Besides occupying spaces, these spaces make us who we are; that is, we shape and are shaped by complex geographies, as both agents and subjects of places. For example, in Western society, youth occupy a specific location in the spatial ordering of society, so we expect to find children and young people in the private and protected spaces of the home or in regulated, institutional set-tings like schools. Therefore, when social subjects like street kids transgress or resist the sociospatial geographies in the dominant mainstream cultures, they are perceived as "out of place" or disrupting the established social order.[5] But simply by being young—a subjectivity "in place" at home or school but not on the street—street kids occupy an inherently contradictory sociospa-tial position. Street youth are transgressively "emplaced" in public spaces. The questions that the movie *Kids* call to mind can be used to qualify what social theorists and critical human geographers have come to describe as the powerful material indicators that make up the routine organization of everyday lives. The social construction of youth and public spaces is integral to understanding how street youth are mapped onto the margins of society while being situated in the center of public spaces.

Framing Street Youth: Why Are Street Youth Both On and Of the Streets?

Society constructs its knowledge about street youth from their material exis-tence, social settings, public spaces, and political, economic, or religious cli-mates. Thus in order to understand the current intersection of street youth, social services, and public-space regulations in New York City, we first need to understand how these young people have evolved as a regulated social and spatial category. Street youth are sandwiched between two powerful social ideologies—the Street (a subjective place laden with concepts of democracy, civil society, danger, romance, chaos, and social order) and Youth (a sub-jective position encompassing social understandings of innocence, develop-ment, freedom, competencies, potential, hope, and fear). These complicated social understandings of what it means to be young and homeless are then materialized through society's treatment of youth and the social services and public aid offered to "street kids."

Societies create social frames for the structure and understanding of social groupings. Indeed, social frames are so important to how societies func-tion that they often appear to be predetermined, leading to social categories that are accepted as natural.[6] The depiction of street youth in *Kids* reflects the ways in which young people and public spaces are socially bound to one another, constructed and framed by interrelated and evolving social ideolo-gies that depict youth as out of control and out of place in public venues. Street youth, in particular, have been socially constructed in relation to vis-ible forms of disorder, corruption, and impurity that shape and reaffirm the idealized social order of public spaces. Next, by reviewing the literature on street youth, I show how the evolution of a category for them contrasts with the development of contemporary conceptualizations of privatized, structured, and observed childhoods and socially sanitized, orderly public spaces.

When social binaries begin to intrude on each other—when the public is in the private or the private is in the public—our view, as social subjects, is challenged. In this chapter, I discuss how street youth have been framed historically as young people, as homeless, and as subjects of public concern. These frames are tightly bound to their counterframes, or what it means to be adult, housed, and private subjects. The current situation of street youth as simultaneously public (street) and private (youth) subjects is a paradoxical social position that has been reified through artificial boundaries of childhood and adulthood and of public and private. The presence of street youth marks a social fissure disrupting modern Western society's imaginary of itself as orderly and just. Because street youth present a type of social dissonance—a ripple in the social stream—social forces over the years have attempted to dislodge, explain away, reposition, reimagine, and erase them.

Shifting Paradigms of Street Youth

Three major paradigm shifts have influenced the social position of street youth and the interpretation of youth homelessness in Western society. These shifts have been neither smooth nor universal. Rather, competing frameworks of youth have overlapped at critical periods in U.S. history, often sparking debate and more social change. The first paradigmatic era dates from roughly the early 1800s to the early twentieth century and in the United States is generally referred to as the "child savers movement." During this era, a redefinition of childhood, including the place and work of children, reflected the spread of normative middle-class values. This in turn spurred a progressive reform movement in the United States aimed at the children of the urban poor. In many industrializing cities, private philanthropic groups enacted these middle-class social norms by creating orphanages and reform schools and through missionary work. This was also the time period when the highly influential Chicago School of Urban Ecology initiated modern urban sociology using "naturalistic" studies of urban communities. Even though social scientists and social reformers had been studying the city for a number of decades, the Chicago School began a systematic study of urban systems, spaces, and people that had long-lasting effects on theories of delinquency, social disorganization, territoriality, and youth subcultures.[7]

The second major era in youth studies, beginning in the early twentieth century, was the spread of developmental and behavioral sciences and the precedence of the science of childhood over the salvation of children. The psychological development and identity crisis of adolescents were framed in individual growth and life cycles.[8] During this time, concepts such as juvenile delinquency and adolescence, which were partly a result of the earlier progressive reforms, were further developed. The early work of social reformers, mapping a moral geography of working-poor neighborhoods, provided the basis for further research and social interventions.[9] For instance, the Chicago School labeled slum areas as "delinquency areas," which appeared in rapidly growing cities as a natural outcome of social competition and disorganization.[10] Newly arriving African American and Hispanic populations were described by the Chicago School researchers as having residential mobility, weakening social controls, and low participation in social institutions such as schools, which were seen as bulwarks of social order. From this environment of "social disorganization" came youth with few moral boundaries or social limits on their behavior: the so-called juvenile delinquent. Research on delinquency in particular introduced new theories of developmental psychology in regard to young people. In reaction to the rapid social change after World War II, delinquency studies expanded and diversified to include structural theories of youth subcultures, counterculture youth, runaways, and youth gangs.[11]

Beginning in the 1970s and 1980s, a third major paradigm shift grew out of the poststructural theories of agency, empowerment, and the social construction of youth.[12] Poststructuralist concepts have significantly added to and diversified the focus on street youth to encompass varying experiences of childhood and homelessness. In each era, what constituted street youth, where they were located, and what type of aid would be provided to them were determined by hegemonic paradigms of childhood and society.[13] When differing paradigmatic ideologies of childhood overlapped, spaces would be made for both the radical reinterpretation of street youths' social position and creative alternatives to established forms of social welfare.

The social construction of street youth in these various paradigms reflects and interacts with the development of social services and public policies addressing youth homelessness. The current provision of services for homeless youth in New York City today is thus a product of more than two centuries of young people interacting with aid workers, social activists, and the public. These social services also are shaped by national trends and local efforts. Street youth have been constructed through these relationships in a number of ways: as souls to be saved, as dangerous and out-of-control members of society, as hurt and endangered children, and as the unfinished building blocks of future communities.

During each era, ideological discourses of religion, politics and socioeconomic conditions have influenced the framing of street youth. In what sense have these divisions determined who would be considered a homeless youth? How has the social construction of youth homelessness become layered through changing social perceptions of age, class, race, and gender? How does the form and type of aid available to street youth vary according to how they are perceived by academics, policymakers, and the public? And ultimately, how is the history of street youth bound up in the evolving ideologies and development of professionalized social services? These questions are important because changing social constructions of street youth have influenced the development of specific forms of public aid for them—namely, street outreach—by socially and physically locating the phenomenon of youth homelessness both *on* and *of* the street. There is no outreach to a place called "homeless." Each of these aforementioned eras had powerful social agendas that shaped the definition of street youth and how they were treated by society. The goal of this chapter is to denaturalize ideological social assumptions by uncovering some of the evolution of what we—as academics, activists, policymakers, and the public—mean when we talk about youth homelessness and street kids.

The First Era: Immigrant Children and the Child Savers Movement

Before the late nineteenth century, aid to street children in the United States was based on religion and funded through the private philanthropy of only a few people. Figures such as Charles Loring Brace attempted to raise awareness of the plight of working-class children living in industrial cities though the work of organizations like the Children's Aid Society, which he founded in 1853. A "child savers" movement in both the United States and England brought attention to the working-poor children in industrial cities. According to an article in the *New York Times*,

> The philanthropic spirit is not dead, nor slumbering in New York. The wretched condition of these poor children, the days and nights of suffering to which they are exposed, the moral contamination inevitable in their present mode of life, and the hope of rescuing them from the doom of the criminal, or the death of the vagrant, have stimulated the charitable dispositions of the benevolent, and led to the rescue of thousands from a life

of degradation and misery. Self-interest, too, has prompted to active effort to prevent these little vagabonds from becoming permanent depredators upon the community, and hence has aided in the establishment of institutions for their reformation.[14]

During the nineteenth century, the urban poor were physically and socially isolated from the middle and upper classes in growing cities like New York. Street children were regarded as a problem of slum environments. The middle classes were concerned about the future criminality of these "dangerous classes," and their proposed reforms were rooted in earlier fears of vagrant and destitute immigrant groups, which led to their isolation from the rest of society. After the Civil War, much of the rural population in the United States moved to find jobs in the rapidly industrializing urban areas, coinciding with the unprecedented wave of immigrants. The first immigrants from Anglo-Saxon, Germanic, and Scandinavian countries generally transitioned through slum and working-poor neighborhoods in a relatively short time period as they established social and economic capital in their new homeland. But the later waves of immigrants from Slavic, southern European, and non-European countries encountered racism as well as ethnic and religious bias, which isolated them in urban "zones of transition," that is, ghettos, for substantially longer periods of time.

Many nineteenth-century accounts describe the squalor and deprivations faced by new immigrants in neighborhoods such as the Five Points and the Lower East Side of New York. By the 1860s, more than 15,000 tenements (narrow, dark apartment buildings affording little light or air) crowded the working-class neighborhoods of Lower Manhattan. Many tenements housed multiple families on each floor. Because there was little public sanitation available, human and animal waste littered the back alleys and streets, and contagious diseases such as tuberculosis and cholera were rampant and devastating. By 1900, an estimated 42,700 tenements housed more than 1.5 million people in New York City.[15] In that same year, 508 newborn babies were taken in by the city's foundling hospital, 170 of whom were found abandoned on the streets.[16] Foundlings, or abandoned babies and toddlers, were a result of widespread poverty and an increase in destitute women.[17] Sociologists later described the crime and suffering in poverty-stricken immigrant neighborhoods as *social disorganization*. This disorganization resulted from "a breakdown in the ability of families, schools, and other community-based groups and organizations to control deviant behavior"[18] and became the basis for explaining social deviancy and street youth behaviors for the next century.

During the mid-nineteenth century in industrializing countries like England and the United States, urban environments began to be studied from a social-reform perspective, which was committed to social action in the city's slum neighborhoods and the moral improvement of the working classes. Newly formed social science societies in England drew members from the educated middle classes who were concerned with social disorder in the rapidly growing industrial metropolis. This middle-class understanding of urban environments was formed by popular attitudes toward the "dangerous classes," which linked the environmental disorganization and deterioration of slum neighborhoods to moral corruption and social disorder within the working classes. This urban geography of poverty was characterized by overcrowding, malnutrition, and disease transformed into a moral geography of social corruption and contagion.[19] Reformers believed that corrupt environments would create morally corrupt peoples. The exterior spaces of the street and the interior spaces of bars, brothels, and tenement buildings were the fertile soil from which grew street kids: thieves, prostitutes, and beggars. It then followed logically that the only way to stave off moral corruption was to remove young people from the slum environment. In a typical newspaper report from the late nineteenth century, the idea of physically removing low-income and immigrant children from their community was widely accepted. Under the subtitle "Boarding Out among Rural Laboring People" the article agrees that children's natures are malleable and therefore salvageable:

> Those who are brought much in contact with the defective and delinquent classes must often doubt the lasting utility of much of the work that is done for them. It sometimes seems as if in a certain number of cases the principal result attained is provision for the survival of the unfit. If such an opinion occasionally finds voice it cannot apply to children. At this plastic age, the inertia of years of physical deterioration and mental, together with moral, slovenliness has not to be overcome. A change to a new and healthy environment will work wonders, even in apparently forbidding material. Hence, any social work for the saving and reclaiming of children is not only hopeful, but far-reaching in its results. The larger its scope, the smaller will be the future burdens of society from the diseased and incapables.[20]

By casting urban working-class children as at risk of "moral slovenliness," social reformers were able to create a subject and a space accessible to intervention, both socially and physically:

"Moral science" was, therefore, a science of conduct and its relationship to environment, both moral and physical. It paid particular attention to standards of discipline; to the morale of the population. It is in this sense that contemporary social reformers labeled particular sectors of the population "demoralized"; they were beyond the pale of social discipline. The task of "moral statistics"—and social science as a whole—was to measure the loss of control over the laboring classes in general, and particular deviant groups within that population. This would provide a basis for remedial action.[21]

In the United States, and New York City in particular, this "remedial action" came in the form of the Children's Aid Society and later the "orphan trains," which removed children from the city.

Paradoxically, the urban environment was viewed as both a morally corrupting force for young people and a "naturally" degraded living state for immigrant and working-poor communities. In studies of Chinese and other immigrant communities, academic geographers describe the racial and class biases of the nineteenth century as supporting the isolation and poverty of new immigrant groups while simultaneously attributing their subsequently poor living conditions and social confines as natural to peoples deemed morally inferior to the Anglo-Saxon middle and upper classes.[22] Images of filthy living conditions, drug and alcohol abuse, and illiteracy in poverty-stricken neighborhoods that social reformers like Charles Loring Brace or Jacob Riis used in their campaigns were often set in opposition to discourses of democratic, saner, and safer rural landscapes. Their arguments were couched in the language of salvation:

> But after all that the best organized and best administered system of public instruction can accomplish, there will remain a considerable residuum of children (it cannot be, today, in the United States, less than half a million) whom these systems will not reach. Their destitution, their vagrant life, their depraved habits, their ragged and filthy condition forbid their reception into the ordinary schools of people. It is from this class that the ranks of crime are continually recruited, and will be so long as it is permitted to exist. They are born to crime, brought up for it. They must be saved.[23]

The child savers worked to universalize a middle-class social ideal of an extended and protected childhood, which the lives of working-class children contradicted and transgressed.[24]

Charles Loring Brace was one of the most influential social reformers of the nineteenth century. Although his work encompassed a wide range of social issues, his primary calling was to end the plight of impoverished children in New York City. His view of the physical and social living conditions of the working poor—a mixture of pity and condemnation—was shared with the child saver movement. Brace's principal written work was entitled *The Dangerous Classes of New York and Twenty Years of Work among Them* (1872) and reflects the belief that children of the poor would grow up to become future criminals if not taken from their degraded living environment. The following is an excerpt from a chapter entitled "The Life of the Street Rats":

> Seventeen years ago, my attention had been called to the extraordinarily degraded condition of the children in a district . . . called "Misery Row" . . . the main seed-bed of crime and poverty. . . . Here the poor obtained wretched rooms at a comparatively low rent; these they sublet, and thus, in crowded, close tenements, were herded men, women and children of all ages. The parents were invariably given to hard drinking, and the children were sent out to beg or to steal.

During the nineteenth century, children working in these quarters were a common sight in the streets, their labor constituting on average about 20 percent of a working-poor family's income.[25] According to childhood historian Steven Mintz, the children of the working poor were an indispensable part of both family's and the city's everyday public life:

> Poor children participated in the informal economy, selling fruit or matches on street corners and scrub brushes and other household goods door-to-door, or peddling loose cotton, old rope, shreds of canvas and rags, bits of hardware, and bottles and broken glass to junk dealers and to papermakers, foundries, and glassmakers.[26]

Occupations such as scavenging were illegal in most cities, however, so children caught scavenging, stealing, prostituting or deemed to be either vagrant or destitute (homeless) were arrested and placed in an adult prison. In 1823, 450 children in New York City were incarcerated for being homeless. Finally, in 1825 the first House of Refuge opened as an alternative to adult prison for destitute youth. The majority of the more than 500 children housed there in the first few years were charged with vagrancy and petty theft.[27] But the children at houses of refuge and reform schools were still forced to work long days and were subject to harsh physical and emotional treatment. Furthermore, most houses of refuge were located outside urban areas, thereby placing children far from their families and in unfamiliar (and sometimes hostile) rural environments. Not surprisingly, the refuge system suffered from vandalism, arson, and rampant runaways. As revealed in their focus on work, these early refuges and reform schools still subscribed to a social reality of child labor while attempting to incorporate a sense of what was acceptable places and types of work for children. The place of work constituted its moral meaning; that is, street or urban work was morally corrupting, and institutional or rural work was morally reforming. These institutions thus "sought to remove wayward children from the moral contamination of the city and transform them culturally through a regimen of moral instruction, prayer, and physical labor."[28]

By the time these children were in their midteens, their income might equal or surpass that of their parents. In addition to participating in every aspect of the street economy (from scavenging to peddling), children worked in mills, mines, factories, and shops. Even though parents had legal claim to their child's income until the age of twenty-one, many youth managed to gain a modicum of economic power. Because working-class children entered the labor market at a much younger age, they also had more physical, social, and economic freedom than did their middle-class counterparts. Indeed, studies of women's labor extending into the mid-twentieth century often concentrate on the work of young women and the remarkable amount of social freedom and privacy they gained when they migrated to cities and worked in factories, dance halls, and restaurants.[29] Indeed, young people helped support the entertainment and shopping industries through their labor in shops, dance halls, theaters, gambling houses, restaurants, and bars.

For these Victorian social reformers, the sight of youth both working and occupying public domains contradicted their middle-class social norms, which demanded a private, protected, and sheltered childhood. Working children were often mislabeled as orphans simply because at a young age, they were highly mobile across the city and occupied in independent tasks away from their parents. Indeed, children working in public spaces were often informally lumped together under the derogatory label of "street arab." The Victorian linkage of street children with a nomadic "other" associated with xenophobic stereotypes of non-Western cultural groups was common by the second half of the nineteenth century. Writers like Horatio Alger and social reformers like Jacob Riis used this term extensively when describing street children in books like *The Story of a Street Arab* (1871) and the chapter "The Street Arab" in *How the Other Half Lives* (1890). Street children were the subjects of horrified popular imagination, depicted as gangs of wily street thieves in novels like Charles Dickens's *Oliver Twist* (1838) and Victor Hugo's *Les Misérables* (1862). Newspapers in New York frequently ran headlines like "Little Street Arabs" (1869), "Reclaiming Street Arabs" (1883), and "Our Street Arabs" (1870),[30] which documented the growing social concern about street children. In these articles, street children are depicted as objects of pity and disgust, sympathy and fear: "a certain proportion each year of misfortune, crime, indulgence, poverty and death which at once sets those little wanders adrift on the currents of the City streets. The little City Arabs are the accidents of a great city."[31]

Although street children are seen as victims of the industrial city—suffering from poverty, overwork, and exploitation—they are equally regarded as urban predators who picked pockets, swindled passersby, begged, and prostituted. Street children were a social paradox, described as both the victims of the chaos of a morally depraved city and the creators of morally decaying landscapes. Charles Loring Brace was a frequent contributor to newspaper op-ed pages and wrote numerous pamphlets that simultaneously fueled a moral panic over street children and created working-class children as subjects of social intervention. In the following excerpt from a letter to a newspaper, Brace sets up a seeming paradox, that children are working in dire conditions on the streets and yet are at risk of succumbing to petty theft, idleness, and vagrancy:

Other children, who were orphans, or who had run away from drunkards' homes, or had been working on the canal-boats that discharged on the docks near by, drifted into the quarter, as if attracted by the atmosphere of crime and laziness that prevailed in the neighborhood. They slept around the breweries of the ward, or on the hay-barges, or in the old sheds of Eighteenth and Nineteenth Streets. There were mere children, and kept life together by all sorts of street-jobs—helping the brewery laborers, blackening boots, sweeping sidewalks. . . . Herding together, they soon began to form an unconscious society for vagrancy and idleness. Finding that work brought poor pay, they tried shorter roads to getting money by petty thefts, in which they were very adroit.

Brace then associates the corruption of child labor with the moral destabilization of society: "The police soon knew them as 'street-rats'; but, like the rats, they were too quick and cunning to be often caught in their petty plunderings, so they gnawed away at the foundations of society undisturbed."[32]

In this view, children are willing and able to work but are easily seduced by "easy work" or into criminality. Brace and others like him believed in child labor, but of a particular kind; farmwork was seen as physically and morally invigorating, but shining shoes was not. Indeed, the geographic romance of the midwestern yeoman farmer infuses the nineteenth-century debates about urban childhood. Whereas the impoverished city child could only become a "street rat," leading to the dismantling of society, the midwestern farm child would become the backbone of American society, independent, thrifty, and law-abiding.

Nineteenth-century social reformers believed that the only viable solution was to move the most vulnerable and impressionable segments of the population out of the urban environment and accordingly social aid programs moved street youth, young mothers, and the mentally ill from urban environments to rural locations. Brace began a program coined the "orphan trains" that shipped thousands of street youth from New York City out to farming families in the Midwest. It was through the creation of a disgust/pity binary that social reformers were able to convince a middle-class public that street children should be removed from the city for their own salvation. By the end of the nineteenth century, moralistic accounts of abandoned and corrupted children like Stephen Crane's novelette *Maggie: A Girl of the Streets* (1893), describing the street prostitution and eventual death of a young homeless woman; photojournalist Jacob Riis's *How the Other Half Lives* (1890), *The Battle with the Slum* (1902), and *Children of the Tenement* (1903); and Brace's *The Dangerous Classes* (1872), depicting the carnal horrors of the streets led to philanthropic efforts to "save" street children.

The removal of urban children from the streets, their families, and their communities in itself represented a form of early urban revanchism. Part of the effort to impose social order on the diverse urban working-class populations was removing what was considered to be the future subjects of social disorder: the children of impoverished immigrant families. Early social workers constructed street youth as dual sociospatial subjects: pity was linked to the status of child (by means of terms like *little, small, waif*, and *tiny*), and disgust was linked to the status of the street and mobility (by means of terms like *guttersnipe, vagabond, wanderers, arabs*, and *rootless*). These discursive constructions formed a framework that naturalizes a type of spatial revanchism. It was necessary to remove children from the urban street for their own salvation. Despite the reformers' persuasive arguments, however, allegations that the predominantly Protestant social reformers were focusing their efforts on the children of Catholic immigrants, stuck.[33] Such efforts contributed to a rising moral panic concerning the criminalization of the working classes and the perceived chaos of working-class neighborhoods.

Congested living quarters were frequently regarded as a basic cause of not only high rates of sickness and death but also of social disorganization among immigrants. It was long assumed that the behavior in many low-income immigrant neighborhoods was socially pathological and directly related to the breakdown of the traditional social organization of rural people in the impersonal and anonymous social environment of the city.[34]

Reformers used sociological theories of social disorganization to designate immigrant community structures as either ineffectual or illegitimate. Even though immigrant communities did have social networks, they were not necessarily acknowledged or valued by those outside these communities. During a period in U.S. history when social welfare was weak to nonexistent, impoverished communities had to support their members through informal ties to religion and family that encompassed young people. In addition, local social networks that aided this integration were often denigrated. For example, one such structure that integrated young people into local communities was the widespread phenomenon of the street gang; in a 1920s ethnographic study of Chicago's poor youth, one researcher identified 1,313 separate gangs.[35]
Social reformers began competing with informal cultural networks when they tried to assimilate immigrant children into mainstream society. Reformers identified children as a more viable option for reformation than nonnative born adults, whom they felt were already "set in their ways." The focus on children was part of the broader discourses of worthy versus unworthy poor prevalent during the 1800s. Based on their perceived innocence, children were deemed worthy poor.[36] In New York City, groups such as the Children's Aid Society, the Five Points House of Industry, the Five Points Mission, and the House of Refuge were mobilized to aid and, more important, to "reform" slum children.[37] Childhood historian Steven Mintz summed up the sentiment that slum children were an unfortunate outcome of growing cities: "Child-saving was driven by a mixture of hope and fear—by a utopian faith that crime, pauperism, and class division could be solved by redeeming poor children; and a mounting concern over growing cities, burgeoning gangs of idle and unsupervised youth, and the swelling immigrant populations."[38]
In its first fifty years of operation, the Children's Aid Society helped approximately 300,000 immigrant children through food and education programs.[39] These programs were so successful that by the end of the nine-

teenth century, the organizations originally formed to help a broad spectrum of slum residents began to focus solely on children. By the 1860s, the Five Points House of Industry, which began as an institution to aid all unemployed and indigent poor, had changed its focus to concentrate almost solely on unaccompanied children. (At this time, a street youth was generally a younger child below the age of thirteen or fourteen. The concept of an extended period of youth between childhood and adulthood was not yet well developed.) The typical street child of nineteenth-century New York City was portrayed as an impoverished immigrant child who, if not saved from the streets, would become a criminal. An article written by Children's Aid Society founder Charles Loring Brace reflects the view that "the class of street children are undoubtedly the rich bed of soil from which spring a fertile crop of vagrants, prostitutes and criminals.⁴⁰ Another article by a prominent social critic stated that "the little girls selling papers around Printing-House square before very long, if indeed they were not already defiled, they would be prostitutes, thieves and vagabonds."⁴¹ These depictions of street youth set up a binary in which homeless children were discussed with equal measures of pity and disgust, for example, "gathering children from the streets[,] though they are little better at the time they are brought together than bundles of rags and filth and vermin."⁴² In this way, social reformers were able to mobilize philanthropic interest in removing children from not just the streets but also the city itself: "The sure and only way is to strike at the root of the evil and take the child before he becomes immured to vice."⁴³

Several methods were used to assimilate street youth. Physically transporting the children out of slum areas—resituating children both literally and figuratively—was one popular method,⁴⁴ and by the end of the nineteenth century, more than 250,000 children from New York City had been transported by the "orphan train" to foster families across the United States.⁴⁵ Disturbing accounts describe young people being forcibly removed from their families, many of whom were adopted by farming families in need of cheap or unpaid labor. The Five Points House of Industry aggressively sought court orders to remove children from alcoholic parents, but only from families in immigrant and poverty-stricken neighborhoods.⁴⁶ The evolving moral discourses strengthened efforts to "salvage" immigrant children from their perceived natural environment in the slums, on the streets, and from their inevitable future occupation as criminals. These discourses reflect a larger trend in the sociospatial placement of childhood from the public to the private (from the streets to homes or schools) and of children from urban environments to rural environments.

In addition to the reinterpretation of children's social and spatial existence, reformers also focused on street youths' temporal existence. During this time, social reformers voiced concerns over young people working in public spaces at night. Although night has been a negative temporal space for many cultures, it did not become a legally negative time-space for children until around the turn of the twentieth century when cities and towns began to enact curfews for young people. In the early 1900s, child labor laws began to address children working after dark. In 1909, the National Child Labor Committee targeted night-messenger boys in New York City, citing concerns that the young boys who were delivering messages to brothels and bars late at night were being exposed to "unsavory" elements and the vice economy.[47]

Several ideological factors stand out from this time. The first is the widening gap between childhood and adulthood in middle- and upper-class society. In the nineteenth century, the industrialization of Western society saw a general shift to formalized education for middle- and upper-class children that lengthened the time spent in the classroom and put off entry into the adult world.[48] In working-poor communities, the responsibilities of adulthood were still granted at earlier ages: based on need and ability, children were expected to work and help support their families. Urban children in working-poor neighborhoods were able to sweep streets, pick rags, and sort junk metal. Boys worked as bootblacks and newsboys, while girls sold apples, hot corn, or matches.[49] These small but vital industries occupied a large part of immigrant children's everyday lives, and their work made them a staple of the street economy and a common sight on the streets of cities like New York at all hours of the day and night.

In addition to the value of children's labor on the streets, the cramped living quarters and poor sanitation of tenement buildings produced an intensive street life in all forms. Everyday activities such as child care, home economics (laundry, washing, repair work), and cooking that in modern society would be conducted in private spaces were carried out in public spaces. Children were thoroughly embedded in nearly every aspect of street life, and their presence as part of the public—out in the streets—was, conceptually speaking, a new middle-class problem. The child savers movement was part of a larger social process that reframed the moral landscape of the streets on which the children were situated. This new landscape caused young people to be both visibly and morally "out of place" in the eyes of middle- and upper-class social reformers, who saw public spaces as morally corrupt environments and children as vulnerable to moral corruption. The reformers of that time practiced an early form of street outreach when they looked for young people engaged in public activities and employment.

Rather than let children remain in public spaces, progressive reformers tried to save children in private, home environments where they could be closely supervised and protected. This ideological frame led to a widespread child welfare reform movement whose purpose by the end of the century was to remove children from their social position in public spaces. It is ironic that the same social trend that placed young people in private spaces simultaneously deprived youth of the privacy and independence they had previously held in public spaces. At the time, a social historian noted, "The benign motives of the child savers, the programs they enthusiastically supported diminished the civil liberties and privacy of youth. Adolescents were treated as though they were naturally dependent, requiring constant and pervasive supervision."[50] Children previously trusted to work in public settings were now conceived as structurally reliant on adults and were understood as being incapable of performing basic tasks without adult supervision.

Progressive reformers went on to start a universal education movement, implement the first child labor laws, and institute a juvenile court system.[51] Whereas universal education redefined the goals and length of childhood and isolated children into private institutional spaces, child labor laws constructed boundaries around the adult labor market, in order to control and prevent youths' access to work. During this time, the "street child" in need of saving was always a working-class child. Jacob Riis, one of the most vocal social critics of this period, described the increasing numbers of street children as an outcome of widespread poverty:

> In a score of years an army of twenty-five thousand of these forlorn little waifs have cried out from the streets of New York in arraignment of a Christian civilization under the blessings of which the instinct of motherhood even was smothered by poverty and want. Only the poor abandon their children.[52]

For Riis and other social commentators of this time, the living conditions of urban poor children stood in stark contrast to the protected, middle-class child of the Victorian era.

The creation of a universal "childhood" based on Western middle-class norms was only one facet of a rapidly modernizing society. What Michel Foucault called "the development of disciplinary societies" was the creation of new institutions of social control, such as the factory and the school, and the subsequent displacement of work from the home.[53] Socioeconomic shifts resulted in the replacement and revaluation of women's and children's work in Western society. Family, school, and work each were assigned their own spaces, logics, and internal structures.[54] These "spaces of enclosure" isolated and controlled the emerging labor value of the working class through the social encoding of spaces based on age, class, and gender. Controlling the social reproduction of the working class—that is, their children—was an ideologically powerful strategy. Children assimilated into middle-class norms and standards would self-regulate, it was argued, because they would have accepted the moral and ethical standards presented to them as the "right and natural" way of living.

As geographer Tim Creswell explains in his book on space and ideology, "Certain orderings of space provide a structure for experience and help to tell us who we are in society."[55] Therefore, social understandings of street kids are constructed in tandem with an understanding of "the street" as an ideological space. The social division of public and private spaces and children's place within them highlight "the role of place in the construction of ideological beliefs concerning order, propriety, and "normality."[56] These spatial ideologies become apparent only when they are challenged by conflicting cultural values. In this case, the "place" of children was challenged by conflicting cultural norms between middle-class social reformers and working-class families. One way to resolve this cultural conflict was to blame the sociocultural context or environments that these families' children occupied.

Geographers and sociologists have used Pierre Bourdieu's concept of *habitus* to better understand the development of youth behavior and identities in relation to contextual sociocultural structures. *Habitus* refers to the relationship of environments and social structures, such as culture, to the body. For example, the actions of street children can be understood only in the social and cultural context of the streets that they occupy. Their actions and behaviors are reproductive of their social existence. Modern-day researchers and social workers understand that when a street child engages in prostitution or theft, these actions can be interpreted as survival strategies tied to the environment that the child occupies. As Bourdieu stated, however, the *habitus* naturalizes practices that allow "one group to experience as natural or reasonable practices or aspirations which another group finds unthinkable or scandalous."[57] In the late nineteenth and early twentieth century, immigrant working-class families understood child labor to be essential to their economic reproduction. In order for middle-class social reformers to classify street children as "abandoned" and to justify their removal from the streets, they first had to define the street as a morally defiled environment, thereby recasting children's presence there as alien and their bodies corrupt. In this way, the revanchist removal of working-class children from the city on orphan trains was normalized as the only just response to an ideologically untenable situation.

Street youth in this era often were young people legitimately occupied with and valued as working members of immigrant communities. Early street youths' social position, however, did not align with the social position of childhood that reformers were building through an ideology of a universal childhood situated in discourses of innocence and isolation. Although there was no doubt that many children were suffering in New York City's impoverished, working-class neighborhoods, reformers regarded all children found on the streets as being neglected and exploited, rather than considering children's street presence as an integral and valued component of immigrant and working-poor communities. Reformers and middle-class constructions of the "street" and street activity emplaced youth as "out of place" in these environments rather than challenging how sociospatial structures could be used to engage with youth. With the morally suspect landscape of the city streets as their only guide, reformers feared that street youth would develop into the next generation's criminals.

The Second Era: Youth Development, Delinquency, and Subcultures

The concept of delinquency emerged from the efforts of nineteenth-century reformers to control working-class youths' behavior. The child saving movement strengthened the social boundaries between childhood and adulthood in an attempt to protect and alter the treatment of street youth. In doing so, they also helped reify a new social phenomenon of delinquency.[58] That is, young people were considered delinquent when their behavior fell outside the social boundaries defined by middle-class standards for children's behavior. This is an important distinction: At first, delinquency did not necessarily entail the breaking of laws. Dominant groups have the power to define what is deviant by setting social norms: "Power is the ability to make rules for others."[59] When the dominant middle-class society of twentieth century set the rules and social expectations for childhood and youth, they also labeled as deviant those marginal groups who broke these rules.[60] Over time, laws were enacted that pertained specifically to youth behaviors considered to be socially deviant, such as street occupations and night work.

Juvenile Delinquency and Gangs

The discourses of the time reflect the social and spatial positioning of street children as marginal and "other." According to social critics, street youth were, through their social construction as urban nomads, conceptually different from other, home-bound youth:

> The Street Arab has all the faults and all the virtues of the lawless life he leads. Vagabond that he is, acknowledging no authority and owing no allegiance to anybody or anything, with his grimy fist raised against society whenever it tries to coerce him, he is as bright and as sharp as a weasel, which, among all the predatory beasts, he most resembles.[61]

Here again the label "street arab" refers to both these children's mobility and their perceived, marginalized otherness. Labels such as "arab," "nomad," or "vagabond" construct street youth in relation to wider Western geographic imaginations of nomadic and mobile populations. These descriptions are seen simultaneously as abnormal or strange and romanticize the perceived freedom and independence of the street children, linking them to the core social values by which they could be "saved" and turned into "useful" citizens:

> His sturdy independence, love of freedom and absolute self-reliance, together with his rude sense of justice that enables him to govern his little community, not always in accordance with municipal law or city ordinances, but often a good deal closer to the saving line of "doing to others as one would be done by"—these are strong handles by which those who know how can catch the boy and make him useful.[62]

By the beginning of the twentieth century, an evolving industry of professionals was dedicated to redirecting wayward youth: "catching" the children to make them useful. What constituted a "useful" child was changing as well. More recently, social theorists have argued that the creation of an age-based social category of "youth" was actually the beginning of a new social class whose productive activities could be entirely controlled (and exploited) by adult-run societies.[63] For the first half of the twentieth century, new institutions of social control provided outlets for professionals such as doctors, lawyers, and teachers to test and debate, through the medium of youth, social policies concerning the poor, immigrants, and minorities.

By the 1950s, delinquency was linked to working-class subcultures, boys, and urban gangs in the popular media and in the developing fields of youth studies and criminology. Youth gangs were hardly a new social organization. In New York City, ethnically and religiously based gangs of Irish and English youth had fought with each other before and during the Civil War and twice had burned large portions of the city to the ground.[64] What had changed socially was not so much the organization of gangs or the behavior of urban, working-class youth but the middle-class norms that viewed working-class urban youth groupings as abnormal and deviant and therefore delinquent. Social scientist saw variations in crime and delinquency as a result of the breakdown of the community and the absence of social regulation. Delinquent youth were therefore an outcome of social disorganization. This shift in interpretation coincided with changes in thought concerning the origins and behavior of gangs from class and ethnic solidarity to paradoxical discourses of individual pathologies and poor social development linked specifically to working-class youth.[65] These studies also explicitly linked working-class street youth to youth gangs to public inner-city environments while simultaneously moving the conversation away from pressing social issues such as poverty, unemployment, and youth homelessness. Scholars in the mid-twentieth century focused on material indications of social and cultural change, addressing youth gangs and other groupings as "subcultures" marked by their language, style of dress, and music.[66]

The 1950s and 1960s were times of large-scale social transformations in the United States, and several excellent examples of youth street gangs represented in the popular culture of that time speak to the social positioning of street youth, especially in relation to race, class, gender, and public behavior. For example, the musical *West Side Story* (1961) depicts rival street gangs divided by racial and ethnic prejudices. In this film, the members of the street gangs are young white and Puerto Rican men—dubbed JDs for juvenile delinquents—fighting over the control of a New York City neighborhood. Whereas the young men spend their time in conflicts with adults and other youth in the public space of the streets, the young women spend their time in the private spaces of shops, bedrooms, or rooftops, reaffirming the image that working-class public spaces are masculine spaces.

In another work from this time, S. E. Hinton's book *The Outsiders* (1967), a group of working-class "greasers" fight it out with a more affluent gang of young men, the "socials." All the girlfriends of the greasers are described as tough and rude girls, while the young women surrounding the socials are described as pretty and well mannered. For its time, *The Outsiders* was remarkable because its author was a young middle-class woman writing about the experiences of a group of working-class men. Moreover, Hinton was just sixteen when she wrote *The Outsiders*, expressing the experiences and feelings of other young people. The authors of both *The Outsiders* and *West Side Story* depict street youth and youth homelessness; the young characters have few adults in their lives, relying instead on tightly knit networks of friends for survival. Most of the important action takes place in public spaces, and much of the plot entails young people acting out or displaying violent, antisocial behavior and then dealing with the social repercussions of their actions. These works contain a beguiling mixture of graphic street experiences (particularly violence and death) and the romantic imagery of self-reliance and freedom found in earlier accounts of street youth.

Just as fictional works on street youth reflected popular conceptions of urban working-class youth, academic studies of street youth reflected the broader trends in youth studies at that time. During the late 1950s and 1960s, youth studies split into developmental and behavioral psychological sciences, on the one hand, and cultural studies, on the other. Developmental studies featured an adult view of a universal childhood consisting of sets of benchmarks and stages on the way to adulthood.[67] It was during this time that the idea of "adolescence" was conceived as a transitional zone between childhood and adulthood.[68] Children were regarded as unfinished adults, with adolescence the transition time when youth could explore, test, and develop an adult identity, as well as a key time of assimilation into adult society and responsibilities. Residential mobility, family breakdown, and weak community regulation all were linked to antisocial youth development. Again, delinquent youth were constructed as the natural by-product of socially disorganized immigrant and low-income communities. Gangs were not acknowledged as a form of social organization. Not until gang studies again gained prominence in the 1990s were the social-regulating work and community building of urban gangs addressed.[69]

In the 1960s and 1970s, scholars began approaching youth studies using cultural studies of agency and the child's point of view. Much of the early work came from the Birmingham School of Cultural Studies, which focused on post–World War II working-class, predominantly male, youth subcultures like the punks, teddy-boys, mods, and rastafarians in England.[70] Accordingly to these studies, youth were in revolt against restrictive middle-class social norms while still caught up in the social dominance and reproduction of their own working-class backgrounds. William Bunge's classic study of Detroit children was exceptional for the time because it situated young people as central members of a wider community and saw them as actors for social justice in their own right. Rather than being part of a "sub" or marginal culture, Bunge saw youths' actions as being central to society and its reproduction. He was therefore able to speak to young people's understanding of their environment and their rights to community places as *youth* rather than as incomplete adults.[71] This change opened the door for other researchers to examine how children perceived the world around them and, in particular, how they dealt with an adult-centric world and paternalistic structures of social domination.[72] Around this time, academics also began discussing how youth cultures developed in conjunction with, yet remained independent of, adult and mainstream cultures.[73]

During this time, sociologists' renewed interest in gangs and other working-class youth revived the studies of youth labor, culture, and education begun by the Chicago School of Urban Ecology in the 1920s and 1930s. These later studies took a structural approach, however, grappling with the role of environment and the forces of social and economic reproduction on young people.[74] Paul Willis's groundbreaking study *Learning to Labor* addressed many of the concerns of this generation of scholars, by interrogating the intersection of youth agency and bonds of social structure in the reproduction of the working classes.[75] *Learning to Labor* uncovers the pressures and decisions that shape working-class youths' engagement with the socioeconomic structures that ultimately tie them to the working class. In Willis's study, young men who "rebelled" against middle-class norms of education and school labor actually lost opportunities to advance out of the working classes, thereby locking them into reproducing the existing social structures. According to Willis, hegemonic class reproduction is influenced as much by forces of consent by individual actors as by social domination. Similar studies of delinquent urban youth also focused on wider structural and environmental processes thought to create a delinquent youth culture.[76] Although these studies took an interest in youth agency, it was not until the next generation that a critical sociology of childhood complicated structural explanations of youth socialization by challenging the idea of a uniform and universal childhood and class-based identity.[77]

To reiterate, youth were studied through both behavioral/psychological factors and the basic premise of subcultures: that young people formed peer networks with their own internal logics and structures, which in turn influenced and socialized younger children into groupings such as gangs. Modern street-outreach models are based on efforts by social workers in the mid-twentieth century to infiltrate youth gang societies. A common perception in the early to mid-twentieth century was that the social phenomenon of juvenile delinquency existed not because there were "bad" children but because of learned behavior from children assimilating into bad social environments. Children were blank slates that readily adapted to their social surroundings. Because street children were conceptually linked to a perceptually negative space—the urban street—their supposed delinquency was naturalized. Another way in which the delinquent image of urban street youth is powerfully naturalized is in opposition to a related but different social conception, that of the runaway.

Runaways

The 1960s and the countercultural revolution saw increasing numbers of white, middle-class, often suburban, and, especially, female youth migrating to urban areas and living on the streets, in abandoned buildings (squats), or on vacant plots of land. Earlier theories of street youth based on delinquency, subcultures, and gangs and rooted in class, gender, and ethnic divisions could not account for these new arrivals. A related but parallel concept of the "runaway" thus was created. In a popular nonfiction account published in the early 1970s and aimed at teachers and parents, runaways were described as "independent, active, strong-willed. If they are frightened, they hide it well—at least in the beginning. Often, they are intelligent, although intelligence alone may not be enough to prepare a vulnerable teenager for the vicissitudes of city life and the struggle for survival."[78]

In popular publications and media reports, runaways were constructed differently from their fellow urban street kids and street gang peers. Whereas working-class youth were seen as an unfortunate but inevitable part of the urban landscape, runaways were viewed as a burgeoning social crisis: good, middle-class kids sucked into the depravity of city street life. In response, in the early 1970s, the federal government enacted the Runaway Youth Act, which provided funds for local organizations to work with at-risk and runaway youth through shelter, basic care, and counseling. Then in 1977 the act was amended to include homeless youth (local urban youth). New York State adopted this amended act the following year, in which money was put aside for street outreach programs explicitly targeting sexually exploited youth. These early programs were fueled by fears of young, white, middle-class girls engaging in prostitution, despite the fact that many runaways were young men. Although running away was eventually made a crime, and runaways were certainly considered delinquent youth, their behavior and subjectivity were often read in opposition to that of urban street youth. In the past, runaways had been situated in an older social mythology of exploration and freedom that differed from stigmatized forms of nomadism. Now, however, runaways were constructed more like familiar, modern-day Tom Sawyers or Huck Finns rather than as strange or exotic urban bedouins. The moral panic over female runaways changed the social stereotype from that of a boy adventurer to that of a sexually endangered girl.[79]

Many runaways were "summer runners," or seasonal runaways, which seemed to support the idea that these youth were going through a temporary and natural stage in their social development. In 1969, an estimated one million young people under the age of twenty-one ran away, and of these, 50 percent were girls with an average age of just fifteen.[80] By the late 1960s, a widespread moral panic was growing around the increasingly visible numbers of young, white, and especially female runaways living in what were perceived as highly dangerous inner-city neighborhoods. The brutal murder of runaway Linda Rae Fitzpatrick in New York's East Village in 1967, for instance, served to coalesce social fears of the hippie countercultural movement, the sexual revolution and the rising tide of runaways.[81] Then in 1973, police in Houston, Texas, arrested a man who had been systematically picking up young male runaways, raping and murdering them, and burying the bodies in mass graves. Police ultimately discovered twenty-six victims.[82] Due in part to these well-publicized crimes, runaways were formally recognized as a national social problem with the passing of the Runaway Youth Act of 1974, which made it illegal for a young person under the age of eighteen to leave home without parental permission and required parents to report children who had run away. In New York State, a companion law, the Runaway and Homeless Youth Act, was passed in 1978, which encompassed both children who had run away and those who had become homeless for other reasons.[83] In the 1970s, a national juvenile delinquency prevention agency and a national runaway hotline were created, and the rhetoric of freedom-seeking youngsters shifted toward a deeper understanding of the domestic abuse and neglect that were swelling the ranks of young runaways.[84] Social services for runaways began operating in and around neighborhoods popular with countercultural street youth, such as San Francisco's Haight-Ashbury and New York's East Village.

A number of private social service organizations also were founded during this time to aid runaway and homeless youth in New York City. In the late 1960s and 1970s, New York City underwent a fiscal crisis that resulted in substantial disinvestment in state-run social services. Increasing numbers of runaway youth were flocking to countercultural venues in places like the East

Village and commercial-vice areas like Times Square. Indeed, the East Village was becoming nationally known for the large numbers of traveling, hippie, punk, and runaway youth dealing drugs and sleeping on the streets. Times Square was drawing attention for the many young people working publicly in the sex industry, both in peep shows and on street corners. In addition, high unemployment, poor social welfare, decaying schools, and the rampant spread of illegal drugs resulted in a rise in working-class street youth becoming involved in street economies and urban gangs during this time.

Grassroots, community, and faith-based groups began once again setting up drop-in centers, shelters, and work programs for runaway, homeless, and street-involved youth in neighborhoods such as the East and West Villages and Times Square. Just as in the previous era, the most prominent of these was a Christian charity organization. Covenant House, a Catholic charity begun in a storefront by a priest, became the largest private organization working with homeless youth in the United States. By the late 1970s, Covenant House was working with both runaways and what it referred to as "throwaway" urban youth in the East Village and, later, Times Square. Covenant House began a far-reaching fund-raising and education campaign in the late 1970s that significantly shifted the social understanding of youth homelessness away from romanticized images of freedom-seeking youth to images of sexually abused and exploited young people. Covenant House also helped direct street outreach efforts toward youth involved in sex work. By the late 1980s, its annual budget, made up primarily of private donations, was $90 million, far exceeding federal appropriations for runaway and homeless youth programs.[85] Like the House of Refuge in the early 1800s and the Children's Aid Society at the end of the nineteenth century, the work of Covenant House is an important example of the influence that private philanthropy has had on both services for street youth and the public perception of youth homelessness.

Several important concepts evolved in regard to street youth and youth delinquency from the 1950s to the 1970s that still resonate today. In early accounts, runaways were constructed along gender divisions that situated male runaways as adventurous travelers and female runaways as vulnerable sexual victims of urban street environments.[86] Most reports of runaways throughout the 1950s and 1960s described male runaways traveling the rural byways of the United States and described female runaways almost exclusively through morality tales of young women being drawn into dangerous urban settings and prostitution.[87] Finally in the 1970s, graphic depictions of young male hustlers, often selling sex in Times Square, began to permeate the popular media. The author of a mass-produced paperback for teen readers, entitled *Young Hookers*, labels young men as "chickens" and their pimps as "hawks."[88] In one chapter, young men from middle-class New Jersey, calling themselves the "Amboy Dukes," sell sex to older men in the movie theaters of Times Square as a way to fund their own youthful desires for peep shows, bars, and young women:

> In the Dukes' early forays, the movie Johns were just opening festivities for the gang, the weekend source of money. The Dukes supported the unique economy of the Times Square area. Their earnings were immediately reinvested into peep shows, rub parlors, food, porn, bars, discos, hookers, and other neighborhood attractions—sexual and otherwise.[89]

In each chapter of *Young Hookers*, the sexual revolution of the 1960s, the lack of good employment for youth, and a general breakdown of social morality lead many youth down the "wrong path." *Young Hookers* is subtitled *The Truth about the Rising Tide of Child Prostitution in America Today*, thereby metaphorically positioning street youth as a destructive force of nature. Many of the kids in *Young Hookers* sell sex for a "lark" or because it is "easy money," whereas the text graphically describes different subsets of sex work clients, predominantly unattractive older men. The book recreates the social binary of pity/disgust that earlier public depictions of "street arabs" conveyed. Many of the young men and women in this book are suburban youth, products of neglectful families who had found their way to the city and prostitution through youthful ignorance and bad decisions. These geographic imaginaries are important because they situated some kids as more out-of-place and endangered than others and therefore more in need of social intervention. At the end, the author of *Young Hookers* states that

> without assistance from society as a whole so that they may grow and proliferate, these attempts to save our children are small lights in an underworld whose darkness is spreading at a frightening rate and swallowing up those who are least able to do anything about it—the youngest and most vulnerable.[90]

Social work during this time evolved to fit the perceived needs of the most vulnerable segments of the youth population. White youth from nonurban areas were given far more attention than were nonwhite youth from urban areas because they were socially constructed as being at greater risk in a "foreign" environment.

Raced and classed understandings of runaway and homeless youth also constructed and (de)naturalized their emplacement on the streets. White street youth or runaways were seen as having hit the streets by choice, as a result of either political rebelliousness or social acting out.[91] For these kids, the central identifier was active: they had actively run from their "naturally" suburban, housed, loving, and affluent environment to the city streets, where they were endangered and out of place, both physically and socially. The social mythology of the white, suburban runaway was presented in opposition to Hispanic or African American urban street youth, who still were often presented as passively situated in their "natural" environment of slum neighborhoods, criminal activities, and dead-end streetscapes.[92] Sociological theories of the disorganization, breakdown of traditional family structures, poor socialization of youth, and construction of an underclass were used to explain the social positioning of urban street youth and the ever increasing numbers of incarcerated youth of color.[93]

Take, for example, the urban youth/underclass label. Some theorists of social exclusion discussed the unemployed urban poor as an "underclass" or social class caught in a cycle of permanent poverty, state dependency, and, ultimately, criminalization.[94] Many social work organizations seeking out at-risk youth identify street youth of color with underclass domestic environments. The definition of an underclass has changed over time and now is highly contentious in that it has been used politically to undermine social welfare and has supported racist and sexist understandings of poverty by placing the blame for social ills on segments of the urban poor. What is rarely discussed in public debates on poverty is that the taken-for-granted indicators of future social ills are grounded in assumptions of youth and not just race, class, and gender. In particular, underclass studies identify young unemployed males, unwed teenage mothers, and youth offenders as the primary indicators of a developing underclass, effectively blaming marginalized urban youth for broader systems of social breakdown.[95] Underclass debates position street youth between stereotypes of individual choice/agency and social/structural inequalities that constrain opportunities to succeed.

In summary, in this second era, urban street youth and street youth of color were constructed through the lens of deviancy and the youth gang. Street youth of color in particular were framed as innately urban, deviant, and violent. Although social services for suburban runaways were organized in the 1960s and 1970s around ideas of aid and counseling, the responses to urban street kids still were often situated in a discourse of criminality, reform, and punishment. These social divisions are important because during the twentieth century, the state accepted more responsibility for homeless youth. The state created, regulated, and funded social programs situated in what constituted common knowledge concerning a runaway, homeless, or street youth. These "knowledges" were grounded in geographic imaginaries that linked young people to moral landscapes conceived through differences in urban and rural spaces. These links between knowledge and social placement serve the "powerful role of social interests in shaping dominant beliefs."[96] Situating street kids in relation to the streets speaks of the proper place of young people and the materialized moral structure of society. How they moved through and between different spaces is erased in a moral framework that considers youth homelessness to be a social problem explicitly located on the streets. As we enter the twenty-first century, social workers and social programs are still struggling with histories of street youth that artificially divide and locate young people into one group or another and into some spaces and not others. Social-spatial divisions of street youth are still resonating in the public consciousness and have materially structured the type and manner of social services available to all street youth.

The Third Era: Street Kids and Youth Geographies

What demarcates many contemporary social science studies of street youth from earlier studies of runaways, gangs, deviancy, and subcultures is the turn away from a generalized homeless youth (or runaway youth or gang member) to a focus on social processes and the everyday contextual experiences common to street youth. Recent studies address diversity within the larger population of street youth by attempting to understand the processes—such as poverty, social isolation, familial abuse, and the breakdown of state or foster care systems—that serve as structuring media for the phenomenon of youth homelessness.[97] These studies parallel similar changes across youth studies, which have shifted to emphasize youth agency, processes of youth identity formation, and the social construction of childhoods.[98]

Contemporary studies attempt to uncover how social opportunities are structured for and by street youth before they become homeless, during their homeless careers, and after (if) they leave homelessness.[99] Other studies have developed knowledge of youth homelessness by observing and discovering how street youth create families and routines through the everyday spaces and situations encountered on the streets.[100] For example, studies have addressed the formation of street families that both reflect and resist conceptions of home and family.[101] In a recent study of San Francisco street youth, researchers found significant differences in African American and Caucasian youths' homeless behavior and survival strategies.[102] Street outreach workers in New York City have long noted that at-risk youth approach homelessness differently, depending on how their home communities understand homelessness and the various stigmas attached to homeless behaviors such as panhandling. Street kids often understand and interpret social stigmas attached to homelessness in different ways.[103] For instance, middle-class, white, homeless youth from suburban environments often panhandle (or "spange"), whereas African American youth from urban neighborhoods shun this activity as being too demeaning or shameful. Everyday situations on the streets may involve contact with homeless adults, other youth, police, the public, or social workers that can tell researchers a lot about how street kids understand their subjectivity in relation to contexts beyond homelessness and the streets.

Contemporary studies of street youth follow current trends across the social sciences that call for increased understanding of agency, ethics, and activism in research with marginalized or vulnerable populations, especially children.[104] The implementation of university IRBs (internal ethics review boards) restrictions significantly affected urban ethnographies with marginalized or deviant populations.[105] Today, current research has renewed its emphasis on gaining youths' permission and respecting their empowerment. By valuing and showing young people's alternative visions of the world, these studies have begun to highlight the marginalization of youths' voices in certain environments, particularly public spaces.[106] Many studies highlight young people's exclusion from design and decision-making processes; the criminalization of public activities popular with kids, such as skateboarding; the control of young people's access to public spaces through curfews; and a variety of youths' transgressive and resistant readings of public venues.[107]

Youth empowerment has also opened the door to street youths' voices found in both popular and academic literature. Larry Clark's film *Kids* is powerful and profoundly disturbing because Clark himself had been a young male hustler in Times Square in the 1970s and because many of the street kids in his film used their own voices and language to describe each scene. Other accounts of youth homelessness have been published by former street kids themselves. For example, in *Runaway: Diary of a Street Kid*, Evelyn Lau compiled the journals that she kept while she was a young runaway in Vancouver, British Columbia. She describes with brutal honesty the everyday experiences, people, and places that created her identity as a street kid. It was often the mundane moments—getting on a bus, a stranger offering help, or passersby ignoring her that profoundly affected her understanding of her own marginality and her ability to survive the streets emotionally:

> A curious thing happens when the bus comes. Watching it stop, I wonder for a split second if the driver will let me on, knowing I'm a prostitute. The sudden degradation is tremendous. The passengers stare as I find a seat near the back entrance; there are no more seats on the bus except the one beside me, yet the people that file [in] ignore it. The man who eventually sits down hesitates, standing and approaching, then stopping, then sitting. . . . Two boys hopping onto the bus grab the seats behind me, and to my horror I hear one of them saying, "No, she's not," and then the other laughing knowingly, "Yes, she's a hooker," and afterwards when I turn around they are staring at me.[108]

The feeling of being ignored and watched, exploited and neglected, are common themes in Lau's memoir and many others.[109] Organizations that work with sexually exploited youth commonly collect youths' narratives and oral histories, recognizing that children's documenting of their own daily life and experiences is empowering and creates a critical description of street life. Lau's experiences of childhood challenge the social understanding of a universal, safe, and protected childhood in Western society.[110] Images of privileged Western childhoods often sit in opposition to underprivileged and exploited childhoods from non-Western countries. Social perceptions of childhood serve to locate youth homelessness as a problem of the Global South while simultaneously obscuring its presence in developed nations.

The surge in international research on street youth has allowed scholars, policymakers, and activists to begin speaking of youth homelessness as a global phenomenon created by economic and political systems of exploitation and exclusion.[111] Research indicates that the global population of street youth is in excess of 100 million,[112] due to various factors from urbanization and poverty to famine, wars, epidemics, and natural disasters. International research with street youth has accordingly highlighted the need for more culturally sensitive and contextual understandings of childhood, family, home, and the streets.[113] Social scientists have productively expanded on social theories of agency and *habitus*[114] to better understand the complexity of street youths' worlds:

> Thus it is now generally acknowledged that children actively construct their worlds, and that street children's worlds cannot be distinguished by

a simple division between "home" and "street," but rather with respect to several "domains." These include public and private spaces; institutions such as the justice and police systems; government and civil society programs; groups of adults such as street educators, market vendors and other street workers; as well as such varied "inside" spaces as prisons, orphanages, cinemas and shopping malls.[115]

In both the United States and internationally, the rise of HIV/AIDS has brought funding for research with street youth. Because this research money has specific policy goals in mind, the research funds are directed at a particular slice of street youths' experiences (sex work, sexual abuse, and health), usually conducted through large-scale, statistically based studies using behavioral, medical/psychological models. Within this body of research, ideas concerning deviancy, delinquency, and behavior modification based on earlier studies may still appear. Much of the behavioral studies literature paints a generalized portrait of street youth as victims of poverty/neglect or as deviant/criminal,[116] what geographer Gill Valentine termed the "angels" versus "devils" bipolarity of youth studies.[117] The ideas of the "child savers" from earlier eras still resonate in the delinquency literature. In 1985, a scholar studying female juvenile prostitution stated at a public meeting in Oregon that the local community would be better served by "stay[ing] away from adult prostitution and put[ting] all of its energy into the kids. Because we can do something there."[118] Youth are not just "savable"—they also are more easily controlled through their everyday spatiality in ways that would violate the basic rights of the adult population. Youth can be the subjects of detainment, exclusions from public spaces, and curfews more readily than adults can. For example, after a recent African American youth "flash mob"[119] in Philadelphia, local police threatened to

step up enforcement of a curfew already on the books, and to tighten it if there is another incident. They added that they planned to hold parents legally responsible for their children's actions. They are also considering making free transit passes for students invalid after 4 p.m., instead of 7 p.m., to limit teenagers' ability to ride downtown.[120]

Curfews and movement restrictions typically are imposed on the adult population only in times of extreme disaster, 9/11 and Hurricane Katrina being recent examples.[121] But children are not full citizens, and their rights are limited in a number of ways, from legal social pressure on parents to curfews and transit restrictions. Moreover, these restrictions do not take into account the many legitimate reasons for youth to occupy public spaces for work and leisure or their rights as citizens to access public spaces. Once these regimes are in place, a teenager downtown in the evening becomes a person out-of-place.

What is particularly noteworthy about both large-scale quantitative studies and the few small-scale qualitative studies that form the current research on street youth is the continued linkage of public space and young people to the phenomenon of youth homelessness. Despite all the evidence that the experiences of street youth involve complex intersections of gender, age, race, ethnicity, class, and sexuality interacting within both public and private spaces, there seems to be a need for ever finer demarcations of "youth" and the "street" evolving in the literature. Several recent studies have organized their subjects of study based on a relatively new division of youth who are *on* the street, as opposed to youth who are *of* the street.[122] The on/of the street division has been used by researchers in South America to account for street youth who worked in the street economy and spent most of their time on the streets but still lived with their families. These young people were on the street because of their daily activities but were not considered of the streets in that they did not identify as homeless. In contrast, street youth who were "of" the street were living on the streets and were assumed to be active in the street economy. While it is good that scholars across many disciplines are addressing environmental contexts—the geography of street kids—they also are limiting their scope by defining which youth meet the criteria for homelessness.[123] Divisions within youth homelessness become critical when they are integrated into public policies on homelessness and structure funding for social services. In a neoliberal environment of increasing competition for funds and accountability in the form of quotas, nonprofit social service providers are under immense pressure to "account" for which youth they serve.[124] Accountability often takes the form of strict guidelines concerning which youth are "really" homeless and therefore eligible for aid. In this way, homeless youth are constructed through the needs of social services to account for their time, money, and practices.

In the United States, similar divisions are gaining popularity as well. Recent studies have tried to separate street kids who sleep on the streets from those who use shelters.[125] Others have created divisions according to tenure in relation to the street, not homelessness (long-term street youth versus new runaways or couch surfers) and public versus private space occupations (those who panhandle versus those who sell sex).[126] The majority of these studies focus on street youths' relationship to the streets in some manner, whether as victims or aggressors, initiates or initiators to the street environment. Research that challenges static binaries is evident in recent work with street youth that combines critical ethnography and memoir. Critical ethnographies of street youth have lately created an opportunity for more of their voices to be heard, albeit through the auspices of academic writing.[127]

The majority of these studies collected data either in the institutional spaces of drop-in centers, schools, clinics, and shelters or through the medium of trained street outreach workers. Despite the assertion that "street children and street activities are by their very nature visible," for researchers and social workers alike, finding street youth on the street presents myriad challenges.[128] More researchers are turning to peer street outreach workers to gain access to street youth populations in public spaces. To date, studies that use street outreach to access data and that call for additional street outreach in policy recommendations do so without addressing the socially constructed history of street outreach or the role of outreach workers in interpreting and defining youth homelessness.

In sum, private and public aid to homeless youth has evolved in conjunction with socially contextual and evolving perceptions of what it means to be "young" in Western society, especially in relation to their place in public. These frames have often set street youth apart from the rest of the homeless population (adults, women, families with small children) and from other youth. These divisions have become increasingly important over time because they have shaped the interpretation and mobilization of aid for street youth. Services for homeless youth have developed and now are socially situated in relation to how street youth were framed in each era. The deployment of powerful, apparently immutable, social binaries is realized in the structuring and provision of social services for homeless youth.

While street youth and social services have long been conceptually yoked together, urban environments and street youth activities have often changed more rapidly than social paradigms of youth or social service provision to street kids. All three conceptual paradigms of street youth and youth homelessness that I have discussed here are active in contemporary social services. The institutionalization of social services has hampered the ability of social workers to adjust services and programs in response to changing urban contexts. The competitive nature of funding for social services today and the general neoliberal trend in social work often have complicated communication and collaboration among different organizations. The need to account for funding also has limited the flexibility of outreach groups to decide which youth are in need of services.

Throughout history, institutional social services have lagged behind social change and the needs of street youth. One benefit to current trends in social services has been the emergence of new and innovative nonprofits. The use of social entrepreneurial models and creative partnerships between private industry and nonprofits has created some opportunities for homeless youth not typically found in state-run social service systems. An example of this is the work of the Reciprocity Foundation in New York City, which seeks "to enable homeless and high-risk youth and young adults to permanently exit the social services system and start meaningful, sustainable careers."[129] By trying to create strong social and professional networks for youth, this organization is breaking from traditional social services that often place young people in low-paying careers with little financial stability. Youth in this program have gone to college and obtained jobs and internships with Fortune 500 companies. One of them even was the first transgendered contestant on the popular TV show *America's Next Top Model*. Another young person obtained an internship with a leading clothing designer. These kinds of opportunities are vastly different from the traditional social service model that pushes youth to take any paying job, regardless of their skills, dreams, and desires.

The Reciprocity Foundation's website states: "We understand that homelessness and poverty cannot be solved solely within the public sector. As such, the Reciprocity Foundation operates as a 'bridging organization' that helps youth connect to creative professionals, leading corporations and academic institutions as partners on their journey to building a meaningful career." By placing social services at gateway points to wider social networks, some organizations are effectively altering how social aid works:

> We believe that one of the root causes of chronic homelessness is related to one's isolation from society. As such, our curriculum is co-taught by industry professionals who mentor and coach the youth throughout their transition from homelessness to independence. These individuals also form the youth's core network as they advance their career and educational goals.

Programs like the Reciprocity Foundation are seeing great success in their work with homeless youth. In a competitive financial environment, however, these programs are generally small and have limited resources. In addition, the people who run innovative social services are often unpaid or under-paid because neoliberalization has shifted the financial burden of social ser-vices away from states and onto the shoulders of a few individuals willing to volunteer their time and effort. Their work often receives little fanfare or acknowledgment, further erasing the cost of addressing youth homelessness.

Currently, New York City street youth are caught between two isolating processes: mobility and social invisibility. Mobility, invisibility, and their combined outcome of social erasure are processes imposed on young people. Mobility and invisibility also are individual coping strategies used by street youth and present challenges for social workers attempting to find and con-nect with them in a variety of settings. The form and type of aid available to street youth have varied according to how youth homelessness is perceived by society and how street youth occupy public spaces and homelessness. These ideologies have set street kids apart from the rest of the homeless pop-ulation, from other kids, and from the communities in which they exist. In the next chapter, I tell the story of one street youth in New York City and dis-cuss how the social construction of youth homelessness and social services has intersected with his experiences.

Blacc, a Street Kid from
Far Rockaway, Queens

When you take the A train from Manhattan to the easternmost reaches of New York City, you have a one-in-three chance of ending up in Far Rockaway. Winding along metal rails set high above the neighborhoods, the elevated A train takes you over a seemingly endless landscape of brick houses, rusting gas stations, and weed-filled lots. Eventually the tracks split, with one long prong heading out toward the Atlantic Ocean and the Rockaway peninsula. Pe ched on the far edge of Queens, wedged between the flat, gray waters of the ocean and the affluent suburbs of Nassau County, Long Island, Far Rockaway is familiar to most New Yorkers only because its name adorns the side of the A train rumbling through more affluent parts of the city. Far Rockaway feels like a world away from the tourists and skyscrapers of Manhattan, yet this is New York City as well.

Over the years, Far Rockaway has changed from neighborhoods consisting primarily of Orthodox Jews and Irish Catholics into more ethnically diverse, working-class communities of African and Central Americans. The gentrification that has transformed some Queens neighborhoods has not reached Far Rockaway. Despite the occasional decaying mansion, the more common sight of multifamily, two-story homes—flat facades covered in weathered wooden clapboard or cheap vinyl siding and surrounded by chain-link fences—are what define the character of the many narrow side streets. As you near the ocean, the smaller homes give way to tall, blocky public housing projects that stand like sentinels staring out over dry marsh grass and gravelly sand. Like many other working-poor neighborhoods in New York City between the 1970s and 1990s, Far Rockaway went through severe periods of unemployment, rising crime, drug use, community breakdown, and physical decay. Thus when Blacc was born to a young single mother in 1985, Far Rockaway was an aging, inner-city neighborhood, far from the heart of the city.

In recent years, popular accounts of homeless youth in New York City have focused on young people who have traveled across the country (usually from California or Florida) and who have ended up living on the streets in Manhattan.[1] These accounts usually center on young people who are part of the "visibly homeless" population, those sitting in parks with all their possessions, dirty looking and panhandling passersby for coins. In reality, though, the average homeless youth in New York City is from one of the five boroughs[2] and rarely looks homeless, in either appearance or behavior. Studies of street youth in several cities across the United States have shown that the majority of homeless youth are "local," despite the visibility of traveling youth and the social image of urban nomadism.[3] In New York, most street youth are from poverty-stricken neighborhoods throughout the city[4] much like Far Rockaway, neighborhoods situated on the fringes of Brooklyn, Queens, the Bronx, and Staten Island. In New York City, about two-thirds of street kids are youth of color, usually black or Hispanic, and range in age from about twelve to twenty-four.[5] They travel the subways into Manhattan to seek friends, find work, escape families and problems, and find help.

Blacc is one such youth. His trajectory into homelessness and his experiences once on the streets and in shelters are typical of street kids' coping mechanisms and behaviors in the broader public, private, and institutional systems. Homeless youth rarely spend all their time "on the streets." Instead, they can be found in many different spaces in the city, and they organize their behaviors and practices both through and in spite of the circumstances of their everyday lives. For the sake of clarity, I tell Blacc's story chronologically, from his early childhood to the present day, in part to highlight the common trajectory of youth homelessness that others have identified in numerous studies[6] of prehomeless conditions, socialization into street life, and engagement with social welfare. A linear narrative also shows how the layering of experiences has brought Blacc to where he is today: a young man who is a competent youth worker and yet who still faces a potential future as a homeless adult.

The Prehomelessness Years

Blacc spent the first five years of his life being shuttled between foster homes. "My mom . . . my biological mom was in Far Rockaway. She had my little brother and my little sister and another one on the way. It was kind of crazy for her." Blacc and his next youngest brother lived in a dozen foster homes. Although Blacc saw his mother from time to time, usually during his moves between foster homes, her appearances followed no logic. "Yeah. She used to come by regularly to give me an ass-whupping for no reason." But he never lived with his mother again, and when he was eleven, she died of cancer. "It's kind of funny 'cause sometimes I hear her call my name or something like that. It's spooky." For Blacc, the few memories that stand out from these early years are the death of a neighbor's child and the closeness that he felt toward his own brother.

Blacc is perhaps unusual compared with other street youth in that he and his siblings were adopted and thus left the foster care system at a young age. Experiences with foster care are a point of connection for many homeless kids. In fact, being a foster child is so common that many of the drop-in centers for street youth gather foster care data as part of the initial intake interviews for entering their programs. Statistically, one in four children who age out of foster care in the United States become homeless within four years,[7] and in the United States, 20,000 to 25,000 young people age out of foster care every year.[8]

In 1990, a couple from Far Rockaway who had known Blacc's mother from the neighborhood adopted Blacc and his four younger siblings. Blacc lived with this family for the next fourteen years, starting and finishing school, making friends, learning to fight, and growing up in their home. Despite the instability of his early childhood and growing up in a community beset with socioeconomic problems, Blacc does not think of himself as a troubled or troublesome kid:

> I would never take off for days at a time. It's just . . . I missed a night once or twice, something like that. But it wasn't like I was a delinquent. I always did go to school, except for when I was misbehaving or something like that. My grades were always good in school . . . then high school, I guess that's when I really started to fight. Because in junior high school I was still a punk. My friends were like: "You know we're not always going to be there for you, you need to know how to protect yourself." From that day on, I started to defend myself . . . I was pretty good at it.

Studies have shown that homeless youth often had trouble in school and at home before becoming homeless.[9] Indeed, Blacc's statement that he "missed a night once or twice" is indicative of kids who are creating an emotional and physical distance from their families before either running away or being kicked out. School is often where at-risk kids can get help from adults, but only if they are recognized as being at-risk. In Blacc's case, his own determination kept him in school until graduation:

I finished high school. Even though I had a dean and she told me in front of my mother: "You're really never going to graduate from high school." From that day on, I was like "Really?" And I proved her wrong. It was just something that I felt I had to do.

When Blacc was nineteen, he had a series of arguments with his adopted mother over his lifestyle and lack of paid employment:

I was acting. I had just finished doing a show—*The Dissenters*. I wasn't working . . . I was just acting, but I wasn't getting paid for it. Which was my mom's biggest thing: "You don't have a job . . . you're coming in at one or two o'clock in the morning. Sometimes you don't even come in . . . it's taking up all your time." Stuff like that. So just a lot of bitching. . . . So one Sunday, we had an argument.

That particular argument was the last; afterward, his father kicked him out:

My father said, "You have thirty minutes to pack your shit and get out of here." Shit, OK. And that was just it. I could have begged, but I was like "I'm not going to beg no more to stay in his house. . . ." So I packed my shit and I left.

When Blacc was kicked out, he was nineteen, but the age limit separating a homeless youth from a homeless adult varies. Although street youth rarely hang out with significantly older homeless people, it is not uncommon for some members of street youth groups to be in their midteens to mid-thirties. Indeed, these kids' connections to other street youth are often a stronger identifier of being young and homeless than is their actual age. For street kids, "life on the street is often intensely social."[10] In contrast, studies of homeless adults highlight the extreme isolation of homelessness.[11] Studies of homeless youth often base their participants' cutoff ages on legal age limits for social services or ethical (informed consent) regulations, which have little to do with how street youth conceive of their own transition from childhood to adulthood.

The age limits of social service programs usually are based on a combination of funding criteria and government regulations. Many programs work with kids from twelve to twenty-four, although the cutoff age for some is sixteen, eighteen, or twenty-one, depending on the services they offer and the regulations of their funding sources. The different programs' inconsistent age limits are confusing for both street youth and social service providers attempting to connect them to services. Many young people do not seek out services until they already have reached the cutoff age. As one young homeless woman told me,

> When I turned twenty-four, I aged out of almost every program in the city [for youth]. . . . The moment you turn twenty-four . . . you don't suddenly just find yourself in an apartment in the Village with a little dog and a great job where you can sit at a desk. I wish. It's not happening. They don't just hand you a key to a nice loft. I get why they do it, but there are still people like me who are falling through the cracks.

Age limits are particularly frustrating to street outreach workers, in that it is difficult to gauge a young person's age, especially for those who have been on the streets for several years and whose appearance often makes them look much older than their actual age. Street kids have an incentive to lie about their age, both to escape attention from police and to gain age-specific benefits from social service programs. Inconsistent age limits also can result in young people's being transferred from social service programs and shelters as they age out of services. Every change in program means a new case manager and, more often than not, a loss of information (due to confidentiality laws). Moving kids from place to place usually means losing progress through the social service system. In sum, age limits present an obstacle for a continuum of care, a problem that Blacc repeatedly had over the next two years.

Again, street kids are often portrayed as urban nomads—sleeping under bridges or in abandoned warehouses—not knowing anyone, taking too many drugs, and losing themselves in the city's "mean streets." This representation, however, presents a spatially and socially static portrait of street youth: they are either "on" the street or "off" the street. This simple binary and its accompanying stereotypes make it difficult to understand the complex, subjective experience of being young and homeless. Street youth can experience many forms and levels of homelessness, from staying with friends and/or relatives to sleeping in cheap hostels, squats, shelters, bus stations, parks, and many other locations. A study of street youth in a West Coast city reported that two-thirds of those surveyed had been homeless more than once, and one-quarter had been homeless more than ten times.[12] In each episode of homelessness, a youth may stay in many different places in quick succession. What connects these young people is their unstable living situations, their lack of opportunities and resources, and their vulnerability to violence, illness, and exploitation (especially in connection to the street economy), and, most important, their nearly total invisibility while homeless.

Homelessness and Socialization into Street Life

African American, six feet tall, and burly, Blacc may not fit the media stereotypes of homeless youth, but his is the face of youth homelessness in New York City today. When I first met Blacc in 2006, he was twenty-one and had been homeless for two years.[13] Between the ages of nineteen and twenty-one, Blacc had moved nearly twenty times. He first stayed with his sister and her boyfriend's family, until overcrowding soon pushed him to live with a friend's family. He quickly moved from there to stay with another friend, whose house later burned down. At that point, having no other options, Blacc remained in the burned-out house, followed by a short stint in a studio apartment with three other people. He then lived on the subway, in a youth shelter, in an adult men's homeless shelter, back on the subway, at an overnight youth center, at a youth emergency shelter, in Times Square, back to the first youth shelter, in a transitional living center for homeless boys, back to the emergency shelter, in Union Square, on rooftops, in empty U-Haul trucks, at a GLBTQ youth shelter, at a gay-friendly church shelter, back to the first GLBTQ youth shelter, and, finally, in 2006, in a transitional living program for GLBTQ homeless kids.

When I met Blacc, he was working as a peer educator and outreach worker for a GLBTQ drop-in center in Midtown Manhattan. I had been hired by the center to train peer youth outreach workers through my ongoing research on street outreach. Amid the crowds of young people pouring in and out of the drop-in center during the day, Blacc stood out because of his calmness. He takes his time when speaking, often measuring his words thoughtfully and carefully. "Blacc" is the name that he chose for himself when he first became homeless.[14]

Becoming homeless is rarely the result of a single, isolated event; instead, a wide variety of events and circumstances can lead to a life on the streets. Youth homelessness often evolves as a series of progressively more tenuous living and housing arrangements. Researchers working with homeless youth have discovered how a progressive engagement with street life, street networks, and street economies determines how and/or when young people come to live on the street.[15] This engagement usually begins with brief stays away from home, extended time spent on the street gaining street friends, becoming involved with street economies and supportive networks, and living with friends or tangential family members (couch surfing).[16] Studies have shown that the longer and more sustained a young person's engagement is, the more likely he or she will experience multiple episodes of homelessness.[17] This was Blacc's experience, too, for after being kicked out by his father, Blacc first went to live with his sister.

> I was living with my sister . . . her boyfriend is a jackass. He's a big-time thief. A very big-time thief. He used to steal cars and sell the rims. Stuff like that. . . . [The police] raided the house and whatnot. Because he beat up a sanitation officer. Half the things that went on in the house, I didn't know about because I was staying with my sister sometimes and then I wasn't staying there sometimes. Because his family was very arrogant toward me. Me and his cousin were like really, really cool. But his other family was, like, obnoxious.

Immediately after leaving his parents' house, Blacc's living situation became tenuous, at best. Not surprisingly, street youths' earlier experiences with domestic conflict and the process of leaving home help determine their subsequent living situations and relationships. Still in Far Rockaway at this point and living only a block from his parents' house, the feeling of being an unwanted guest led Blacc to spend more of his time with friends and their families. Next, he moved in with two different friends, still out in the Rockaways.

> I stayed with another friend. . . . I celebrated Christmas at my friend's house and that was the best Christmas I ever had. There was no gifts. . . . It was just very fun. We woke up and had a water fight. It was cold as shit, but we had a water fight. I think that's like the best day I've ever had that was actually celebrating something. Out of birthdays and Christmases . . . that was the best day, that water fight. I tell people that to this day and they're like, "How can you have a water fight on Christmas?" But what else was there to do? You're a bunch of poor people. So you have a water fight . . . it was good. But after a while, I didn't want to intrude on their space and then my friend started going out with this girl.

During this time, a physical altercation with a man who had assaulted one of Blacc's friends resulted in Blacc's being arrested. After he was released from jail, he moved in with a different friend. That, too, lasted only a short time.

> He [the friend] left the house to go get some money from his father one night. And his father called him gay. Because me and him was sharing . . .

like sleeping in the same room and whatnot. And his father and was like "chi-chi mon" . . . he was Jamaican. So he took out a blade and he was cutting his father up.

After this incident, Blacc's friend set fire to the house where they were living. "Yeah, because he thought his father was going to call the police. It was me, him, two other roommates. So he did that craziness. . . . I could have been asleep when he did shit like that."

For several nights, Blacc and his friends went on living in the burned-out shell of the house. Then one of the girls who had been displaced by the fire was able to get a small studio apartment and invited Blacc and his girlfriend to stay with her.

I was staying with a friend. Actually she became my friend after the friend that I was living with burned down the house. So we was actually living in the burned-down part. Then her landlord helped her get a studio temporarily. She was like, "You can come stay with me." So at the time, it was freezing cold . . . there was two inches of snow on the ground, so I was like, "Fine with me." It was me, her, her boyfriend, and my girlfriend. So she accepted me and my girlfriend. She looked after me. I'll never forget her name. It was Melissa. She was a struggling artist. She brought us both in. So we stayed there about a month or two. Then he [the landlord] locked us out. He knew that me and my girlfriend were staying there, and he locked her out of the place. . . . But he didn't give her any warning that he was going to lock her out.

That night, Blacc and his girlfriend, along with Melissa and her boyfriend, tried to get into a homeless shelter in Brooklyn. But homeless shelters admit people as individuals, not as family groups (with the exception of mothers with minor children), and are separated by gender. Although most shelter workers understand that street youth form strong familial relationships with one another, there are no supportive structures for keeping street families together in institutional settings. Because Melissa was pregnant and did not want to be separated from her boyfriend, the couples decided to stick together[18] and opted to sleep on the train instead.

We went to this shelter. I forget the name of it . . . it's in Brooklyn. And she was pregnant at the time so she didn't want to leave her boyfriend. And I'm allergic to cats and there was a cat running around the dorm room. So we left there . . . we all decided to leave. So we slept on the train that night.

When Blacc and his friends left the shelter, they decided to ride the same A subway train that runs through Far Rockaway. As one of the longest subway lines in New York, the city's homeless population sometimes refer to the A train as a moving hotel. From its start in Far Rockaway, the A train travels through three of the five boroughs (Queens, Brooklyn, and Manhattan) before it turns around and makes its way back, nearly two hours from end to end.

> That was the only [subway line] I knew at the time . . . like the back of my hand. So I was like "I'm not going to stray from it." . . . So we slept on the train that night. During the day we had separate business to take care of and we were supposed to meet up, but we missed each other.

Street youth have a difficult time keeping contact with one another. Although many use prepaid cell phones and the Internet to stay in touch, when they do not show up at a prearranged meeting point, there is almost no way for their friends to find them. As a result, many street youth spend a large portion of each day finding, missing, and losing their street friends. Outreach workers are often used as contact points and informal message carriers for street kids. Blacc searched for his friends for several days, going back to the first shelter and searching at a local adult Christian shelter. While he was at the Christian shelter, the staff there contacted a volunteer group that helps the homeless. By then, he had heard that his friends were at an adult shelter, but he thought he was too young to get into it. The volunteer group eventually took him to the largest youth homeless shelter in New York City.

> We went to the YMCA to look for my other friend . . . for the girl. They called Volunteers for America. . . . We were too young to go to where they was at. We went to where they'd stayed that night . . . we went there the next night and a guy down the block that was actually a minister . . . he told us that they were over there because he sent them over there [an adult shelter]. And they had moved somewhere else . . . but I was at Covenant House and then I lost their cell phone number.

Run by a religious charity, Covenant House was founded in the late 1960s in New York City to house and care for homeless youth aged eighteen to twenty-one. Currently, of the 300 emergency shelter beds for homeless youth in New York City, 270 are at Covenant House,[19] so most homeless youth in New York City eventually have some contact with this shelter. Any young people without identification who are picked up by the police at the city's bus or train terminals are brought to Covenant House. According to Blacc, the youth shelter was "a hellhole. They just was like . . . they're shady . . . staff don't talk to you with respect . . . you know, some shelters are better than others." Covenant House's reputation for its poor treatment of gay and lesbian street youth is well known to other social service providers, who estimate that of the roughly ten thousand homeless kids trying to survive each year on New York City's streets, 30 to 40 percent are GLBTQ.[20] Of these, the majority are youth of color, like Blacc. Even though many youth use Covenant House's services without incident, those who encounter problems have few other options for shelter.

Blacc stayed at Covenant House for just over a month. It was winter in New York City, and he was willing to put up with uncomfortable conditions in order to avoid sleeping outside and alone in the freezing cold. During this time, Blacc met other street youth and, through them, found work in both the informal (street) economy and the legal, formal economy. Covenant House requires that all its residents be either employed or actively seeking employment. But with little education or job training, most street youth can, at best, find only short-term, minimum-wage work. Only recently have some social service providers questioned the long-term efficacy of favoring immediate employment over career building and mentoring.[21] In any case, most street kids find that they can make more money in the illegal street economy.[22]

Street kids have four main ways of making money while homeless: sex work (prostitution), drug trade, theft, and panhandling ("spanging" or "spare-changing").[23] While some also have jobs in the formal economy, most are minimum wage and do not provide enough to rent an apartment in New York City. Blacc and his friends chose the third option (theft), by "bending" subway cards. They would pick up spent Metro cards, bend them in a particular way so that they would work again and then charge people money to swipe them onto the subway:

We would bend Metro cards and swipe. We would find them on the ground. We would bend them until they worked and then we would swipe people in with the Metro cards, onto the train . . . it would be really crazy. . . . If it was a local, you'd make a dollar for a two-dollar ride . . . because they know. But if it was a tourist, you'd get the whole two dollars. Or you'd say, "I'll swipe all four of you on for six dollars." So you'd be giving them a break, but you'd be getting them out of the way to get to more customers.

Blacc and several other street kids would work in teams so that one of them could keep an eye out for police while the rest were bending Metro cards.

> When we saw cops, we would hit it. We'd have somebody looking out for the DTs [police] in the train station. There were a couple of times that they got a rein on us, but they couldn't find anything on us. I would throw it down with a pile of Metro cards . . . and then the police would have to go through all the Metro cards, and who wants to go through all that?

Although Blacc was never ticketed for bending Metro cards, he and his friends certainly came to the attention of police while in the subway stations. One police officer approached him and said, "Oh, you think you're a smartass, huh? Come here—let me see some ID." Though not challenging the police officer directly, Blacc thought at the time, "Yeah. I wasn't really saying that, but in my mind, I'm like 'well, yeah.' It's all about skill."

Another time, Blacc was bending cards on his own and was approached by a police officer:

> I'll never forget; this black cop approached me . . . he says, "Get the fuck over here. You think you're slick." I had just gotten down there. I was going down there to do it by myself. So he was like "Get the fuck over here." Shit. And I had a Metro card in my hand. He was like "Let me see the Metro card." But I hadn't bended it yet. So he was like "You down here selling swipes?" I said, "I wanted to get on the train . . . is there a problem with that?" So he swiped the card. . . . "This says invalid." So I said . . . "Well, shit, I gotta buy a Metro card." So he said, "Don't let me see you down here again." I was "whew"! I beat that one.

Blacc and his friends had to learn the patrolling officers' patterns in order to pull off their scam day after day. At $200 a day, bending Metro cards was more lucrative than panhandling and less dangerous than sex work or drug dealing.

> Basically, we knew when they would change their shifts. I couldn't tell you when the cops go down there now, 'cause I haven't done it in a while. But we used to go when they'd change their shifts. We knew the best time to go . . . two o'clock was a hot time. You'd go down there and rack up so much money . . . but it was hot. Two in the afternoon . . . everybody wanted to go down to SoHo. We were like the MTA's . . . information center. People

wanted to know, "How do I get this place?" We'd be like, "Listen, don't go to the machine . . . I'll swipe you on . . . you take this to that."

In order to increase the demand for swiping, Blacc and his friends would also block up the Metro card machines.

> You know, you have some stubborn assholes; they always want to use the machines. . . . So what we'd do is, we'd block up the machines. You'd put the Metro card in the money slot. It would shoot it back out on the bottom, but if you leave it there for a couple minutes, it will suck it back in. Or what you do is you bend the Metro card and put it in the credit card slot. . . . But then any time we'd jam up a machine, the MTA people would come fix it. Then I got out of it because I had gotten a job. I always make it a habit that when I have a legal job, then I don't do anything else illegal. So I stopped swiping.

I met many youth during my fieldwork who had similar views of employment. Some of them saw legal work as a point of pride, while others saw it as a way to avoid the police's attention or even to deny the police the perceived pleasure of arresting them. Blacc had a series of low-paying jobs in the formal economy, ranging from call centers to temporary office work. But despite having a job and making some friends at the shelter, Blacc was kicked out of Covenant House after a month because of a fight with another resident. He was then sent to the city-run men's adult homeless shelter in Brooklyn.

The Bedford Men's Shelter is housed in an old armory dating from the late 1800s, which was converted in the early 1980s to house hundreds of the city's swelling adult homeless population. Rising housing costs, unemployment, and the closing of numerous state mental hospitals all fed into a population of nearly 30,000 people seeking shelter each night in New York City. At one point, the men's shelter was sleeping 900 single men on the floor of its old drill hall. Eventually though, dangerous conditions, theft, fighting, and drugs convinced many residents that it might be safer to sleep on the streets. Then in the 1990s, the neoliberalization of the welfare state in the United States shifted away from large warehouse-like, city-run shelters to smaller, privately run shelters and transitional housing centers, usually specializing in one or two "problem" issues, such as drug abuse, mental illness, or work readiness. By the time Blacc arrived there in 2005, the men's shelter held just 350 beds, and drug use, fighting, and theft were still rampant: "My stuff hasn't ever been stolen when I was out on the street. But the second I go into a shelter, all my stuff disappears." Blacc spent nearly two months there after he was kicked out of Covenant House. By this time he was twenty years old.

Because he had already been barred from the city's primary under-twenty-one youth shelter, Blacc had little choice but to stay in an adult shelter until his six-month suspension from Covenant House was over. Although there are a few small shelters for homeless youth in New York City, most contain fewer than six beds and often have long waiting lists.[24] Because conditions in adult homeless shelters are often chaotic and frightening for homeless youth, his other option was to hit the streets again.

> This guy who had HIV, he was HIV positive, one day he cut his wrists and put blood all over the place . . . all over people. I was like "No, I don't want to deal with that." Yeah. I'm not going to go through my life like that. . . . But like I said, anywhere you go, if you're homeless, you're going to find someone who's going to watch your back and you're going to watch their back. I guess that's the rules of the streets. From the men's shelter, I was on the train again with some friends that I knew from Covenant House.

According to Blacc, the first rule of the streets is sticking with your friends, as finding and keeping friends may mean the difference between surviving and not surviving on the streets. Because the childhood of many street kids is marked by chronically broken trust, they often form closely knit street families, with each member assuming particular roles and responsibilities. But because shelters are designed to serve individual homeless kids, their regulations often break up these street families.

The second rule of the streets for most youth is to not appear homeless:

> Through it all, when I was sleeping on the train . . . you would think that I was just a guy that fell asleep on the train. You wouldn't think I was home-less. Through my whole sleeping on the streets . . . I always took care of myself. I never looked like I was homeless. Even today, you'd never know I was homeless unless I told you. People look at me . . . I don't tell them. They can make whatever assumption they want to make.

Not looking homeless is an important survival strategy for many young peo-ple, and they often ask outreach workers for information about showers before food or even shelter. In Blacc's case, not looking homeless was both a survival strategy and a point of pride: "I've got too much pride to let myself go that far. Streetwork has a washer and dryer and I used to keep a locker there. I would put clothes in there. And they have showers, so you're pretty good." Being identified as homeless can draw dangerous attention from police or other authority figures, drug dealers, and pimps and can attract ridicule from the general public. The principal exception to this rule of the street are gutter punk and "traveler" homeless youth, who are the only visible segment of the street youth populations (and indeed account for the popular stereotypes of all street youth as counterculture youth). Nonetheless, regardless of physical appearance, according to Blacc, keeping a positive sense of self is a herculean task for homeless youth: "If you forget who you are, you'll end up on the streets forever."

Traditionally, aid for street youth has centered on an identifier of homelessness that structures young people's subjectivity according to what they lack: a narrowly defined home. Recently, progressive social service providers have begun to implement programs based on other facets of street youths' lives and skills. In fact, the reappropriation of the term *street kid* refers to the value placed in the resiliency and knowledge of youth who survive the streets.

The third informal rule of the streets is to keep moving. By the time Blacc was sleeping on the A train again, he had been living for a year cycling from street to shelter. His fellow street friends offered a kind of security, and the A train was familiar territory.

> I used to stay with them on the train because they didn't have a place to go. I had a bed at the men's shelter. I really didn't like it, but it was a bed. I would have kept the bed if I didn't know that they were sleeping on the train. I was like, you know, "You guys are sleeping on the train. I'll sleep on the train, too."

Once again, the importance of street networks and relationships is clear. Through informal networks of other homeless youth, street kids find out about shelters, jobs, places to get a free meal, and innumerable other bits of survival information.

After another short stint on the A train, Blacc entered a small, nonprofit youth shelter that he had heard about from other street kids. He stayed there for about two months: "I used to drink a lot. I came in drunk. . . . So I got discharged." From the small youth shelter, Blacc spent a week in an emergency shelter in the Bronx before heading back to Manhattan and his friends, some of whom were sleeping in Times Square:

> We used to hang out up there. Cop a squat by the ticket booth . . . we wouldn't go to sleep until the streets were dying down . . . there was always

something to do, somewhere to go. We would just like hang out, talk to people, flirt . . . all kinds of things. It was just me and my friend Offwhite. We called him Offwhite because he was this Jewish kid and he was, like, really, really black. He smoked weed and everything. [Offwhite] knew this guy "Ace." . . . He used to make sure that me and Offwhite had something to eat and stuff like that. When you're homeless, you always have to find somebody . . . and you always have to look out after each other. You know what I'm saying?

After a while, Blacc decided to try Covenant House again. "Well, I went back last year . . . I had to have a job in order to get back in. So I had this job, but they said no." The staff instead referred Blacc to a transitional living program for homeless youth in Brooklyn, but he stayed there for only a few months:

The kids there were, like, crazy. . . . I got discharged from there for fighting. I had a fight with this kid. Over gang matters and whatnot. I used to have anger problems. Now I can leave it. He was Blood. I'm Crip. He touched something he wasn't supposed to touch and we started scrapping. It's a boundary matter.

Both Blacc and the other kid were discharged from the transitional living program and sent to the same emergency overnight shelter in the Bronx. By this time, Blacc had been sent there so many times that the staff let him stay for several nights instead of the twenty-four-hour limit. The young man with whom Blacc had fought also was at the emergency shelter for a few days.

So after a while, I spoke to him. . . . I'm not one who is going to hold a grudge. We talked, "get over it." . . . So we was man enough to put it behind us. Like I said, when you're on the street, somebody is going to have to take care of you or you're going to have to take care of somebody . . . so we had that little buddy system going on and it actually worked out pretty good.

Unfortunately for Blacc, the six-month suspension that he received from the transitional living program would be up four months before his twenty-first birthday, the age at which he had to leave the program: "I didn't want to sit there and waste my time if I was going to age out in two months." The emergency shelter in the Bronx once again tried to get Blacc back into the adult shelter system. "They thought I was in the men's shelter because they give you a referral to the men's shelter and I was like 'OK, I'll go.' But in all actuality, I was sleeping on the train . . . .because when I did go to the men's shelter . . . it was like . . . hell." Sending youth to adult shelters presents a significant problem for social service providers.

Most of social workers that I encountered during my fieldwork felt that adult shelters were the last option for street youth, and they would go to amazing lengths to find alternatives for their young clients. Inevitably, however, older street youth are regularly sent to adult shelters. One outreach worker (who had been conducting outreach for more than ten years) told me that the young person who haunts her the most was a young man that she had to escort to an adult shelter a few years ago. When they arrived at the waiting room, the young man began to cry and asked her not leave him there.

Another problem is that most city-run adult homeless shelters (and, increasingly, youth shelters as well) have been relocated to the fringes of New York City. Street youth who are transported to these shelters are thus isolated in unfamiliar and potentially hostile neighborhoods, far from their street networks, youth drop-in centers, and outreach workers. Then in the early hours of the morning, they have to find their own way back into the city when the shelters discharge their occupants. One social worker told me about a young woman whom she had driven up to a shelter in the Bronx but on arriving there decided not to stay. The young woman then ended up walking out of the shelter toward a subway in the middle of the night and in an unfamiliar neighborhood. Another social worker told me that she would tell young people to sleep on the subways before sending them to certain shelters. She was not alone. One of the first young people with whom I conducted outreach talked about "good" police officers who would drive street youth to a downtown adult shelter on cold nights and then would watch as the young people walked out of the shelter (literally a revolving door) and toward the nearby subway entrance. After one of the more popular Manhattan drop-in centers for street youth closed in the evening, a staff member would walk young people to the subway and swipe them on for free using a group pass. This was nominally so that youth could reach an outlying shelter, but many kids opted to stay on the subways.

Blacc stayed in a number of places besides the A train. He tried living in Union Square, another popular street youth hangout, but decided that there was too much drug dealing and too many police there.

When there was a lot of drug use going on back there. . . . I guess [the police] scoped it out . . . then they shut things down . . . like, you know,

"You can't sleep here" and it's like 11:30 p.m. We would just move over to where the tables and benches are and sleep there. But most of the nights I would stay up and watch the skateboarders do their tricks, 'cause that's what interests me. . . . I was just there for a couple of days . . . a week at most. They were all assholes. I really didn't like Union Square—those kids were fucking crazy. They live on acid trips or whatever. They'd start throwing around rats and shit. I'm like, "This ain't the place for me." But yeah . . . when they started throwing around them rats, I was like "oh, no." Then from Union Square I started sleeping in staircases over in Chelsea.

In both Times Square and Union Square, Blacc was with other street youth, the sort of group that often attracted the police's attention, often in the form of orders to move along and out of public spaces:

"You're out of here." You know what I'm saying. "Before I take you in . . . I'm going to lock you up." You want to avoid that, so you just move. There was nothing to really keep you there . . . so back then, we didn't have cell phones . . . so we'd be like, "I guess we got to meet them [friends] somewhere else." You know what I'm saying. "If they don't meet us back there, they'll come to this place . . . if they don't come to this place, we'll just see them later on that night."

But street youth do not form their entire identity around homelessness and often have a range of street friends who are both on and off the streets. These extended networks of youth can lead to creative ways of finding other forms of shelter.

And I would stay on Twenty-fifth Street, in one of the project buildings near Tenth Avenue. I had some skateboarder friends . . . you know, we used to go over there, get drunk, whatever. I think that's the biggest thing you do when you're homeless . . . go with the coolest things. It seemed like the coolest thing. You stay drunk to run away from problems. Not really because you have the money, but to get away from problems. Then I met up with another friend that was sleeping in the project buildings . . . I stayed in there. Up at the roof. . . . It was just cold and there wasn't enough room for two people. Nothing that I would do again. . . . Then I was going to sleep in the U-Haul trucks. Which most homeless kids used to do. . . . It's just a parking garage where the U-Hauls used to park their trucks. But since a lot of kids would sleep there, it was locked. They moved them to a different location. I had slept in the U-Hauls before. So I figured that I could do it again. But then I went to Sylvia's Place to use the bathroom, and they asked me was I in here for intake, and I was like "Yeah!"

Housed in an old Protestant church on Manhattan's West Side, Sylvia's Place was the first GLBTQ youth shelter to open in New York City. On any given night, about a dozen young people crash in the back room of the church.

It's a sauna. It gets awfully hot in there. It's a very crazy environment. It could be a very cool environment. It depends on how you are and how you interact with other youth. It's just a big open space, full of cabinets . . . there aren't really beds . . . we sleep on cots. But in the summer, most of the kids sleep on the floor and whatnot. It's more comfortable.

After a few months at Sylvia's Place, Blacc was transferred to an affiliated center at another church in Queens. A newly formed volunteer group in New York City—the New York City Homeless Youth Alliance—began a program in 2005 in which several gay-friendly churches across the city volunteered to shelter six homeless youth at a time over the winter, on a rotating basis.

This was a new and creative alternative to formal shelters,[25] and for social service providers, it marked a small but real victory in changing public opinion about homeless kids. Some social workers also spoke of this program as an important step for the adult GLBTQ community to accept responsibility for the welfare of GLBTQ homeless youth, incorporating those young people who had gravitated to gay neighborhoods but who had continued to be socially marginalized by the adult gay community. A social worker joked with me at one point that any contact between street youth and the adult gay community that did not involve sex work was a step forward. Each church supplied a bed, a locker, and dinner provided by two volunteers. A recent e-mail announcement marked the beginning of the winter efforts:

In January and February, The Church of the Village is partnering with Sylvia's Place to host a temporary emergency winter shelter for six homeless Lesbian, Gay, Bisexual, Transgendered, or Questioning Young Adults at 48 St. Mark's Place. The Church needs your help to staff the shelter facility with two trained volunteers each evening.

It is an inconvenience, and perhaps even a sacrifice, to forgo a night's sleep in our warm beds at home to sleep instead on a cot, and lose half of a regular night's sleep. However, without volunteers willing to do this for the benefit of these often-neglected youth, they may have no bed or safe shelter at all. Sylvia's Place (the only year-round Emergency Shelter for GLBTQ Youth in the city) is already over capacity, and the cold temperatures and inclement weather of winter have not even begun. Shelter guests will be referred from Sylvia's Place on an as-needed basis.

Thank you for helping us to show these youth that God cares—and we care—about every Child of God.[26]

Even though many street youth are resistant to contacting religiously run social service programs, those who have stayed at the temporary church shelters have been satisfied with them. Yet clearly, this is a small-scale and short-term solution. Moreover, informal shelters may be inconsistent and are not regulated. The Queens shelter was closed after only a few months owing to rumors of altercations between the youth and a priest. The shelter was shut down quickly and quietly, taking social workers by surprise. Several weeks after it had closed, there was still confusion over why it had closed and if it would ever reopen. In the meantime, Blacc went back to Sylvia's Place, which was now overcrowded, as it was housing both their regular residents and the youth coming from the closed shelter. Blacc had been at Sylvia's Place for about a month when I met him in the summer of 2006.

When I met Blacc through my work training peer outreach counselors, he had been working at a GLBTQ drop-in center for a few months. Housed in a gray stone, twelve-story office building in Midtown Manhattan, the drop-in center offers counseling and social services to young GLBTQ homeless. The majority of the center's clients are young black men aged thirteen to twenty-three. Part of Blacc's job at the center was to watch the front door on the nights when the youth had dances and social events, making sure that none of the members were harassed when entering or leaving the building. The other part of Blacc's job was to go out and talk with other street kids, telling them about the center's services and handing out free condoms. Peer outreach seemed to come naturally for Blacc, as he had been looking out for other homeless youth for years. His jobs at the center also gave him time to take a step back from his life, from his homeless self. Being on the streets has been a hard transition to adulthood for Blacc:

I've learned how to be a hell of a lot more independent. I've learned the city more. . . . You learn a lot . . . but I miss my bed. I miss a bed. Out of all the things that I miss, I miss going home . . . all the things that you take for granted when you're there.

But Blacc does not envision going home: "I think about living [in] other places. I do want to leave New York for good. And I think about where I would go. Because I don't want to go where I have to start this bullshit all over again. . . . Homeless is not fun at all. It's very hard." Blacc sees himself getting off the streets, but maybe not in New York: "I might come back every year or something like that, but I've gotta get out of New York for a while. Just for a little while. New York is just too hard." By the end of 2006, Blacc was hoping that a construction job outside New York might offer the dual benefits of employment and getting him out of the city for a while.

A month after that conversation, he was kicked out of Sylvia's Place for fighting with a staff member. A social worker told me later what she knew about the incident:

> Basically, a staff member assaulted a client. He pushed him out of an office, hard enough to throw him against the wall of the adjoining hallway. This client was a friend of Blacc's. When Blacc confronted the staff member, the staff member became irate, screaming insults at Blacc. The staff member told Blacc that he had to leave for the night. When Blacc turned to leave, the staff member continued to yell and insult Blacc, following him out into the vestibule. At this point, Blacc turned and threw a cup of apple juice onto the staff member. The end result was that Blacc was suspended for a week.

Blacc was eventually allowed back into Sylvia's Place, but within weeks he was transferred to a long-term transitional living program for GLBTQ youth in Harlem. In this program, Blacc shared a small apartment with several other young people, where he stayed for a year.

It is tempting to try to summarize Blacc's experiences with the "mean streets" and the hopelessness of street youth fighting their way through a system that seems designed for failure. The strengths rewarded on the street are rarely the qualities rewarded in the shelter system. Fighting and lying low, staying independent, and sticking together may seem like contradictory strategies for surviving the streets, yet homeless youth manage to do this with grace while shifting their goals and expectations to manage what few opportunities they find to improve their lives. All too often, the lives of street kids are disruptive, violent, boring, fragile, and short. Blacc's story and the stories of others like him are always continuing, as being off the streets is a fragile state. Social workers often expressed the sentiment that in some sense, street youth never leave the street.

Street Outreach

> Street youthwork is about . . . geographies of everyday life of cer-
> tain groups of youth; it is about how geometric space becomes
> lived-space and the life-worlds of site, venue, and locale; and it
> is about how these geographies work as calls . . . for some kids—
> as well as some adults, including youthworkers—and how they
> respond by taking on existing street roles or creating new ones.
> —Michael Baizerman, Foreword to *Caring on the Streets*

Outreach is the practice of contacting socially marginalized populations in their physical and social environments. For outreach focused on
homeless youth, this typically involves efforts by social service providers to
reach out and engage kids "on the streets." Because of past abuse and fear
of adult authorities, many street kids are hesitant to seek out help on their
own. But what does "reaching out" mean? What is the social landscape that
street outreach workers enter when they seek out youth on the streets? How
do outreach workers enter, occupy, and conceptualize these spaces? Are outreach interactions on kids' terms or structured by adults? How do outreach
workers understand their role on the streets, with youth, and with other
social service providers? How do they identify and engage with homeless
kids, and how do young people understand and interpret outreach workers'
actions? Finally, what are outreach workers' opportunities and restrictions
when trying to broaden the resources for street youth?

In the past, the federal government defined street youth as runaways and
homeless children, but this definition was recently expanded to include any
young person involved in such street economies as sex work or drug dealing.[1]
These youth are also at risk of homelessness, exploitation, illness, and abuse.
The U.S. Department of Health and Human Services oversees the Administration for Children and Families. Housed within the Administration for
Children and Families is the Family and Youth Services Bureau, which in
turn oversees its Youth Development Division (YDD). The YDD runs the
Runaway and Homeless Youth (RHY) programs for the federal government.

These programs consist of funding and regulating four services: Basic Center Programs (BCPs or drop-in centers), Transitional Living Programs (TLPs), Maternity Group Home Programs (MGHs), and, finally, Street Outreach Programs (SOPs). In New York City, funds for these four programs are allocated through the Department of Youth and Community Development (DYCD) in a competitive grant system for nonprofit social service organizations.

In 2004, $14 million in federal outreach grants was distributed among 128 youth programs in the United States. In 2006, however, federal funding for street outreach had fallen to slightly more than $13.5 million distributed to 140 programs.[2] The funds for street outreach are given to community-based and nonprofit groups to conduct outreach at the local level. The goal of federally funded outreach is to meet immediate needs (food, shelter, medical care, clothes) and to build trust, with the ultimate goal of reducing the sexual abuse and exploitation of homeless and runaway youth. Street outreach is not limited to federally funded programs, of course, as it is a popular activity of small, faith-based groups and independent nonprofits working with youth, which often work in relative anonymity.

Street outreach has been called both a vital direct social service and a marginal entry-level job. In practice, it is both. Street outreach is a performance, a process, and a model for engaging with street youth, and over the last fifty years in the United States, outreach has been shaped by political, social, and economic trends. Its practitioners often constitute a social service subculture, and they bring their own identities, agendas, and histories to the outreach process. Despite the complexities of outreach, academics and policymakers who work with street kids are increasingly using street outreach workers to gather data and are recommending street outreach as a temporary, ameliorative fix to some of the problems faced by social services for marginalized populations such as street youth.

On the surface, street outreach is a simple process of reaching out to people who may or may not be accessing traditional social services through other means. In concept, outreach is meant to act as a bridge between young people on the streets and the shelters, clinics, and drop-in centers where they may receive aid. In practice, outreach is a competitive process. Outreach counselors tactically engage youth who are simultaneously interacting with and reacting to the rest of the street population, which includes drug dealers, pimps and johns, store owners, police, and the general public. At various times and locations, street outreach has also been used as a form of surveillance of street youth or other public agents, or as mediators between differing groups.

Street outreach is as diverse as the street environments, adults, and young people involved. Outreach has an agenda and is not a one-way relationship between adult counselors and youth clients. The outreach process is a power-laden social performance by both street youth and street outreach workers. That is, while the street outreach workers are attempting to project a calm, caring facade or maintain a friendly face, at the same time they are trying to persuade young people that accepting social services will be beneficial in the long run. Street youth, who may have had adults abuse and exploit them, often wonder what outreach workers want from them. Indeed, figuring out what adults want from them is how many street kids stay alive. In turn, street youths' performances have layers of meaning that can range from coura-geous bravado to lost helplessness or from friendly joking to angry glares. Thus the needs and desires of both street kids and outreach workers play off each other in a socially powerful dance.

The Philosophy of Street Outreach

The philosophical foundation of street outreach is not readily apparent in the academic or professional literature, in part, perhaps, because street outreach is often used as either a starting point (those studies that use the existing out-reach data uncritically) or an ending point (those studies that recommend street outreach as an unexamined solution). The exceptions are outreach-training manuals, which tend to concentrate on the practical and tactical components of outreach and not the philosophical assumptions underlying outreach practices. As a starting point, street outreach is commonly used as a medium for data collection in broader studies of street youth and is often pre-sented as a seemingly uncritical methodological tool.[3] Street outreach also is frequently recommended as a solution to a range of issues identified by differ-ing studies of homeless youth and social services.[4] Those studies recommend-ing outreach as a "fix" for social service provision tend to regard outreach as a neutral process and fail to clarify what type of outreach they recommend. In these instances, "the street" is seen as a place where social aid can be provided, yet one remarkably devoid of power or conflict between street kids and street outreach workers. For example, some studies recommend that "all services for street children should be provided by street workers, on the streets, with chil-dren having the right to assess and accept or reject services offered by street workers."[5] In many contexts and instances, however, street kids cannot accept aid or workers cannot engage with a young person. Moreover, these studies rarely discuss the problems, limitations, and power relations involved in street outreach, giving them an uncritical tone. The few studies explicitly concerned with street outreach models are nearly always practical applications of better or more efficient practices for professional youth workers.[6] These works generally focus on the "how" of street outreach, not the "why." In my own experience conducting street outreach with a variety of different groups and in reading both formal and informal training manuals for street outreach workers, I found a way of thinking that unites various outreach methods and tactics.

The current street outreach in the United States corresponds to the social science paradigms of the 1950s, 1960s, and 1970s, and thus outreach philosophies reflect the popular conceptions of marginality, exploitative social relations, and empowerment that were central to political and social debates during these decades. In his book *Pedagogy of the Oppressed*,[7] Paolo Freire's intellectual work and philosophical challenges have widely influenced street outreach to homeless youth. Freire spent most of his career working on literacy outreach to indigenous populations in South and Central America in the 1960s and 1970s, in which he saw the marginalization and oppression of various peoples as a mutually supported relationship between oppressors and oppressed in modern society. Consequently, the liberation of oppressed peoples must be a mutually engaging process by both the powerful and the powerless. Freire defined oppressed peoples as those social groups denied opportunities for participation in and access to the mainstream society's resources, believing that only through an awareness of their position in the hierarchical society and their subjectivity in relation to broader structures of power could they begin to work toward their own liberation.

Freire hypothesized that oppressed groups were submerged so deeply in oppressive structures that they were unable to see their own oppression. In order to "see" their position as marginal, they needed spaces in which they could begin to ask and answer questions about their position in society. According to Freire, an outsider from a nonoppressed group could enter and create a space in which to facilitate a dialogic process of self-realization within the oppressed group. In other words, an educator could go into a poverty-stricken indigenous community and, though a problem-posing model of teaching, would act as a catalyst for political and social change. Freire believed that an outsider/educator could help broaden the understanding of the structures constraining the range of opportunities and stimulate a discussion about the workings of power in society. But only the oppressed people themselves could mobilize social change.

Freire's work had a wide-ranging influence on social work and social outreach in North America. Social workers in underserved communities used his ideas in the form of philosophies of care that sought to empower communities at the local level. In practice, Freire's ideas were used for clients' agency, flexibility of service, and the reduction of harm. For example, "both street-based services and those provided in drop-in centers are designed so as to give youth as much flexibility as possible, focusing particularly on needs identified by the youth themselves and working at a pace that is also in large part determined by them."[8] In order to formulate services that were partly defined and initiated by young people, the social work industry tried to create spaces and media for dialogue and communication between social workers and youth.

Street outreach methods exemplify Freire's philosophy in that the outreach process strives to create a temporary space in which street youth can understand and critically reflect on their lived experiences through a dialogic encounter with outreach counselors. In this space and process, outreach counselors can facilitate change, but it can be mobilized only by the youth themselves. In addition, while street outreach counselors do go to where street youth are located, they do not seek to become "insiders" in the street youth community but instead hope to become "conscious outsiders." In the social outreach model, only by situating themselves in the center of street youths' lived spaces can outreach workers engage with street youth and create spaces where youth can step back from their daily struggle for survival and reflect on their past, present, and future condition. This, of course, is an idealized conception of street outreach that flows from a rather romanticized and sanitized understanding of care, work for others, mentoring, and empowerment. The actual experience of street outreach is more diverse, more ethically gray, and a lot messier.

The History and Development of Street Outreach

Although the concept of street outreach began in the 1800s, research on it has not progressed very far. In the various iterations of street outreach work, "reaching out" has been represented as a process, a metaphor, and a philosophy, as reflected in the many designations for outreach work, such as "detached youth workers," "gang workers," "area workers," "street workers," "corner workers," "extension workers," and "street gang workers."

Street outreach began more than a century ago in the United States as an informal, disorganized practice, primarily the work of religious leaders and missionaries. Many of these early "child saver" progressive reformers used street outreach methods to find children who were working on the streets in poor neighborhoods. The goal of early street outreach by missions and religious reform institutions was to remove children from the street environment (often forcibly), thus rendering both the street and the street youth as mostly passive agents. Simply by separating children from the supposedly corrupting influence of the streets, reformers sought to halt their involvement in street life and negative behaviors. This method, however, ignored the street youths' complex supportive and skilled relationships that helped them survive on the streets and their incorporation of those experiences into lived identities. As a result, children who were forcibly removed from the street environment often returned there as soon as they could, which they still do today. To break this pattern, outreach groups now try to move young people off the street gradually, over a period set by the youth themselves. In street outreach today, a long-term engagement with the street environment is a key component in reaching out to youth.

Street outreach first became a profession in the 1950s through detached youth work with urban gangs.[9] These preliminary programs followed up on the early, experimental outreach efforts in the 1920s, which had not been widely publicized or adopted.[10] Youth belonging to urban gangs were increasingly coming to the attention of police and community members through their turf wars and public vandalism (particularly in the later form of graffiti "tagging") after World War II. Again, before the early twentieth century, the public did not generally perceive youth gangs as socially abnormal.[11] For example, many turn-of-the-century youth gangs were regarded as working-class social and sports clubs. It was not until the concept of juvenile delinquency gained wide acceptance that young people in gangs were seen as a social problem linked to the individual pathologies of urban working-class youth and the social disorganization of working-poor neighborhoods.[12]

Gang youth in particular were not easily accessible to social service providers, in that they did not frequently visit institutions like community centers, churches, and schools. In the 1950s, however, street outreach became more common, with individuals reaching out physically and socially to young people in their own spaces, activities, and times. Though institutionalized through different government-funded programs, these early outreach workers usually operated alone and had some history with or ties to the neighborhoods in which they worked. In the 1950s, a number of cities across the United States experimented with "detached youthworker" programs,[13] with New York City being one of the first to fund such outreach efforts through its Youth Board. The goals were to "reduce gang fighting" and to "provide a series of real experiences for the group that might result in changes in their general world-view, as well as in the standards by which they judge their own behavior and that of their friends."[14]

Studies of early street outreach programs showed a wide variation in how street outreach workers approached kids. Nevertheless, early assessments showed that the presence of an outreach worker seemed to decrease public antisocial behavior (violence and vandalism), although it had very little impact on private behaviors (drugs, drinking, and sex). Conversely, one study recorded an increase in antisocial public behavior as street youth vied for the attention of the outreach worker.[15] Local communities took a "better than nothing" approach to early outreach efforts, which had some limited utility in that they exposed young people to adults who were interested in their well-being and social success. Outreach workers could provide some measure of social connection to basic services, education, and jobs, whereas in street environments, youth often interacted only with adults who regarded them as exploitable resources.

Whereas early outreach efforts to street youth focused on urban gangs, street outreach later was extended to encompass young people involved in all segments of the street economy and street life, whether or not they were sleeping on the street or belonged to a gang. Outreach itself has largely been professionalized, with job expectations, street quotas, and budgets determining the types of street outreach being practiced in the United States today.

Processes, Expectations, and Limitations of Professional Street Outreach

Street outreach is a kind of social service provision in which social workers go out into public spaces, find where street youth hang out, and directly engage them on their own turf. As a result, understanding the location of that turf, the other actors present, and how those spaces are controlled is critical to their success. Indeed, street outreach programs succeed when outreach counselors are familiar with their territory, both socially and physically. Workers can consistently go out and find the same kids, in the same locations, night after night, month after month, because they know how the kids and public spaces are situated in the broader community's geographies. In some communities, street outreach workers are able to establish a presence on the street as a recognized entity in much the same way that beat cops or local priests have publicly recognized roles.

The outreach relationship is not easy and requires a lot of time. Outreach counselors need to be able to find the same young people over and over in order to gain their trust. Although outreach work generally is done at night, paid outreach workers often are on call at all times. Street outreach workers typically combine their work life with their social life, in part because their work space is not strictly defined but extends to a multitude of places. For example, outreach workers escort young people to shelters, emergency rooms, and job sites. Outreach work can be carried out on in the street, on a rooftop, in a hallway, or over the phone. As Michael Baizerman[16] pointed out, the work of street outreach situates the worker in spaces that are socially constructed both physically and mentally, and as such, outreach work may have more porous boundaries than traditional social work does. These fuzzy job boundaries can make outreach confusing and discouraging. Outreach workers often feel as though they are being invited into a young person's performance when an outreach is going well. Getting back out again, however, can be more difficult, and many outreach workers have difficulty knowing when to end an outreach or to convey to a young person that the outreach is over.

Outreach work can also be a solitary and frustrating job. Street outreach and outreach workers are sometimes seen as being on the margin of other forms of social service provision. In the 1950s and 1960s, street outreach workers reported that other social service workers and supervisors were condescending to them, that they were not given a voice in policy decisions, and that they were regularly given policy ultimatums. Little has changed in this regard. When changes in funding and regulations alter outreach patterns, outreach workers must nonetheless adapt, even if it means disrupting fragile street relationships. In late 2006, New York City reallocated its street outreach funding for four different drop-in centers. As a result, one center that had conducted outreach in Upper Manhattan and the Bronx for several years was given only one month to change its outreach territory to Lower Manhattan and Brooklyn. Outreach workers were left with the task of letting youth know that they would no longer be showing up in established areas but would be scouting out an entirely new "turf" with which they were largely unfamiliar.[17]

Most programs rely heavily on their outreach workers' common sense to handle rapidly changing situations. Street outreach is an open-ended process in which the tactics change along with the behaviors of the street youth and the environments in which the outreach takes place. As one outreach worker explained,

> We used to do more outreach in Lower Manhattan, but gentrification sort of killed all of that. There used to be a lot more sex work in places like

the Meatpacking District. You could walk along a certain block and find five or six trans workers.[18] We haven't seen a kid down there in probably a year now. Whenever we were parking along Christopher Street or near the piers, residents would send angry letters to the director [of the drop-in center]. Our van is very noticeable. So now we park near Washington Square Park and walk over with some outreach material. There are fewer kids that hang out on the piers as well. Kids are getting scared away—if you're being harassed, you're not going to hang around.[19]

In this regard, street outreach models are more flexible than the services located in institutions. For example, moving a drop-in center from one location to another requires a lease, zoning permits, and a huge expenditure of time, materials, and labor. Outreach workers, however, can decide in real time to check out a new location based on information gathered from kids they encounter during their work. Indeed, street outreach requires a flexibility that is hard to document or be formally controlled by social service agencies, policies, or communities.

As a profession, outreach workers are low-pay, low-status social workers, so street outreach is often viewed as an entry-level position requiring only rudimentary training. Furthermore, outreach workers' high burnout rates have a detrimental effect on street relationships and consistency:

> There is a high burnout rate for street outreach—it's much better to have part-time outreach workers. A young person can see someone's bad mood very quickly. You have to genuinely want to be there, and you can carry over stresses from your other jobs or life into the outreach. I've sent people home that were having a bad day.[20]

Outreach workers are often former street youth themselves. A common perception is that former street youth make good outreach workers because they are more likely to be knowledgeable about the "turf" in which they work and are accepted by the subcultures that they are attempting to interpret and intercept.[21] Accordingly, the social alignment of street outreach workers with the marginal position of street youth is not uncommon.

In sum, outreach workers do not have the same status as other types of social worker: "The status of agencies often reflecting the status of the people they serve also appears to apply to the status of detached youthworkers within those agencies."[22] The professional status of street outreach workers still is often marginal. But some agencies now require that case managers and social workers regularly perform some outreach in addition to their main duties in clinics, drop-in centers, and shelters. This helps mitigate the "us-them" mentality that arises between those who work with youth on their own turf and those who encounter them in settings structured by professional caregivers. This is not to imply that the street outreach encounter is youth structured. One way that outreach groups are addressing outreach performances and power imbalances between adults and youngsters is through the incorporation of peer workers.

Peer Outreach

Beginning in the 1990s, a progressive paradigm shift in the social sciences in general and in social work in particular emphasized youths' agency and empowerment.[23] For social workers, this heralded a renewed interest in kids as active, participatory individuals rather than traditionally limited, passive service recipients. A wide variety of organizations in New York City instituted youth advisory boards, peer educators, mentors, and other youth-led activities.[24] The young people who protested the policing of Hudson River Park and showed up at meetings to have their voices heard all were members of a youth organization committed to youth empowerment. As part of its mission, FIERCE! spent several months teaching street kids how to speak for themselves at community board meetings and other public events. In addition, they trained youth members to begin conducting peer outreach with other kids on the streets. Indeed, peer outreach has become a common component of many youth agencies in the city.

The incorporation of peer outreach into an existing outreach program usually means street kids doing outreach with other street kids. In most cases, the staff at the drop-in centers or clinics ask older kids to become peer outreach workers. Less often, youth who have not been homeless but are connected to the street scene serve as peer outreach workers. Certainly, young people may conduct outreach on their own by praising a shelter or drop-in center or by showing other street kids where services are located. This sort of informal information flow is how young people build relationships and networks on the streets, and peer outreach workers try to formalize and build on these networks. In some cases, those young people who frequently bring other street kids into shelters are asked to do formal outreach. At one shelter in Midtown Manhattan, youth requested their own outreach cards to give out and then were paid for giving other youth referrals to shelters. This program was unusual in that young people initiated a formal, peer-run, outreach program.

They had no training, set hours of operation, or supervision. By contrast, in most peer outreach programs, an adult social worker trains and supervises the kids, who go out in small groups to established sites at set times.

Among other duties, peer outreach workers are expected to "provide information on locations for where youth gather and hang out."[25] Hiring homeless or formerly homeless youth to point out street kids who may or may not present themselves as homeless to the public or social services creates some obvious conflicts of interest and ethical concerns.[26] Inevitably, peer outreach workers run into old friends, boyfriends/girlfriends, and enemies while doing outreach work. In fact, one outreach group had to suspend its peer workers when they had difficulty separating their street life from their outreach work. As one social worker termed it, "You can't pick up a date when you're on outreach." Yet outreach spaces are the same spaces where kids survive in the street economy, and it is this knowledge on which social workers hope to capitalize. Separating their street identity from their social work identity can be extremely difficult for these youth and, in some cases, was counterproductive. Asking kids to forgo a street contact that may bring them a place to sleep for the night is problematic when only three hundred shelter beds are available for youth in the city and they are usually filled.

Toward the end of my research for this book, I had the opportunity to train six young people for peer outreach from a Midtown GLBTQ drop-in center. At first the kids were fairly enthusiastic about doing outreach. One quiet, thin young man observed, "It's easier for kids to do outreach with kids, you know," and a tall and outgoing transgender woman pointed out that outreach works better "with other gays." They did not see a problem doing outreach in areas that many social workers are hesitant to enter, such as public bathrooms, dark alleys, or wooded parks, since these were locations with which they all were familiar from their involvement in the street economies of sex work. The only problems that they initially brought up were that some kids might not want to talk or be the objects of outreach, and they were not sure what they would do if the other kids were rude to them in their new roles as outreach workers.

The youth whom I trained for outreach had a number of issues concerning identity and role negotiations. Even though all the young people in my particular training group were extremely knowledgeable about the public spaces where the drop-in center wanted to conduct outreach—in this case, the West Village and Hudson River Park—several of them noted that it would be strange to run into their friends and street acquaintances. One young woman was able to map out where different groups of street kids hung out in a particular park, broken down by sexuality, gender practices, age, and tenure. This was a far more sophisticated understanding of the street kid geography than most adult outreach workers had. She also understood the social dynamics of this park and was able to devise a strategy of starting with the older kids and working her way down to contact with the younger kids. In contrast, when working in a new location, many outreach workers unknowingly disrupt street kids' power structures. Detailed local knowledge from the kids themselves therefore can be invaluable and is part of the attraction to implementing peer outreach.

After a long session during which the kids mapped out the details of where and with whom they would do outreach, one young man stated that he would be happy to do outreach in other parts of the city, just not the neighborhoods where he had been homeless. A big African American kid with a tough demeanor, he thought it would be easier to do outreach with out-of-town, white runaways in the East Village than to risk running into kids that he knew around Union Square or Christopher Street. During the mapping exercise, these kids were able to point out which bathrooms were hookup sites for sex work, where drug contacts were made, and where different groups of street youth hung out, not just in the West Village, but in parts of Upper Manhattan and Brooklyn as well. All this knowledge came from their active and ongoing participation in the street scene. Moreover, becoming a peer outreach worker may be dangerous when he or she had previously been involved in illegal activities such as sex work or drug dealing.

My peer outreach workers had both successes and difficulties, and in the end, only two of the six went out on outreaches. They enjoyed getting out of the drop-in center and roaming around as part of their job. They also offered a wealth of knowledge about the street environment as well as a willingness to talk to a variety of young people. But they ran into difficulty when encountering familiar people. We therefore ended up doing more outreach outside their traditional stomping grounds, but there we could not benefit from their local knowledge. The two peer counselors told me that it was harder to do outreach in neighborhoods where they were still hanging out or known as street kids, and they eventually drifted away from outreach.

In addition to the stresses of taking on a secondary street role, many service agencies require that peer workers become actual employees, which necessitates their distancing from or ending their position as a client in need of services. As another outreach trainer expressed it,

Because peer outreach workers are models for other kids, they have to be very careful about setting up boundaries. In order to be a peer outreach worker, a young person has to be stable enough to cut ties with the drop-in center because it would be a conflict of interest. They can't merge those two roles.[27]

Stability for many street youth is irregular, however; they may be stable one week and back to couch surfing or sleeping in the subways the next. Thus owing to the regular chaos of their everyday lives, it was difficult for the peer outreach workers to maintain consistency with their outreach work.

Street youth who conduct peer outreach may also not be emotionally or socially prepared for issues that are brought out in the open by the outreach process. As one outreach worker explained:

> The van staff is generally composed of a driver, a social worker, and a peer youth worker. When they first started, there were four peer outreach workers, a driver, and a social worker, but this became too much. The social worker sometimes had to spend as much time dealing with conflicts between the peer outreach workers or issues that were brought up during outreach that the peers had not resolved themselves.[28]

Peer workers also may find it difficult to counsel a young person involved in sex work when they themselves have not yet come to terms with their own sexual exploitation while homeless. Indeed, peer outreach workers are expected to be "responsible for culturally competent outreach, crisis assessment, education, and referrals."[29] This is an enormously difficult task, made harder if a young person has not begun to work through his or her own experiences. In addition, outreach can be an exhausting and stressful exercise in boundary maintenance for peer outreach workers. The use of kids for street outreach therefore relies on young people's being able to negotiate a dual identity as insiders (street youth) and outsiders (outreach workers). Peer outreach is an excellent example of how insider-ness/outsider-ness is practiced though the strategic maintenance and manipulation of social boundaries, identities, and performances.

Training manuals for outreach work recommend that when doing outreach, peer youth workers have some sort of highly visible marker (a bright T-shirt or bag) of the agency that they are working for to use as a preliminary boundary. Peer outreach workers need to demonstrate more clearly than adults that they are working and therefore are playing a different role. Peer workers, though, often feel that an outreach "uniform" makes them stand out too much, especially to other actors in the street economy and to the general public. For street kids, standing out is often to be avoided at all costs. In addition, outreach appearances may not reflect the youths' own style or personality, which is their main connection with other street youth.

Peer outreach workers' histories and experiences on the streets are both strengths and detriments. For instance, they find it very difficult to refer other kids to a center or shelter where they themselves have had conflicts. For example, all my peer outreach workers had had problems at Covenant House, and all of them refused to send young people there, despite its being the only twenty-four-hour, walk-in youth shelter in New York City. They also said that they would never refer an older youth to an adult shelter because of the horrible stories that they all had heard about kids being harassed or even attacked in city-run adult shelters.

Nonetheless, the outreach process offers peer outreach workers a structured way of transitioning out of their street youth identity while making use of the knowledge gained through those experiences. For young people getting ready to transition out of homeless youth services, peer work can be an important step toward adulthood and self-sufficiency. It can also give them a sense of pride and giving back to both the street and the social work community.

This process requires a great deal of conscious "self-work" on the youth's part, and it can backfire if it is not done with the support and mentorship of adults in the broader organization. Unsupported peer outreach work can leave young people feeling used by social services. Social service agencies therefore must struggle to negotiate outreach goals that are supportive and understanding of peers as youth and that address the capacity and limits of outreach.

Despite these problems, youth organizations feel continued pressure to use peers because of the economic consequences of neoliberalizing social services. As budgets shrink and are revised, peer workers offer a beguiling combination of cheap, flexible labor and expert knowledge. That, in combination with an ethos of youth empowerment, will continue to place more of the labor of social services onto kids themselves, whether or not it is empowering for them.

Volunteer Outreach

Cutbacks in state services have also increased the demand for volunteer and faith-based social services to fill the gap. Volunteer outreach is perhaps the oldest form of street outreach in that religious organizations have traditionally relied on it. In fact, with few exceptions, volunteer outreach now is almost entirely faith based. Volunteer outreach with the homeless in the

Western world is predominantly Judeo-Christian, although there are some exceptions with Buddhism and other Eastern religions (for instance, members of Hare Krishna give out food to street kids in the East Village nearly every week). The ethos of a faith-based outreach to the homeless is apparent in many aspects of modern Christianity, from homeless shelters and soup kitchens run out of church basements, to Christian missions and orphanages in many countries throughout the world. A philosophy of inclusion and aid is even evident in many popular modern hymns sung at most Catholic masses in the United States and in a wide variety of religious literature.[30]

Public statements of faith help shape church members' understanding of both their religious philosophy and their practice, that is, how members realize their faith. Focusing on commonalities and creating a common space are part of a larger ethos of faith-based caregiving to the homeless. Paul Cloke's research on volunteerism in British homeless organizations found that the overriding motivation for service was faith based, and a significant subset of the volunteers he questioned said that they were "giving back" to the communities to which they had earlier belonged, such as recovering drug addicts and formerly homeless people volunteering in these communities.[31] As Cloke and others have explained, peer outreach is a complex practice that involves the past and present experiences of each volunteer, enacted in a way that is "significant in terms of the ethical freight carried by the volunteer into their practices and performances."[32]

Despite the long history of volunteer outreach that predates the professionalization of street outreach, professional outreach workers are often either wary or dismissive of volunteer outreach efforts because of the histories and agendas of religious organizations. They also are concerned that volunteer outreach workers may not be consistent or sufficiently trained to be working with homeless kids. Finally, professional outreach workers worry that their work may be "de-professionalized" if funders or institutions believe that the same job can be done for free by volunteers.[33] For marginalized, low-paid, and low-status social workers, these fears can cause real animosity toward volunteer outreach groups.

There certainly are many challenges for volunteer outreach, including turnover, training, commitment, and consistency. As one volunteer outreach trainer and recruiter stated,

> There are a lot of people who are well intentioned and want to help, but that isn't necessarily what is best for the kids. The fact that volunteering is often temporary and that there is such a huge learning curve is work-

ing against us. And the kids don't see enough consistency in outreach. We have a hard time being that consistent face that they can recognize.[34]

Several volunteer trainers told me that their main frustration was the inconsistency of volunteer labor. While groups often ask volunteers to commit to a minimum of six months to a year, they more commonly leave after two or three months. In my experience, a volunteer trainer may spend anywhere from eighteen to forty hours of their own volunteer labor training a new outreach worker, only to have that person quit before having spent even the same amount of time in outreach.

These are issues that all street outreach groups—professional, peer, or volunteer—face on a regular basis. The low pay and long (and late) hours of professional outreach lead to a high turnover rate as well. By definition, peer outreach is a temporary job, as the youth are expected to mature and age out of their "peer" status. Volunteer groups must cope with the additional challenge of constructing a "rewarding" experience for outreach workers that is not based on monetary or career considerations. As one worker told me when I first started outreach:

Outreach is generally not as rewarding as people think. The process of not seeing kids, of wandering around for hours is hard. Especially as a person who has trained new volunteers and you know that there is the expectation of seeing and helping kids. You really feel the weight of volunteer expectations when there are six people standing around you, bored and disappointed.[35]

Indeed, my first outreach experience was spending several hours walking the streets of New York City in December without speaking to a single kid. At the very end of the outreach, our group of four new volunteers and a trainer found a young woman asleep in front of a record store. Because part of the training for this group discourages waking kids who are asleep, we debated and then left an outreach bag next to her in the hope that it would still be there when she woke up.

Volunteers decide to become involved in outreach for many reasons. For faith-based groups, the reward of street outreach may be spiritual, cultural, or communal. For secular or non-faith-based volunteer outreach, the emotional rewards often are difficult to assess, as they may be personal, emotional, social, or professional. In any case, the difficulties of conducting outreach can outweigh the rewards. All three types of street outreach (professional, peer, and volunteer) suffer from a high turnover, which is detrimental to the street outreach goals of consistency and relationship building necessary to move young people off the streets. Turnover also means a nearly constant loss of outreach knowledge and experience, as few organizations keep good records of outreach locations and clients. Whenever a veteran worker leaves, new workers usually must become familiar with the street scene without the benefit of expert knowledge. And knowledge of outreach, kids, and public spaces is critical to successful interactions and interventions in a highly dynamic urban landscape.

Performance and Outreach

Various theories of performance have gained prominence in the social science literature over the past decade.[36] Indeed, the metaphor of performance provides a conceptual tool to explore and understand the practical, everyday actions carried out in human society and the construction, maintenance, disciplining, and manipulation of identities, power, knowledge, and structures brought about and shaped by these actions.[37] Everyday life and the practices that structure our experiences of society are key loci of social power because they influence how individuals express and act.[38] In other words, social power is produced through practices carried out in a variety of modes and, moreover, can be challenged, reproduced, normalized, or hidden in everyday actions. Performance theories can be used particularly well with ethnographic research methods because of their focus on everyday actions and the body as a site of knowledge.[39] Furthermore, critically addressing performance in street outreach opens up avenues for resistance and change to hegemonic power/knowledges that are often experienced as a prerequisite when working with homeless kids on the street.[40]

Performance theories stem from a number of understandings of practice, agency, subjectivity, and power. Work on performance in the social sciences covers a range of topics from institutional organizations, to literature and movies, to racial and gender identities, to tourism.[41] Scholars like Gabriella Gahlia Modan and E. Patrick Johnson have used performance in urban ethnographies as an analytical tool to address social interactions within urban communities that surround the negotiation of power and race. In these works, identities are developed through the performance of one's "place" in society, and performances can be used to strategically challenge boundaries and social regimes. For instance, performance theories have been used to understand how kids in gangs negotiate the complicated interrelations of self, community, and the street economy.[42] Performances in public spaces can shape street kids' sense of moral identity that reflects wider social structures and regimes of control. For instance, many street kids avoid actions that are identifiable as homeless activities in order to escape unwelcome attention associated with the stigma of being homeless. However, these actions also shape youths' own understanding of their unhoused state; that is, many street kids do not consider themselves to be homeless because they do not *act* homeless. Performances shape street youths' understanding of their social state, just as their social position mediates their public performances.

What unites these diverse uses of performativity and performance theories in geography is an interest in how spatial practices intersect with agency, subjectivity, and social structures in forming sociospatial identities. Geographers currently draw on several different understandings of performance in this literature.[43] In this section, I discuss the different theories of performance and how each can be used to deepen our understanding of street outreach practices.[44] In turn, these theories lead to new questions about the roles of individuals and social structures in outreach and the creation of outreach spaces in the context of regulated public spaces.

Goffman's Performance

In my own field of urban geography, one popular use of performance comes from Erving Goffman's work on theatrical performance, or the study of social interactions and the public. Using a conceptual model of theatrical performance, Goffman addresses how people present themselves to others as well as what these actions mean to the people presenting them.[45] This conception of performance situates a consciously acting performer in relation to a receiving/interpreting audience, thereby separating performer, performance, and audience. Goffman also conceives of subjects as creating and using a series of masks, each of which can be used in various social contexts and situations. As social beings, we all play a variety of roles.

Outreach workers often train by using role-playing, which allows them to practice the performance of outreach and to envision reactions to different practices before they go "on stage." Typically in this role-playing, several new counselors try playing the role of "counselor," and an experienced outreach worker plays the role of "street kid." A series of scripted interactions are then performed in which the "street kids" give the counselors a wide range of responses, from mundane to traumatic. For instance, counselors practice conversations in which kids tell them that they have just been raped, robbed, attempted suicide, do not feel like talking, and are not homeless. The point of the role-playing is to give new outreach counselors practice at hearing disturbing or upsetting information and making an appropriately nonjudgmental, understanding, and supportive response, or giving out the correct information for services. Role-plays are also a time when new counselors can practice their body language before interacting with youth. It is important not to intimidate the kids they approach on the street. Often, if kids are sitting on the sidewalk, the outreach worker might inadvertently loom over them, blocking off escape routes or blocking a kid's spanging sign. In turn, interpreting a youth's own performance (identifying those engaging in sex work, drug dealing, or theft) also is key to a successful outreach. Outreach should not be initiated at a time or in a manner that will harm the young person or the outreach worker. In sum, outreach workers are trained to script, think through, and analyze their performance.

Outreach as a conscious (and often extremely self-conscious) performance is then carried onto the streets. As Robert Broadhead and Kathryn Fox describe in their work with AIDS outreach workers in San Francisco, the first step in this performance is establishing a "credible" street identity that takes into account the varying audiences, which include drug users, community members, and police.[46] It is important that all the audiences to the outreach process interpret the workers' behaviors as "third parties," in that they are neither insiders or outsiders. That is, outreach workers are neither part of the drug community nor cops, but they must be able to navigate between the two if doing outreach with youth involved in the drug economy. Creating this credible identity limits the outreach worker's behavior. For instance, in Broadhead and Fox's study, the outreach workers decided not to wear phone beepers (pagers) because they were commonly used by drug dealers and so might be misinterpreted. The inability to use beepers, however, hindered the outreach team's communication with one another and their administrative home bases. In addition, most outreach workers dress in street clothes that will not make them stand out from the communities in which they are working. Dress is a key component of the performance of street outreach but can often lead to the police's misidentifying workers as part of the street community being policed. In another example, the outreach workers realized that they were handing out bleach bottles by flashing the bottle at leg height and then "palming" them off to their clients in a manner very similar to a drug deal. By doing so, they were adhering to social norms of the street economy of being discreet when handing out drug-related material, but their actions would look much like a drug deal to a police officer or other members of the community.[47]

How outreach workers enact their roles on the street closely follows Goffman's conception of performance, in that the subject who is preformed then performs in a scripted and controlled manner. Such a performance is readily apparent in street outreach. Commonly, when an outreach team spots a young person, they stop and have a long discussion about whether or not to approach and about how to engage that young person before making any contact. For an experienced outreach team, this discussion is often a quick shorthand of gestures and words, but for a new team, this can be a five- to ten-minute discussion and review of engagement strategies. Once the outreach is initiated, the team must continue to communicate to one another about how the outreach is going, without necessarily verbalizing that in front of the kids. Outreach workers also need to be able to discern when to break off a performance, even midway through it, as demonstrated in the following example:

> Standing back and assessing the situation, watching what kids are present and what they're doing is important. You need to be able to read the vibe of the scene and get a feel for what is going on in that moment. When you approach a kid, it's good to be general—let them know who we are and ask them if they "know anybody" who might need assistance. Sensitivity to body language and leaving if a kid is giving off signals that they don't want to talk to you is important, too. Kids do this by turning their backs to you, by putting a lot of personal space between you and them, or by not responding to questions and ignoring you altogether. During one outreach, a group of grunge kids in [the park] just completely ignored the outreach workers, shutting them out verbally. We began speaking with two females; the only two in the group of seven. They both stated that they were "stoned" and were laughing for no real reason. The other volunteer was asking them questions concerning where they were from and if they had a place to go to. One of the males, I believe, was being protective and sat next to them while we were speaking to them. This changed the atmosphere and brought the conversation to an end. We left after that.[48]

Outreach workers often learn on the job, ad-libbing their performance as they watch and respond to the street kids' reactions. Part of the outreach training is to recognize and interpret other people's performances, to remain an outsider while simultaneously involved in social action. An underlying assumption is that the street kids' actions are not conscious. But most veteran youth workers realize that kids manipulate adults in a variety of ways, from telling them what they want to hear to enacting particular stereotypes of youth behavior. This understanding of performance seems to follow both the belief that individual subjects construct and control their performances based on preexisting identities and that "identities are in some sense constructed in and through social action."[49] This second understanding more closely adheres to the conception of performance that Judith Butler described in her work on sexuality and normative social organization.

Butler's Performance

According to Butler,[50] performativity is "the citational practices which produce and subvert discourse and knowledge, and which at the same time enable and discipline subjects and their performances."[51] In the previous example of AIDS outreach, workers knew that handing out bleach bottles "under the table" was not illegal but that it looked suspicious to the police. In the end, social norms in the street economy persuaded the workers to hand out legal needle-cleaning material on the sly, following Butler's discursive conception of performance: Through speech, subjects are formed that then perform in particular (particularly normative) ways, including through gendered practices. Another example is the outreach workers' heteronormative interpretation, rather than through other identifiers, of the male street youth protecting the two female street youth. That is, the outreach workers assumed that the male youth was protecting the female youth from a pair of nosy adults.

Performativity is a powerful engine that shapes identities and practices. Performances reflect underlying and unaddressed normative structures with productive and disciplinary effects.[52] A more concrete example is that street youth are nearly always identified by their actions, experiences, and performances. Indeed, they are identified as "street youth" based on preset assumptions of youth, childhood, race, gender, age, and homelessness. The identities of street kids are formed by the productive and disciplinary forces of performances that are structured by social ontologies. In Butler's conception of performance, the subject has limited agency, which is reflected in more traditional social service engagements with homeless kids. Part of street counseling is to help youth disengage from their street identities, to understand that what they had to do to survive on the streets does not make up the whole of their being. So while street outreach workers are trained to perform (in Goffman's conception of performance), they themselves are shaped by the street environment, as their practices follow social norms of subtlety and invisibility. Outreach workers also are trained to expect street youth to have internalized and be products of their own performances, with little ability to see or change their performance without help.

Other Performances

A third cohort of performance theorists uses psychoanalytic approaches derived from the work of Jacques Lacan, whose work centered on the interplay of performance and performer.[53] In his psychoanalytic conception, the performer and the performance are one. Older models of street outreach (particularly early religious models) are grounded in a similar philosophy. According to them, street youths' actions shaped their subjectivity (souls) as innocent (blank slate) young people, morally staining them through criminality and exposure to the streets. Because no conscious social agent is in place before knowledge is gained, the acts themselves construct subjectivity. Therefore, rather than the subject's putting on a mask, as Goffman would have it, or the mask's creating a subject, as Butler believed, the mask and the subject are irreducible. In early outreach, the goal was to "catch" a child before he or she was irreversibly damaged by the contaminating street environment.

Most current street outreach groups disagree with this concept of street youths' identities and performances, but the idea that street youth are "unrecoverable" or "bad kids" has lingered. Social workers worry that the label of youth homelessness can haunt kids throughout their lives. One social worker at a GLBTQ drop-in center was conflicted when a photographer wanted to take pictures of local street kids for a news story. Although she believed that educating a wider audience was important, she was equally worried that the kids telling their stories could later be identified through an Internet search and stigmatized as formerly homeless by future employers.

Performing Identities of Street Youth and Outreach Workers

All three conceptions of performance are apparent in street outreach interactions; indeed, they sometimes are a veritable comedy of errors. One example of this is the "cat and mouse" effect of street outreach. Street kids engage in a variety of survival activities while living on the streets, ranging from the socially unacceptable to the clearly illegal. As a result, part of the performance of street kids' identities may involve being strategically invisible while under the public gaze.[54] Furthermore, being strategically invisible may be as simple as not looking homeless or moving around in order to divert attention. In contrast, street outreach strives to be visible to street kids by anchoring outreach spaces to the streets at particular places and times. Street outreach workers also need to be able to identify the subjects of their outreach and vice versa. Performances of visibility and invisibility, mobility and stillness, by street kids and street outreach workers often conflict in the rapidly changing street scenes. Because each of these performances is embodied—practiced, felt, lived—when street youth are "seen" or "out-ed" when they are attempting to stay invisible in plain sight, a young person may feel exposed or violated. Of course, this is in direct opposition of what outreach workers hope to accomplish.

Ordinary everyday actions assume different meanings and significance when embedded in a conscious stream of performance. For many outreach counselors, passing through or even sitting in a public space can be a normal part of their nonworking day. But during outreach, these actions have a qualitatively different meaning, even though the visible action is not apparent to the general public. For example, when sitting at an outreach point in one of the larger squares in Lower Manhattan, it is not uncommon for vendors, homeless adults, or other individuals to walk up and ask for something from someone sitting still for any period of time. I was approached many times when doing outreach by a lot of different people who were not part of the street kid/outreach worker performance. It is jarring and disrupts the outreach performance. Outreach counselors often tell someone who randomly approaches them that they are "working" and cannot speak just then. But they do not elaborate, so as to reduce the attention drawn to the outreach or to try to resume the outreach role more quickly. The result is usually confused looks from people who saw the outreach work performance as a private individual relaxing, not someone working. Outreach workers thus present a "disruption in the everyday," in that the "ethos of the performative movement" of outreach (the universal elements that connect differing forms of outreach) can be easily misread by the public.[55]

The role of the outreach worker is not just a spatial identity (as, arguably, all identities are) but rather is a consciously spatialized identity. When outreach workers "reach out," what is the space into which they are moving? How do outreach workers conceptualize the spaces that they create with street kids in the outreach moment? Even though space is explicit in the performance of outreach, it is strangely unfixed. Nicky Gregson and Gillian Rose argue that until recently, the element missing from theories of performance was space. They suggest that "space too needs to be thought of as brought into being through performances and as a performative articulation of power"[56] and that, furthermore, these spaces are complex and unstable. Outreach spaces are further complicated when merged with street kids' spatial realities. That is, outreach workers attempt to create what Henri Lefebvre called a "counter-space" or a temporal space where the dominant social arrangements of space are challenged.[57] In outreach space, street youth temporarily have the power to shape their own public space through their engagement with services in the form of outreach workers. Lefebvre posited that all space is socially produced, created through the construction of meaning, values, and symbols. From these socially produced spaces flow particular social arrangements, practices, and perceptions of power in society. Public spaces are generally produced through powerful, normative understandings of the social order, which are held in place informally by the mainstream society and supported by formal regulations that determine the behavior in and the use of these spaces.[58]

Outreach workers understand that what they are producing is not just a service but a space in which street kids can access services. One outreach worker summarized this when describing her difficulty in explaining the utility of outreach. She had been asked if she had ever personally gotten a kid "off the streets" and had given an uncomfortable reply that the focus of street outreach for her was different: "That wasn't what street outreach was about . . . we really were out there to let kids know that someone still cared about them. Even if it was just giving them a new pair of socks." The practice of outreach qualitatively changes the spaces that street kids occupy, if only for a moment. Her discomfort at deconstructing outreach practices reflects the complex nature of outreach performances and the spaces produced. Outreach is focused on knowing the street environment, and the space of the street represents its own power relations. Although "getting a kid off the streets" was the ultimate goal, it could be achieved only through a long process of engaging with youth in public, private, and institutional spaces.

Another useful way to understand the meaning of outreach spaces is through Michel Foucault's concept of a *heterotopia*.[59] Foucault's heterotopias describe "othered" spaces that conform to their own rules, logics, and regulations and, in some way, subvert accepted rules of space. Public spaces are often thought of as spaces of visibility (the binary opposite of private or unobserved spaces). Street kids' presence in public spaces is now typically not noticed, however, owing to policing. Outreach can bring a visibility back into the spaces that street kids occupy. When outreach performances are at their most powerful, not just pimps and drug dealers take note; the police and local residents also "see" that a different space has been created. In some instances, these groups act accordingly by temporarily leaving outreach workers and street kids alone. However, as Foucault warns, "Visibility is a trap." Outreach workers have been threatened and challenged by local groups, accused of enabling street youth, and told to move their outreach efforts elsewhere.

In cities like Atlanta and Las Vegas, outreach practices of giving out food to street people have been made illegal,[60] and more cities are following suit. Because outreach work and street youth disrupt the dominant social arrangements of public spaces, both street youth and outreach workers often must render outreach spaces strategically invisible. One veteran outreach worker explained how he viewed the inherent tension between visibility and invisibility:

> I think that it is a protective stance for both you and for the young people. I think it's smart to not necessarily go out there with bright red jackets or names on your backpacks. And that's not because of any sort of shame . . . it's for safety. Young people who are homeless tend to get preyed upon. Not that they don't know how to use people around them, but they can be victimized a lot more.

Here the outreach worker encapsulated the sense that street kids have their own agency in performances—they can play to particular audiences—but he felt more responsibility to not endanger or disrupt these performances. But being visible is not always in the best interests of outreach workers or youth, and unfortunately, in the public eye, the strategic invisibility of social work perpetuates the public's ignorance that homeless youth exist in the United States. The plight of homeless youth and the labor of outreach workers stay out of sight even as organizations struggle to educate the public about youth homelessness.

Reaching out changes and challenges the access and boundaries of spatial identities and the influence of the spaces themselves. Outreach workers struggle with tactical boundary making, which is at the center of the outreach performance. They do so in part because the creation of outreach spaces continues throughout the disruption of existing, overlapping spaces of public order and street economies. These spaces of the public and the street also are not preset but are created along with other ongoing performances. In order for boundary making to move from the tactical to the strategic (boundary marking), outreach workers need to stake both a social and a physical claim to their outreach spaces. It is this outreach space into which they are inviting street youth on the basis of their actions and words. Interestingly, the spatial power of performance and performativity harks back to Freire's concept of social outreach.

These examples demonstrate that public spaces are more than just a backdrop for the performance of street outreach. The street influences how outreach workers and street kids inhabit the outreach space. During outreach interactions, spaces are created affectively—acted upon in the moment, emotionally—rather than changing the landscape over the long term. Affective outreach spaces produce the stimulus for building networks, responses, and relationships. Outreach workers and street kids strategically use stillness and motion, boundary making and boundary crossing, to create spaces of outreach. Social workers have two ways of discussing outreach spaces. The structural metaphor commonly used by institutions is of outreach as a "bridge" between the kids on the streets and the services housed in institutions. The more common metaphor used by the outreach workers themselves is that outreach is a sport or a competition in the public milieu.

Outreach as a Bridge

One way of understanding the complexity of performances and performed spaces is through a simple visual metaphor. For example, outreach is often presented to funders, new counselors, and others not familiar with outreach practices as a bridge between the youth on the streets and the social services. It makes sense that in a society that regards street kids as endangered and lost, they would need a guide or a mentor to "find their way off the street," both mentally and physically. Street outreach workers thus act as a bridge by connecting to where youth are in their lives and building a path that they can follow from that place. The stability and strength of the "bridge" rely on the stability and consistency of the outreach performances in space. One veteran outreach workers explained it this way:

> There was a young man that was using the [drop-in center]. He was about seventeen, and I met him the day that he found out that he was HIV positive. He came into the [drop-in center] to tell people, and he was threatening to kill himself. Part of our outreach is transporting kids who need psychological evaluations. I ended up sitting with him in the emergency room for six and a half hours while we waited for him to be seen. He was the most open and honest and raw that I've ever seen a kid. He wasn't holding

anything back. I still see him once in a while, and I still feel like we have a strong connection because of that night. It also made me realize how important it is to have enough staff in the van. While I was with this kid in the emergency room, the driver and the peer outreach worker were able to still do our regular outreach route.[61]

Outreach can also serve as a link to unseen street youth through their friends. Outreach workers often cannot go into squats or gang- or drug-controlled buildings that street kids may be occupying, but they can pass materials and resources through other youth. Nonetheless, it can be emotionally difficult to realize that there are many kids they simply cannot reach.

[Seth] stood out in my mind, primarily because he seemed so completely fucked. He's got nowhere to go, he's not getting off the street, and it's only going to get worse. But despite all that, he was saying that he would bring any extra food he got back to the squat for some other kids. So he seemed totally alone on that street, but he's still connected to this invisible community of other kids.[62]

A common outreach approach is to ask kids to pass outreach information to other kids who may need services. This is a less confrontational approach for many kids: they are not being asked directly if they are homeless; they are merely being asked to spread the word about help for homeless kids, which has the added benefit of spreading resources around their networks. The foundations of the outreach bridge are therefore not located in one discrete, physical, public space. Instead, the entrances to the outreach bridge are located at many points in the street youths' network. These connections can be maintained only through the ongoing performances of outreach.

The metaphor of street outreach as a "bridge" can be highly misleading, however. A "bridge" implies a fixed structure, with one foot of the bridge planted in established institutional spaces of social services and the other foot planted in the public space of a park or square. In other words, a bridge implies a stable, fixed path from one point (homelessness) to a desired destination (shelter). The image it evokes is one of street kids safely rising beyond a dangerous current of social strife to reach the safe harbor of a shelter. This is far from how outreach is experienced by counselors or youth, however. In 2010, New York City had fewer than three hundred emergency shelter beds for kids, despite estimates of four thousand to ten thousand needing shelter annually.[63] Outreach workers are therefore forced to counsel kids on how to sleep in public spaces without being harassed and can only hope to find the same kid again, unhurt. Indeed, the dearth of social services for street kids can make outreach workers feel like they are building a bridge to nowhere.

Outreach as a Competition

Outreach workers themselves do not often refer to outreach as a bridge. From their perspective, outreach feels more like a sport, a competition, or a game with an endless variety of locations, players, setbacks, rules, and fouls. Street outreach counselors sometimes say that they are "hunting" for kids or that they feel like they are "stalking" street youth as part of the "approach, assess, and engage" model of outreach. Because the outreach performance is just one performance among many, achieving outreach (be it talking to a young person, giving out condoms, or providing a safe space) can be a fast, tense, frustrating experience. Outreach workers told me the following series of stories when I asked them what was difficult about outreach. In nearly all my conversations with outreach counselors, the issue of competition and the outreach performance was an important feature. Often the competition is between outreach counselors and adults in the community that exploits street kids:

About a month and a half after I started with the van, we were out in Hunt's Point [Queens] around 11:30 p.m. There were two young women leaning against a fence, pretty obviously waiting for work. We don't normally get out of the van, but when these girls walked over, I realized that they were really young—maybe thirteen or fourteen years old. They still had baby fat in their faces, you know? So I asked them if I could get out of the van to talk to them. They said yes, but once I was out of the van, I could see their pimp hurrying over from across the street. I realized that I had about forty-five seconds to do some meaningful outreach and that was it. You can't pick them up and throw them into the van, even though you may want to sometimes. This was a hard experience for me. They were very young, they had almost nothing on, and it was late at night in mid-September. It made me realized that you need a whole different set of skills to do outreach. There are so many factors and things happen very fast. There are a lot of uncontrollable variables. There are other youth, adults, sex workers, pimps . . . you have to be able to read the situation and react quickly. And you have to be able to sit with other people's pain. We got them to take a ton of condoms before their pimp got there, though.[64]

At other times, the competition is over the presence of outreach workers in a neighborhood. Some groups feel that providing social services attracts and enables street youth to occupy certain neighborhoods. In this case, the competition is over space and presence: "We've had multiple run-ins with the Guardian Angels in the West Village. They will just surround our van and stand there."[65] It also is common to feel the dynamics within street youth groups work against outreach performances:

> It's partly cultural, but it's almost impossible to get groups of girls to talk or to take condoms sometimes. They think taking condoms means that you're a "ho," but then they're having sex anyway. We definitely need different tactics with girls. The guys will often surround the outreach workers and ask for condoms, but the girls will hang back outside the circle. We've been working at getting one of the outreach workers to break away and go talk to the girls. You have to be subtle about giving them condoms, though. One girl said that if her boyfriend caught her with condoms, he would think that she's cheating on him, since he would never use a condom. So you have to be able to do assertiveness training with them as well, but in the three minutes that you have their attention. We don't have the luxury of having these kids in an all-day workshop; we have to do what we can right then and there. You can really only learn this through experience— no amount of role-playing in training is going to be realistic enough to mimic how hard outreach can be.[66]

> If there are too many kids around, we have a hard time engaging their attention. If we just say our piece and have to move on, that's not very successful. The lack of privacy for talking to kids is a problem. When there are large groups of kids in a small space, we can give out bags efficiently, but it's not very effective for connecting to the kids. Also, having to go through older kids or adults to access the kids that we want to talk to isn't ideal because it doesn't do much to empower the kids that we want to help. Kids like Chucky are trying so hard to look cool in front of the older adults and street kids; that is a hard interaction to negotiate.[67]

Street outreach can be physically and mentally grueling as well, which adds to the feeling that outreach workers are struggling toward some elusive finish line. The metaphor of the outreach bridge is qualitatively very different from the actual experience and performance of an outreach "in the moment." Part of the quandary of performance is that by definition, it is unfixed; rather, it is a movement, an event, or an action. The relationships and spaces created by performance also are complex, unstable, and difficult to "fix" outside practice.

Calling Attention to the Performance

In light of the history and social context of street outreach presented here and the ideas of critical geographers concerning space, performance, and practice, I would like to revisit the quotation from Baizerman that opened this chapter:

> Street youthwork is about . . . geographies of everyday life of certain groups of youth; it is about how geometric space becomes lived-space and the life-worlds of site, venue, and locale; and it is about how these geographies work as calls . . . for some kids—as well as some adults, including youthworkers—and how they respond by taking on existing street roles or creating new ones.[68]

Through his analogy of street outreach and the street evoked through "calling," Baizerman is talking about two important points. First, he is talking about the power that infuses street outreach through practice. Outreach is a spatial practice that creates a disruption or counterspace within the city, if only for a short period of time. Power is materialized by actions, by going out, by doing something called outreach. But this power is not stabilized or permanently sited. Rather, the act of going out is experienced anew every time the outreach is performed. The social context of outreach is fluid and variable. Outreach spaces are created in the moment, with no outreach ever the same. There is no stable representation of outreach space or the outreach process, despite efforts to visualize it in terms of "bridging." Moreover, outreach spaces are created in a dialogic performance with street youth, who themselves have a powerful role in shaping the outreach interactions and the spaces produced through these performances.

Second, Baizerman points out that performances and performative spaces are always relational; that is, outreach spaces exist in relation to other practices. One geographer described spatial relations in practice: "Places come into being through 'the effect of the folding of spaces, times, and materials into complex topological arrangements that perform a multitude of differences.'"[69] For street outreach, the interplay of differences, performances, and spaces is experienced as boundaries erected and dismantled in the outreach process. If street kids are not in a mood to talk to outreach workers, if they have just had a fight and if there are drug dealers or pimps nearby or police present, then often they will ignore or move away from outreach workers. Outreach space exists in a fragile and highly mutable context of street activities.

Nonetheless, despite the complexity of the street outreach performance, outreach workers do not receive much training or recognition for their work. Just as street youth fly under the radar of much of society, street outreach work also is carried out in relative anonymity. Although outreach workers think of creative ways and means of improving their work, these tactics are rarely recorded, used, or passed on to new workers. The frequent turnover of outreach workers creates a nearly constant drain of talent and information and slows the goal of consistency and relationship building. Yet despite the limitations and frustrations of street outreach, it still is needed. While public funding for street outreach is declining, the need for street outreach continues to increase.

StandUp for Kids and
New York City Outreach

> Where do you find these kids?
> —New outreach counselor after three
> hours of unsuccessful outreach

On a freezing night in December 2004, a group of new volunteer street outreach workers hit the sidewalks of New York City. StandUp for Kids, a nationally based volunteer organization, had tried once before to start an outreach program in the city. Despite fifteen years of successful outreach to homeless youth on the West Coast of the United States, they failed to maintain an active outreach group in New York City. That previous spring and summer, in a second attempt to revive volunteer street outreach in the city, experienced outreach counselors from the West Coast spent four months training new outreach workers to identify and connect with homeless kids. New counselors completed eighteen hours of class work and role-playing to identify and engage street kids, based on a model developed for San Diego street youth.

But on that evening in early December, the group again was unsuccessful. The outreach counselors walked around for several hours, staring intently at each young person they passed on the sidewalk. They searched parks and vacant lots trying to find kids in need of help but did not manage to speak to a single homeless youth that night. The one visibly identifiable street youth they encountered was a small, skinny white girl wrapped in a sweatshirt and curled up asleep in front of a record store. She was dirty and hunched over but so fast asleep that even an uncomfortable sidewalk and the chaos of Union Square could not wake her up. Their training had taught them never to wake up a sleeping youth, as kids living on the street often react violently to being woken by strangers. Instead the counselors left a black plastic outreach bag full of drop-in center cards, granola bars, toiletries, and clean socks next to her, hoping that she would wake up and see the bag before it was stolen or thrown away. They debated whether an older homeless person would take the bag from her while she slept. At the end of that evening, just before the volunteers went their separate ways, one person asked the obvious: "Where do you find these kids?"

Over the next year, StandUp for Kids learned that identifying homeless kids was only the first step in a delicate and difficult process of providing social services in the public eye. Street kids' geographies and street outreach performances are situated in multiple layers of fluid urban territories. Social geographies can influence the type of street outreach that homeless youth are open to accepting and also whether outreach groups can even identify certain young people as homeless. Outreach spaces themselves are created through interactions that are difficult to establish and even harder to maintain. Both volunteer groups and professional outreach workers have difficulty learning and navigating the lives of street kids and the geography of the city that they inhabit, as outreach is situated in the interrelated territories of the streets and public spaces, street kids' worlds, policing, local actors, and social service domains.

Although I used a wide variety of data for my research, the heart of this book is my two-year involvement with volunteer outreach as part of StandUp for Kids—NYC. I joined this group as an observant participant when I began my ethnographic fieldwork on street youth and street outreach.[1] Wanting to combine my commitment to activist research with traditional ethnographic methods, I began my study of street kids and outreach workers by doing street outreach. Initially, my involvement in street outreach appeared straightforward. I trained as a volunteer outreach worker, which included basic orientation to street kids' hangouts and activities, and began performing outreach twice a week for a few hours each time, always with a small group of other volunteers. Little did I know how much the outreach process would reveal about the city's distinct and problematic geographies of street outreach, the street youths' access to social services, their marginalization in society, and the difficulty of conducting research in interlocking social systems. I found that the experiences of homeless youth in our society and the work of social services in increasingly regulated and privatized public spaces offered an exceptional context in which to study the spatial operation of power. I based my case study in this chapter on five different geographies of power: the geography of public spaces, the police, the public, street youth, and street outreach and social services. It is at the meeting point of these geographies of power that street outreach either occurs or does not occur.

Youth Homelessness in New York City

New York State is now ranked thirty-eighth of the fifty states for childhood homelessness, a ranking based on the number of homeless children, risk of childhood homelessness (because of factors such as poverty, median rental rates, minimum wage, and education), and services provided for homeless children. New York State is currently tracking more than 45,000 homeless children under the age of eighteen, the majority of whom are under the age of thirteen. The number of shelter beds for homeless families is 15,000 for the entire state. Moreover, homeless children have three times more overall health problems (including asthma) than do middle-income children who are not homeless, four times more emotional disturbances as housed children do, and less than a 25 percent chance of graduating from high school.[2] Statistics like these, however, account for only those families who have received aid from social service agencies, and most homeless teenagers are independent of their families and therefore are not included. In addition, the homeless youth population overlaps both the child and adult homeless populations in terms of services, which means that they often receive no aid or attention from either.

Social workers believe that there are approximately 10,000 homeless youth in New York City annually.[3] A survey of street youth in 2007 counted in one month 3,800 youth who required services. The median age of those surveyed was twenty. If the average age of a runaway is fifteen and the typical age for a throwaway youth is eighteen, why were the youth surveyed on the streets and in shelters older? The answer is how youth act and present themselves in public spaces. Street kids try to remain invisible and are usually quite successful. Then as they age into the adult homeless population, they often seek out social services and become more visible to social institutions. Because the majority of street youth are difficult to identify visually and count in surveys, even though nearly four thousand kids were counted in the most recent street youth census, professionals in the field believe that the true number of homeless youth is far higher than that figure.

The new outreach counselors that night in New York City were thus not alone in their inability to identify homeless youth, because most of them do not "act" or "look" homeless according to our modern stereotypes. Indeed, a recent newspaper article entitled "Time Square's Homeless Holdout, Not Budging" declared that only one homeless person remained in Times Square but then described a small group of older, drug-addicted panhandling men as "the homeless."[4] These pervasive stereotypes of chronic adult homelessness serve to erase the existence of many experiences of homelessness, including that of most youth. Because of police crackdowns and negative stereotypes of adult homeless people, most New York City street kids no longer panhandle, which is what counselors had been taught to look for on that first night of outreach in the city. New York City contains a number of street kid subgroups, all of whom engage in the street economy, homelessness, and street life in different ways.

In addition to local homeless youth, a number of street kids from other regions come to New York City in the summer as part of a circuit that stretches from Florida to Canada and from Los Angeles to Philadelphia. They generally arrive by May and depart by October.[5] However, most of the city's street kids are from New York's five boroughs, northern New Jersey, Long Island, and Connecticut, with New York acting as both a transportation hub and a social, economic, and cultural magnet for youth trying to escape unsafe and unhealthy living situations. The 2007 State of the City report, compiled by a coalition of New York City social service providers, categorized the city's street youth as 74 percent male, 63 percent heterosexual, and equally divided among Caucasians, Latinos, and African Americans.[6] Because of the dynamics of street communities and public spaces, it is difficult to find youth who represent these statistics in any one area of the city. Far more often, young people form groups according to race, sexuality, community of origin, or subcultural affiliation. Each group has its own public spaces and social scenes where kids struggle to maintain control and survive, sometimes to predominate and sometimes to hide in the social geography of New York's streets.

Understanding the geography of street kids was the new outreach group's first step to finding and providing services to them. Three public spaces in Lower Manhattan exemplify the territorialization of youth street communities.[7] On the east side of Manhattan, the East Village is an area dominated by white, suburban street kids. The Union Square neighborhood is in the central area of Lower Manhattan and contains a mix of African American, Hispanic, and Caucasian kids, mostly from New York's outer boroughs and working-poor neighborhoods. On the West Side of Lower Manhattan, along Christopher Street in the West Village and the West Side piers are primarily gay, lesbian, bisexual, transgender and questioning (GLBTQ) youth of color who are generally from Harlem, the Bronx, Queens, and northern New Jersey. Even though street kids can be found in many other public spaces across New York City, most homeless youth are familiar with the street kid communities in at least one of these locales. With the exception of motorized outreach in Harlem and the South Bronx, the vast majority of street outreach is on foot in these three neighborhoods.

The East Village

The East Village is an odd mix of old and new New York: newer, rather tacky, modern fast-food joints and multistory, glass apartment buildings, as well as old Irish pubs, Polish breakfast counters, and rows of brick tenements from the past century. Small shops and restaurants dominate the ground-level streetscape, which is similar to that of other Manhattan neighborhoods, but here the storefronts are a bit more scarred and covered with graffiti. Tompkins Square Park is in the center of this historically bohemian and working-class neighborhood, which became well known for its punk and homeless squatter communities in the 1970s and 1980s. In 1988, the eviction of a homeless squatter settlement in the park sparked an antigentrification riot that brought hundreds of neighborhood residents into conflict with approximately 450 police officers.[8] St. Mark's Place (Eighth Street), which acts as the main east-west corridor into the park, is better known as the birthplace of punk in America and the location of Andy Warhol's studio. Today, the surrounding neighborhood is still a mix of antiestablishment coffee shops, bars, and bookstores, side by side with fast-food chains and Hispanic grocery stores. Gentrification over the past decade, however, has significantly altered the feel of the neighborhood. New condominiums have filled many of the spaces once occupied by Puerto Rican community gardens, and New York University has built a number of high-rises for student housing. Some of the more famous remnants of 1960s and 1970s youth counterculture still exist, but more as objects to be passively consumed on a T-shirt or a mug than as sites of radical change. Avant-garde theater performances still are held in the church at St. Mark's Place, which is now down the block from Starbucks and McDonalds. Rents have gone up and chain stores are slowly encroaching on the eclectic mix of thrift stores and bodegas. Although community gardens still are scattered across the eastern flank of the neighborhood, most of them have been "cleaned up" to reflect the tastes of their more gentrified, middle-class occupants. Currently, the East Village looks like a countercultural neighborhood that has been taken over by college students and young professionals.

After the riots in the late 1980s, Tompkins Square was redesigned to include restricted walkways and single-use, planned-activity areas—playgrounds, handball courts, basketball courts, and a dog park. The remaining green spaces were gated off and are rarely open; today they are the domain of squirrels, rats, the occasional feral cat, and the homeless kids who jump over the fences to sleep on the grass. When I was a graduate student in the city, I supported myself by walking dogs in the East Village. Although French bulldogs still mix it up with chain-collared pit bulls in the newly renovated dog park at the center of Tompkins Square, the human battles seemed to have moved elsewhere. Street kids are drawn to the cultural past of punks and squatters, music and politics that at one time marked the East Village. These kids are a common sight, crouched outside the McDonalds on First Avenue. The dollar menu there offers them both an affordable source of food and a large number of people with small change that they might be willing to hand over to kids outside the front door. Both the memories of past countercultural youth and also the current realities of drugs, free bathrooms, people with small change in their pockets, and cheap food draw street kids to the East Village today.

The homeless youth who occupy the East Village and Tompkins Square Park are primarily members of the punk, "gutter" punk, squatter kid, and traveler[9] kid subcultures. Most of these youth are in their late teens to mid-twenties, usually male, Caucasian, and not originally from New York City. During my first year with StandUp for Kids, I encountered street kids in and around Tompkins Square who had traveled from locations throughout the entire eastern seaboard, as well as Texas, Louisiana, California, and Canada. The punk and gutter punk subcultures are highly visible, their members dressing in worn and dirty clothes of primarily army green, black, and brown. They usually carry their belongings with them, in backpacks and old army duffels. Often one or two kids have a dog on a rope leash. The street kids in this neighborhood hang out in groups of five to ten, creating their own social spaces by laying out their belongings around them and all sitting facing in the same direction or inward. While this space is not fixed and is easily disrupted by police orders to "move on," it is a visible claim to space and outreach workers nonetheless hesitate to intrude into it. When outreach workers first approach these youth, they always have a sense of interrupting an activity in progress, of unsettling the space itself.

Many of the young people that I met in this area were well versed in political and anarchist philosophies; they were vehemently antiestablishment and subsisted mainly on "spanging"[10] and the drug trade. During two years of doing outreach around Tompkins Square, I encountered a large number of kids from all over the country. Many would arrive in the late spring and find places to "squat" out in Brooklyn. By 2005, the squats that made the East Village famous were long gone. Most of the new runaways and traveling homeless youth who came to the city spent time in the East Village connecting with other street kids who would show them places to crash outside Manhattan. A number of kids were using an area of abandoned houses in Brooklyn that they referred to as the "Bat Caves." Most of the kids I spoke to around the park were quite forthright about their drug use and complained bitterly about police sweeps and regular drug searches. Tompkins Square Park is in fact a center of heroin use among youth and adult homeless, and the majority of the Tompkins Square street kids are involved in the drug culture, as sellers and/or users. The social service provider that has had the most contact and success with this group is a full-service, progressive drop-in center that is also one of the few needle exchanges in New York City.

The kids in Tompkins Square Park represent, for the media and most of the public, the stereotypical image of homeless and street youth: drugged-out, grungy white kids from the suburbs, always asking for money. But this image belies the abuse that drove most of these youth to the streets. Several local newspapers, among them the *New York Times*, have written profiles and special-interest pieces on this subgroup of homeless kids,[11] and studies have shown that the majority of street kids do not have a safe home to return to and chose the street only as a last resort.[12] Such stereotypes also mask the dangerous and demeaning effects of homelessness on individuals.[13] Because of these street youths' high visibility, it is common to see New York City police as well as private park security driving slowly along the walkways of the park in regular sweeps, ticketing kids, and pushing them out of the open spaces. Young people hanging out in larger groups with visibly disheveled appearances also attract the attention of police and the public. They often are hanging out with older gutter punks (in their twenties and thirties) with whom they are engaged in the street economy. This combination makes it particularly difficult to single out teenagers, who do not want to talk to social workers in front of older street people.

Because of the police sweeps that keep the kids continually moving throughout the neighborhood, it can be difficult for outreach workers to locate them, despite their easily identifiable appearance. The threat of arrest and their lack of long-term ties to New York City (these kids often do not have networks of non-homeless friends or relatives in the city to fall back on) make them one of the most mobile of the street kid groups. They usually stay for a few weeks in New York and then move on to Boston or Philadelphia, only to circle back to New York before the end of summer. This type of nomadic behavior makes it especially difficult for these young people to maintain consistent contact with social service providers. In effect, they must start the process of using social services over again in each location, only to move on long before they can make their way through the paperwork and waiting lists that usually accompany any sort of public aid.

The West Village

The West Village is occupied by a second distinct group of street kids. Christopher Street runs through the heart of Greenwich Village, ending at Hudson River Park and a series of renovated piers. Since the inception of the gay rights movement and the Stonewall riots in the 1960s, the West Village, and Christopher Street in particular, has attracted gay and lesbian youth from all over the world. Today, it is the primary social hub of GLBTQ youth of color in New York City. A recent survey of youth on the piers and Christopher Street found that 69 percent identified as Hispanic or African American, 88 percent identified as GLBTQ, and 46 percent had lived in more than two locations over the past year.[14] On summer evenings, two hundred to three hundred young people congregate on the reconstructed piers that jut out into the Hudson River. The young people who meet here are a mixture of housed youth, kids who "couch surf" or stay with friends, those staying in shelters and group homes, and occasionally young people who sleep in the park or with sex work clients. Social service providers estimate that across New York City, nearly 40 percent of homeless youth are GLBTQ.[15] Moreover, GLBTQ youth of color are particularly likely to run away or be thrown out because of conflicts in their families and home communities over their sexual identity.[16] For a person growing up in an impoverished neighborhood in the Bronx or Queens, being openly gay can be a dangerous social position. The majority of kids surveyed stated that the West Village was the only place in the city where they felt safe. While these young people flock to the West Village to explore and develop their sexual and social identities among their peers, they also engage in survival sex, finding clients among the neighborhood's adult male population.

The homeless young people in the West Village spend a lot of time on their appearance, dressing in the latest urban fashions, carefully styling their hair, and applying makeup. This is partly because of the social scene in which they take part (on a Friday night in summer, it can resemble a junior high dance gone out of control, with young people exuberantly laughing and dancing to portable radios) and partly because the homeless kids in this area are more likely to be involved in sex work.[17] As one street outreach worker noted, for homeless youth involved in sex work, a clean, attractive appearance is central to obtaining "dates" and charging more money. In turn, sex work provides access to money, clothes, and shelter (either their clients' apartments or by renting their own with other kids). Street kids in this area are almost never found "spanging," and unlike homeless youth in the East

Village and Tompkins Square, they carefully project a "not-homeless" image. They tend to move around—strolling—and appear to occupy space owing to their sheer numbers rather than marking out fixed spaces as individuals. Outreach groups that have been successful in this neighborhood often use former street kids and peer outreach to engage with young people.

Union Square

The Union Square neighborhood is located in the heart of Manhattan. The square itself sits over a hub of subway lines and is surrounded by luxury hotels, upscale cafés, and New York University's buildings. The square attracts a dizzying mix of shoppers, tourists, office workers, students, political protesters, performers, and street kids. On a sunny afternoon, it is common to find more than a thousand people in a fairly small area around the square. In my time collecting data on homeless youth and public space, this location was consistently both the richest (in the sense that so many different people and actions were coexisting) and the most difficult to describe. A wide array of young people use this space, and their social interactions are frequent and intense. This is the only place where volunteer outreach workers saw kids fighting. It is also the location that Blacc described as "crazy" in his narrative of living on the streets, the focus of chapter 3 in this book. However, unless young people behave in a way that explicitly marks them as homeless—such as spanging—they can blend easily into the crowds of high school and college students, skateboarders, and people watchers. After a year of continuous outreach in this neighborhood, the volunteers in New York's StandUp for Kids chapter were regularly able to find only a few homeless kids in the crowds.

For street kids, the Union Square neighborhood is a rare crossover space for the street youth groups from the East and West Village social scenes. It also hosts kids, like Blacc, who try to stay away from these scenes altogether. Most of the street kids who live in and around Union Square are from New York City. They represent the largest age range (twelve to twenty-five) of any of the groups; they are a mixture of African American, Hispanic, and Caucasian ethnicities; and they exhibit the widest diversity of subcultural styles. Most of the kids in this area hang out in small, mixed-gender, and mixed-race groups. They play music, eat, joke around, and generally look like any group of teenagers relaxing with their friends. Careful observation of these groups, though, reveals a number of adult drug dealers and pimps in and around the social groupings of young people. Because outreach workers are trained not to approach youth who are transacting with adults in the street economy or who are engaged in criminal activities, outreach is especially difficult here. Even when outreach workers are careful to observe youths' behaviors before approaching, they often feel that they are interrupting something. The number of different people and activities makes these spaces difficult to read. In one instance, outreach workers were handing out granola bars without realizing that a street kid was being arrested only a few feet away.

Street Outreach in New York City

In New York City, the outreach workers' turf is often in the center of parks or squares, near major tourist sites, inside fast-food restaurants, on the piers along the Hudson River, under bridges, and along well-known prostitution strolls. The street outreach reports for New York State in 2005 (the majority of programs being in New York City) show an active exchange of goods and information between outreach workers and street youth. In 2005, outreach workers made contact with more than 163,000 people under the age of twenty-one and handed out food, information, and hygiene products to more than 100,000 youth.[18] In New York City, the Department of Youth and Community Development (DYCD) regulates most of the professional outreach to the city's runaway and homeless youth (referred to as the RHY population). In 2005, the DYCD allocated $31,195 to three street outreach programs in New York City,[19] for staff training, professional staff, outreach vans, supplies, and insurance. But by the summer of 2009, DYCD was funding only a single organization to provide outreach in all five boroughs. This organization, Safe Horizon, received the grant on July 1. Because this organization was new to outreach, its workers had to undergo a month of basic outreach training and were not able to begin their full outreach services until the first of August of that year. Safe Horizon's outreach workers are now responsible for all five boroughs and use a combination of vans and walking. They go out Monday through Saturday from 9 p.m. to 5 a.m., handing out information about youth services, condoms, food, water, and other basic items. The information about street outreach on the DYCD's website consists of only one short paragraph:

> DYCD's Citywide, vehicle-based street outreach service is focused on areas where youth are known to gather at night. The role of each street outreach worker is to distribute information about services for vulnerable youth and transport youth to a safe environment—be it their home, another

safe environment, or a Crisis Shelter. Runaway and Homeless Youth Street Outreach Services operate between the hours of 9:00 p.m. and 5:00 a.m., 7 days a week.[20]

The link at the bottom of the page directs readers to Safe Horizon only if they search for "Manhattan" outreach, and the Safe Horizon website lists nothing about street outreach and no information about where the outreach workers will be on each night of the week. Several other groups conduct outreach in the city, using private funds or smaller grants to work with sexually exploited youth, but to date, there is no central location to find out about outreach services for youth in the city.

As I have emphasized, social service work with homeless youth is made even more difficult by the bad experiences that many street kids have had with adults. Before deciding to live on the street, the average homeless youth has experienced sexual, physical, or emotional abuse.[21] For a young person who has been abused and fears being returned to a dangerous domestic situation, voluntarily walking into a clinic or shelter can be a terrifying experience. As a result, many outreach groups have instituted street outreach programs as a way of approaching young people living on the streets. Effective street outreach requires that adult counselors consistently reach out and contact kids in the urban environments in which they are struggling to survive: streets, parks, and vacant lots. For new runaways, street outreach counselors often are their first contact with social services. StandUp for Kids thus was not just finding its place on the streets with homeless youth; this small volunteer organization was also working out its position within a broader field of professional social service providers. These outreach counselors needed, too, to develop relationships with drop-in centers and other institutional settings to which they could refer young people.

The city has developed a continuum-of-care model of social services for street youth, which is a system of street outreach, drop-in centers, emergency shelters, and transitional living programs designed to propel youth from the initial contact (street outreach) to housed self-sufficiency (long-term transitional living programs). In NYC's street outreach model, "van services and outreach workers will reach out to youth living on the street and in locations where such persons tend to congregate in order to make referrals to appropriate services."[22] Street outreach is important because it serves as "one of the main points of entry to DYCD's RHY system."[23]

Drop-in centers and shelters compete for funds in order to add outreach to their services. Because outreach contracts are reassessed annually, which organizations conduct outreach, what materials and information they supply, and the actual location of outreach can change suddenly and drastically, and young people are often left in the lurch. In 2006, an outreach team that had provided transport from the street to shelter was reallocated funds to provide only safe-sex outreach. Because of the regulations put in place by this funding change, outreach was altered in only a little more than a month. Many young people were thus left not knowing why the services had changed or where to find new outreach providers who could offer transportation to shelters. Because outreach is based on a tenuous trust between counselors and youth, sudden disruptions in street outreach services only confirm youths' perceptions that they cannot depend on or trust the adults in their lives. Youth who have encountered a revolving door of outreach workers and services that seemingly change at random are less likely to open up to a new counselor or to seek help. In 2009, when the city's budget for street outreach services was cut in half,[24] the budget for all children's services was reduced by more than $72 million.

During my fieldwork from 2004 to 2006, eleven organizations in New York City were conducting street outreach to homeless, runaway, and street-involved youth. Two of these groups operated mobile medical vans; eight outreach groups used some combination of professional and peer outreach; and only one was run by volunteers. My selection of outreach groups to observe and join thus was limited to those allowing people who were not social workers to have contact with young people. Accordingly, although I was able to shadow three professional organizations, the majority of my participant observation was with a volunteer outreach organization.

StandUp for Kids

StandUp for Kids began in the early 1990s as a small group of volunteers seeking out homeless youth in the tourist areas and abandoned buildings on San Diego's waterfront. By the late 1980s and early 1990s, increasing numbers of runaway youth were congregating in Southern California, in part because of its mild winters, so StandUp for Kids chapters began opening in other western cities. By 2005, thirty-one chapters, more than 1,000 active volunteers, and four drop-in centers were operating in fifteen states, and by 2009, StandUp for Kids had 4,500 volunteers, a small number of paid staff, and an operating budget of more than $1 million, most of which is collected through private donations and corporate partnerships. The organization has a decentralized structure, with each chapter responsible for raising funds and training volunteers: "Each city functions as an independent cell, managed and operated by local volunteers with loose oversight from a small national body."[25] StandUp for Kids had become the largest street outreach organization in the United States and was attracting attention from philanthropic corporations and other large funders. In 2005 it became the official charity of Virgin Mobile, a major source of funding and publicity. As a volunteer organization, StandUp for Kids filled a needed gap in social services for many cities undergoing budget crises and service cuts.

With the exception of StandUp for Kids, street outreach groups in New York City are generally affiliated with drop-in centers, shelters, or advocacy groups that specialize in particular segments or needs of homeless and runaway youth subpopulations. These organizations often compete for public funding and must meet strict DYCD guidelines for the continuum of care and the quotas of youth served. The city-funded youth outreach currently has a quota of forty contacts for each outreach, six days a week. In an eight-hour outreach shift, this allows only twelve minutes per youth. Then once the preparation of supplies and travel time to different neighborhoods are factored in, each outreach can last only about five minutes. Outreach groups are therefore forced to focus on areas with large numbers of kids, such as public-housing projects, rather than areas where the kids may be scattered or more at risk of violence. Youth living on the streets also hang out in small groups, which takes even more time for outreach. One outreach worker expressed his frustration that he "doesn't ever get that much time to talk." Requirements that the kids sign a contact sheet and give such basic information as name, age, and social security number are time-consuming and rarely accurate: "Signatures are illegible, and no one prints their names. The entire effort stifles effectiveness and wastes staff time." In addition, the regulations for street outreach are a morass of institutional accountability combined with the chaos of the street. Even asking a young person to sign a sheet of paper can break the fragile rapport that street outreach workers strive to create.

The neoliberalization and professionalization of social services for youth have fostered an environment of competition and stricter accounting of which young people are eligible for services. This does not mean that outreach groups would deny young people services or try to stop them from using a different social service provider. Indeed, youth who fall outside one group's service population often are referred to another organization. For example, one outreach group may provide legal advice while another works with young people on safe-sex education. Since StandUp for Kids is not affiliated with any neighborhood-based or professional youth organizations, the outreach counselors are free to choose where they attempt outreach. In contrast, outreach groups associated with shelters and drop-in centers often have catchment areas mandated by their funding that they must cover during each outreach. For instance, a group may be receiving funds to do outreach in Lower Manhattan. But the street kids there can easily move to Brooklyn either by subway or on foot, crossing over on one of the many bridges connecting the two boroughs. Then if there are more street kids in Brooklyn, there is often a lag time during which outreach workers have to negotiate changes in their outreach zones in order to seek kids in new areas. In addition, for those groups with quotas of street kid interventions, having to engage with twenty to thirty kids each night severely limits the amount of time they can spend with any individual youth. As a nonprofit, volunteer organization, however, StandUp for Kids has fewer restrictions regarding the structure, location, and duration of outreach. Rather than counting just the number of kids engaged during each outreach, StandUp for Kids tracks the number of volunteer hours spent on the street.

Outreach experiences mirror the street youths' experiences in that outreach workers spend long periods of time (usually several hours) either hanging out or wandering around neighborhoods with a lot of street activity. Outreach workers may occasionally stop and observe a street scene while resting on a bench, leaning against the side of a building, or sitting on a curb. These extended periods of "hanging out" are punctuated, however, by short periods of intense outreach with a young person. On a typical winter outreach, my case study group could spend hours walking up and down chilly streets, entering and exiting the same parks several times with no success in finding kids, only to encounter two or three kids in need of first aid, advice about shelters or showers, and free legal aid in the last five minutes of an outreach. After an intense burst of activity, the kids would be gone and we would be left standing around wondering whether we had given them as much as we could in that flurry of handing out granola bars, condoms, names, and outreach cards.

This flexibility permits StandUp for Kids' counselors some creativity in adjusting their outreach routines in accordance with the social dynamics encountered in the field. Street outreach is a social-spatial performance shaped by a number of seemingly minor and everyday interactions between street outreach counselors, street kids, police, and members of the public, all acting in spaces that are both formally controlled through ordinances and laws and informally shaped by social mores and customs. This flexibility was tempered by the outreach workers' mandate to establish an outreach pattern that allowed homeless youth to look for counselors. The first page of the StandUp for Kids website contains its mission statement:

The mission of STANDUP FOR KIDS is to help homeless and street kids. We do this, every day, in cities across America. We carry out our mission through our volunteers who go to the streets in order to find, stabilize and otherwise help homeless and street kids improve their lives . . . all facets of our mission are guided by the mandate that our volunteers shall tell kids they care about them and then, at every point, prove it.[26]

For outreach counselors to build trusting relationships with young people, they first must learn how to identify and make contact with street kids. Trust is built over time, not in a single outreach session. As I pointed out in chapter 4, consistency is critical to street outreach. Outreach workers are marginal insiders to the street scene in that they are known participants in the street, engage in street activities, and base their own street identities on their interpretations and assumptions about the street environment. Yet street outreach also involves the conscious performance and maintenance of exclusionary boundaries through relationships and trust formed with street youth. Street kids continually test the outreach workers' performances, and an authentic and consistent performance and performer can culminate in this trust and, ultimately, the outreach bridge discussed in chapter 4.

I chose StandUp for Kids as a case study because it is a general outreach group whose volunteers try to establish contact with any young person in need of assistance. General outreach consists of providing food and hygiene packets and information about services available to homeless youth. As an all-volunteer, privately funded organization, StandUp for Kids also was not competing with other professional social service organizations for money. This helped mitigate the difficulties that volunteer organizations have with organizations that have doubts about the long-term efficacy of volunteer outreach.

Volunteer groups, nonetheless, have their own problems maintaining consistency in what is an extremely difficult occupation. Outreach work is stressful, underfunded, and low-status social work, with a high rate of turnover and attrition. There was nearly always a new counselor on each of my outreaches, so I often was able to observe other counselors settling into the outreach and the street environment. All the counselors in my case study group were volunteers and came from a wide variety of backgrounds and experiences. There were both women and men, from several different ethnicities, and ranging in age from eighteen to fifty, as well as various class and educational backgrounds. We spent a lot of time getting to know what motivated each of us, both the volunteers and later the professional outreach workers whom I shadowed on other outreaches.

Because StandUp for Kids began in the coastal Southern California cities, the formative outreach sessions for the organization were performed mostly with white, teenage runaways living in squats and spanging in tourist areas around San Diego. As a result, the training concentrated on the visible identification of this subgroup. New outreach workers were taught to look for kids hanging out in tourist areas, wearing dirty or torn clothing, displaying countercultural markers (particularly squatters' rights symbols), carrying old backpacks, and asking for spare change. Although the StandUp for Kids training manual discusses other groups—those who survive through sex work and the drug trade and those who couch surf instead of living rough—it provides few suggestions for identifying and conducting outreach with them. Instead, outreach counselors are advised not to approach youth engaged in illegal activities, for both their own safety and that of the young person. For example, young people conducting sex work may have an adult pimp nearby whom the outreach worker does not see. Interrupting their activities could result in the youths' being hurt by their pimp for attracting an outreach worker's attention. In fact, volunteer outreach workers often did not make regular contact with young people who fell outside the classic "squatter kid" image in the beginning. This may be because squatter kids or gutter punk kids are more visibly homeless, and they also tend to be Caucasian and from suburban areas, like many of the volunteer outreach workers themselves, thus lending a sense of familiarity. But youth of color and those from New York City rarely present themselves as homeless and often congregate in groups with nonhomeless youth or even adults in the street economy.

Because StandUp for Kids had little contact with other outreach groups when it started, we learned much of the social landscape as we went along. Many outreach groups spend years adjusting their programs in response to gentrification issues, policing, and the public. Outreach in one community thus may be very different when conducted with the same kids and the same outreach counselors but in another location. The expression and expectation of public behaviors and interactions are shaped by public-space regimes regulating how public spaces are accessed and used by the public.

Initial Outreach in New York City (December 2004–December 2005)

Given the national training and background of StandUp for Kids, it is not surprising that the initial outreach encounters for its New York City chapter were with countercultural white youth hanging out in the East Village and, occasionally, the Union Square neighborhood. The subgroup of street kids for which the StandUp for Kids outreach counselors were trained to look were also the youth most likely to travel south, out of New York City, in the winter. Accordingly, in the first six months of outreach, the New York chapter found relatively few homeless youth. The few kids that outreach workers did find were usually sitting alone, spanging along the sidewalk. These are the simplest situations in which to approach a homeless youth. The young person has already identified himself or herself as needing assistance through the action of spanging and has set up a space along a building, which they have marked out for this activity. Most sit on the sidewalk with a cardboard sign describing their situation. Outreach workers must be careful not to block either the sign or the change cup while talking to the young person, but generally these types of outreaches are the most straightforward. A lot of the kids who panhandle in New York City over the winter are older ones who have been on the streets for a few years, have past histories with many of the social service centers (and usually have been banned from some of them), and are involved in the local drug scene. It was therefore in the winter that we would encounter more kids out in the sidewalks who were mentally ill and chemically addicted (MICA) and who were often in and out of treatment programs every few months. These kids seemed to have a harder time finding places to crash, staying in residential programs, or joining up with other youth to head to southern cities for the winter.

I can still remember the young man who told me he was a MICA, long before I had heard a social worker use that term. It was in late January 2005, and my outreach partner and I had been walking around on a brutally cold, gray day for a few hours, circling from Union Square to Madison Square Park and back down along Broadway. In two hours, we had found only one young man, in his mid-twenties, sitting on an old milk crate and panhandling near a subway entrance. After chatting with him for a while, he mentioned that a young pregnant woman might be spanging a few blocks away, so we veered off our typical route. Although we never found her that day,[27] we did find a pale, red-headed, blue-eyed, and freckled young man curled up in a sleeping bag in a building alcove, reading a fat paperback copy of *Gods and Generals*. He was sitting on a square of cardboard, a second sleeping bag wadded up next to him and a half-full cup of change set just past his feet. After doing a double take (we had almost walked past him), we swung around and, as an opener, asked him how the book was. Matt turned out to be one of the most open and forthright of the kids with whom I did outreach with over the next two years. He told us that he had been homeless for about three years. The previous year he had tried to stay in squats in Williamsburg and Red Hook in Brooklyn, ending up sleeping in the offices of the abandoned Domino Sugar factory, a colossal industrial wreck sitting on the banks of the East River: "It was creepy there . . . and freezing. But I could climb in." We asked him if he knew about the drop-in centers, and he said, "Sure—I'm a MICA, so I've been to a few." He went on to explain that he was bipolar and hooked on heroin and had been to several of the social service organizations in Lower Manhattan. He was currently between programs and trying to spange without the cops noticing him. (He was tucked back from the sidewalk and was not verbally soliciting change from passersby, which can be construed as "aggressive" panhandling. He had simply set out a change cup and assumed that people would know he was homeless.) He observed that it was much harder to find squats that year and that the police were "way worse" than in the previous year, so that the young woman we had been sent to find had probably been "moved on." After giving us some leads for other places where we might find kids, he went back to reading his book. We did not see him again for six months. When we finally found him, he was spanging just a block from where we had first met him. He had been in a methadone clinic but had left because of problems with a counselor. Although he looked healthier than when we had first met him, six months had passed and his material condition had not changed—he was still addicted, living on the streets, and rapidly aging into the adult homeless population. But Matt did become the kid that I was always "looking" for when I did outreach. All outreach workers have certain kids that stick in their mind: a girl with scabs from spider bites on her legs, a boy with an infectious laugh and a dream of designing video games, a kid who likes the same music that you do or who refuses an outreach bag because he thinks another kid might need it more. These are the kids who haunt outreach workers and keep them searching just a little longer, looking around just one more corner in the hopes of finding them again.

The group's outreach notes during this period usually describe the kids encountered and the amount of materials given out. For instance, for Matt, we noted his physical appearance, where we encountered him, what he was doing when we saw him, how he behaved when we approached (first annoyed when he thought we were shoppers, then confused, then happy to see us), what social services he was familiar with, and any details of how he was surviving on the streets. We also asked each kid if he or she could direct us to other kids needing assistance. If we could not find any, we often offered some outreach to adult homeless people and asked them whether they had seen any kids around. Sometimes this method yielded new kids, but more often than not, adult homeless could only offer reasons why the kids had disappeared from the streets that day. My outreach notes from April 2005 describe these early near misses:

> We started in Union Square, but then went the loop up Park Ave to 23rd St. and then over and back down Broadway. We saw a guy spanging on Broadway in the mid-20s. He looked a bit past our age range, but we thought he might let us know where the street kids were at if we offered him some outreach. He was spanging with a cardboard sign, white, scruffy, with reddish brown hair. He said that he had been homeless since last October when his wife kicked him out. He is from New Jersey. He said that cops have been getting more aggressive in the past few weeks, moving street people on every hour or so. The street kids are moving to get out of the way of the cops. While we were speaking, a street kid that I had seen last summer and over the winter up on 7th Ave, stopped and asked for an outreach bag. He said that he and his wife are usually up around 37th St. on the West Side. He looks to be early 20s, dark (almost black) fuzzy hair, white, bearded, grungy. His wife isn't with him, but I remember that she is also white, with short reddish blonde hair and is quite small.[28]

Before a new outreach, we read over and discussed our notes from the previous session. At the end of every outreach, the workers also discussed how the outreach fared on a personal level and took extensive notes; this is often called a "debriefing" or "decompression." In addition to talking about what kids they interacted with and how the young people presented themselves, the workers talked about how the outreach could be improved and how they felt about their own performances and reactions. In this way, outreach workers actively assess their own actions as a performative act, something that could be critiqued and possibly improved, a system of reflexivity built into most outreach models that is more extensive than what most student ethnographers are taught. Outreach work has a collaborative and communal reflexivity; it goes on even when you do not feel like being reflexive. Since we all were on the "front lines" together, we also would rehash the experiences together.

The following is an outreach log I and other volunteers compiled after a typical outreach session. In an outreach, two to six volunteers meet at an agreed-on place with materials (bags of food, hygiene products, etc.). We then separate into pairs and walk to different parts of Lower Manhattan where we might find street kids. Along the way, we usually discuss and decide whether any youth we pass on the street might be homeless. We would look at their physical appearance, how they are acting, and where they are located in the public space. In this particular outreach, the entire session was with kids in Tompkins Square, at midday on a weekday. We approached and spoke to kids on the "knoll" after walking around outside the fence once to scope out who was there and to make sure that the police were not nearby. Of note, all these kids were different from those we had seen during the previous week's outreach. By midsummer, the turnover of kids around the park was very high, and we would be lucky to see the same kids more than once.

1ST KID: Caucasian, male, late teens, said he was from Philly but later changed it to New Jersey. He had been in the city for only 3 days and already has to go to court for an open container ticket. He's got dark hair and a black-and-red tattoo on his right bicep. We told him about the legal services at The Door and gave him a Door card.

2ND KID: African American, male, early 20s, says that he is waiting for a friend that goes to Cooper Union to come back into town so that he can stay with him/her. He mentions being on a quest or journey and has a vaguely totemic-looking necklace on a long leather strap. He has short dreads and looked in pretty good health—hasn't been living on the street for long. He said that he just got to NY from Chicago.

3RD KID: Caucasian, female, mid-teens, has a dog/puppy with her. Puppy is a shepherd mix. Dark hair and eyes, tiny, looks like Mila Kunis from *That 70s Show*. She's from Jersey as well.

All the kids were hanging out or sleeping when we first approached them. They had backpacks and a tarp that they were lying on, clearly marking out a space as their own in this park. While we were chatting with the first group, two more kids came up by, jumping the chest-high iron fence that surrounds this part of the park.

4TH KID: Caucasian, male, early 20s, gutter punk, very dirty, blonde hair, blue eyes, broken teeth. First thing he says after we offer him an outreach bag is that he's not hungry because he's coming off heroin. I asked if he was from New York and he said no but that he keeps coming back here year after year, despite "the police and stuff." He asks, "Is there is any water?" and we give him a bottle.

5TH KID: Caucasian, male, early 20s, gutter punk, dark hair, doesn't speak or give us his name. The other kid that he was with seemed to dominate their conversations.

6TH KID: African American, biracial, male, early 20s, shaved head. He came up to ask us who we were and I told him that StandUp does outreach with "street kids." He said, "That's me, I guess," and took a bag.

This particular outreach was interrupted when a police cruiser parked nearby, causing several kids to wander off and the others to occupy themselves with eating and other casual-looking behavior. Street kids often try to look as though they are doing something "legitimate" in their space when the police are observing them, actively performing for the police and the public. Part of this performance is getting up and moving, if only to walk around the block and sit back down again. At this stage, it was not uncommon for outreach workers to spend three or four hours walking around the outreach areas, but to speak to only a handful of young people. We constantly had the feeling, though, that the kids were just a block ahead of us or were circling the other side of the park because there had just been a police "sweep." This particular outreach was considered very successful, even though we rarely encountered any of these kids again. But several weeks after this outreach, we saw the young man with the black-and-red tattoo again, although the long gap in time made it difficult to build much of a connection. The following is an excerpt from a second outreach in the same location but with a mostly different group of kids:

Some of the kids were feeding pigeons rice right out of their hands, and most of the group was focused on that. Two of the kids were sleeping half under one of the benches just to the side of the group: a white couple, the guy with brown hair and the girl with blonde dreads. One kid said that he had worked with "Project Stay," and they all seemed familiar with outreach. I don't think I recognized any of them from previous outreach up here, though. It's become clear that the kids are not in the mood to talk today, and the older adults are being really disruptive (one is drunk) so we start to leave. Just as we're leaving, "Jim," the guy with the red/black box tattoo on his arm and a cane, came up. I had met him during an outreach in Tompkins a few weeks back, but with a totally different group of kids. We gave him a bag, but he seemed quite out of it and was clearly more interested in joining the larger group.[29]

In this case, Jim only vaguely remembered us and did not know where any of the other kids had gone. At the beginning and end of each outreach, the different groups of outreach workers compared notes on which kids they had encountered during the outreach. It was exciting when kids' names came up repeatedly and they became "regulars," although being known to outreach workers does not necessarily mean that they remember us. The following example illustrates the difficulties of building a relationship with a street youth when the contact is limited and sporadic:

At Union Square it was also pretty dead. Our walk from the front to the back didn't yield many kids. "Ben" was sleeping on a bench with his guitar—this is same kid that we had done outreach with before, in front of the record store with another traveler kid, "Jon." Ben is a thin, pale young man with long, straight, dark brown hair. On the way back around to the front, it had started to rain and Ben had waked up and moved. We tracked him down about midway through the park, just outside the dog run. We reminded him who we were and asked him if he was still out in the SRO[30] in Brooklyn and what happened to Jon. He seemed to barely remember Jon. Ben said that he's thinking of moving out of the SRO and back onto the streets. Apparently there is a lot of fighting and drama at the hotel, and he thinks the streets would be quieter. We told him about some bad dope[31] going around and said that he should contact the people at StreetWork if he wants to know more. We didn't know the street brand names of the bad batches yet. He complained a bit about the kids hanging out at Union Square. He thinks that a lot of them are out there for fun and that they could go home at the end of the summer. He seems bitter that he doesn't have that option. After this, the rain increased dramatically, so we called it a day.

We saw Ben several more times over the next month, but on at least half of those occasions, he was too wasted for us to do any outreach with him. He was always dressed in the same cargo pants and dark T-shirt, sometimes with his guitar and always looking tired. We finally connected with him when he mentioned one day that he had two upcoming court appointments, one for a heroin bust and one for theft at Barnes and Noble,[32] which were scheduled for the same time. A former foster kid with needle track marks up and down his arms, Ben was caught with twenty bags of heroin in a friend's backpack, was arrested, was sent to Rikers Island for a few days, was bailed, and was given a court date in a month's time on the same day as that for his earlier arrest for theft. That day, we sat around on the grass at Union Square and tried to connect him to free law counseling. After an hour of phone calls to *pro bono* lawyers and discussions about his public defender, he finally admitted that his plan was to leave the city before his court dates. He had already traveled across the United States more than once as a homeless kid. He was not optimistic that this would get him out of trouble, however, and was fairly resigned to getting jail time. He thought that even if he ran from the charges, they would eventually catch up with him anyway. He said that he would probably be picked up for something stupid like an open container a year from now in Los Angeles and that they would run his name and he would be in even more trouble. And indeed, we did not find him on any subsequent outreaches after that day.

To repeatedly meet young people who were not receiving many services or were not getting off the streets was frustrating, and not finding the same kids again began to worry many of the volunteer outreach counselors. Long outreaches, with little to show for in the end, led to the volunteers' giving up, which this young outreach group could ill afford. Training new volunteers took time that would normally be spent on the streets with youth. We all were aware from the social service reports, surveys, and meetings with drop-in center staff that there were thousands of homeless youth in New York City, and we were frustrated by our inability to find more than a small handful of them or to find them more than once.

After several months of outreach with limited results, the StandUp for Kids counselors began making serious efforts to meet and learn from other outreach groups in the city. This was in part to become familiar with the drop-in centers and shelters to which we hoped to refer street kids. Because StandUp for Kids was solely street outreach, the volunteers had to refer young people to services run by other groups. As part of this referral process, we visited and assessed a variety of drop-in centers and other social service providers. Early on, we had been told by our national headquarters to be careful which groups we referred youth to, as there had been reports of abuses at some shelters. We had met with workers at two of the larger drop-in centers in order to get informational cards to hand out during our outreach. During these meetings, we asked for referrals to other social service groups, hoping to gain more contacts and knowledge. We also expressed our frustration at finding so few youth to do outreach with. When one crisis clinic worker finally asked us to describe what we were looking for, he laughed and pointed to well-dressed African American kids hanging out at his center: "All these kids are homeless. You can't figure that out just by looking at them."

Instead, we had been using a model of youth homelessness that captured only a small subgroup of gutter punk kids and older white youth who were panhandling. Finally, a counselor at a popular West Side drop-in center for homeless youth recommended that the StandUp counselors approach any group of young people hanging out at midday at certain locations around the Union Square neighborhood, regardless of their appearance. After months of outreach and frustration over not finding street kids, the volunteers were ready to try anything. The outreach counselors first tried this method on a group of four Hispanic and African American men sitting at a picnic table, eating. The following is an excerpt from our outreach notes:

> "Hi, we're street outreach. . . . " Outreach counselor approached youth, approximately 20 years old, male, Hispanic, wearing dark clothes. The kid turned to his companions, said loudly: "Outreach is here." He gestured for one of the kids to come forward. We told them that we have outreach bags and asked them if they knew about the drop-in centers and services for street kids. They have heard of 2 of the drop-in centers. One kid volunteered that he had regularly used one of the drop-in centers for a while. He offered to take an outreach bag for a pregnant girl sleeping in the grass in the interior of the Square.[33]

The young people that we contacted during this outreach were long-term street youth, from New York City. They knew about the social services and were deeply involved in the street economy of the surrounding neighborhood. They also fit none of the popular visual descriptors of homeless youth and could not be singled out from any of the hundreds of other young people using this public space. The other outreach volunteers and I might have passed by these young people dozens of times in the preceding six months. One kid that we met that day, "Jason," turned out to be our guide to the Union Square street kid population. Over the next year, whenever there were too many kids and things were chaotic or adult drug users were hanging out with the street kids when we got to the Square, we could always find Jason and ask him which kids most needed counseling that day, who needed an outreach bag, who was new to the scene, and who should be left alone just then. Many of the kids were on drugs, and violent fights would sometimes break out. Jason would act as an unofficial outreach worker, steering kids to us or steering us away from problems. Our "regular" kids at the Square became our primary way to identify new runaways and kids who rarely looked homeless. Our outreach logs reflected these dynamics:

We reach Union Square, still no kids. The front is fairly empty; again the weather is driving people indoors to hang out. The back platform just has some adult homeless-looking guys hanging out by themselves. We decide to sit back there in the shade and wait to see if any kids come by. We sat on the steps for about half an hour. A few kids started arriving—two African American girls—whom we didn't think quite looked homeless. I hadn't seen them around before either. They were both clean, with jewelry and no bags. Then four African American boys showed up, including "Max" and "James" (James is native American, the Motley Crue T-shirt guy). I didn't remember James's name at first, but I told him that I remembered him by his band T-shirt and the other kids laughed. I asked if he had cut his hair and Max gestured to show how much shorter it was (about 8 inches). The two original girls were part of this group; street kids can really blend in this city. We would never have picked out the two girls as homeless, but both were familiar with outreach.

We asked Max if the police were bothering them this week, and he said that they were getting woken up and kicked out of the Square at night more but that they could usually sleep on the back platform for most of the night. The police would wake them up around 6 a.m. He said that it's not fun to be woken up by being prodded with a huge flashlight.

At this point, the kids were passing around a joint, so we asked them where the rest of the regulars were. Max said that he had just seen Jason at the front of the Square, so we decided to head up there and left the kids at the back to their activities.[34]

The following is an excerpt from an official outreach summary that the volunteers of the New York City StandUp for Kids chapter sent back to the national headquarters in San Diego at the end of this time period:

Over the last nine months we have been steadily doing more outreach in the Union Square area with homeless youth. We have seen kids ranging from twelve to thirteen years old up to kids in their early twenties, usually hanging out in mixed groups of guys and girls and of all races. In the mornings, there are usually small groups of two to five kids, with some kids sleeping by themselves on the grass or benches. By midafternoon there are larger groups of kids hanging out (five to fifteen kids), often around the statue and benches. Smaller groups of kids migrate between the front group and the back platform area at the square[35] and to the different fast-food restaurants, bookstores, and record stores in the area. On warm nights the group of kids at the back platform can expand to twenty to thirty kids. The kids that we do the most outreach with spend upward of fifteen to twenty hours a day in and around Union Square, with a small number sleeping in the Square itself at night. That said, the typical kid that we're doing outreach with at this location is in his late teens, male, Hispanic or African American, and from New York City (usually the Bronx or Queens). Many of the kids say that they are bouncing between relatives' and friends' homes, spending nights on the street more in summer. They report high instances of harassment from police. The kids seem to know the city quite well, and some have heard of services like The Door. However, only two of the kids that we have spoken with, have actually used The Door at any point in time.[36]

Over the next six months, the number of street youth that StandUp for Kids outreach workers were able to engage quadrupled, and soon the limits to outreach became apparent. Many of these young people were involved in an ongoing drug trade that counselors had to avoid interrupting. Police would regularly sweep through, scattering kids to other parts of the Square and the neighborhood. We occasionally arrived just after or during an arrest that had disrupted the scene, making it nearly impossible to engage with the kids. Older homeless men and nonhomeless actors in the street economy were continually filing in and out of the scene. During outreach, street youth either did not want to be singled out or were more interested in participating in the street activities than they were in talking with outreach workers. A typical outreach log reflects these issues:

At Tompkins today there was the usual mixed group of gutter punk and traveler kids as well as older heroin addicts. It's been difficult lately to do outreach with this group because it's hard to get the kids at all separated from the adults. When we walked up, we identified ourselves as "street kid" outreach and asked if there was anyone under twenty-one. This is the only place that we have to use this opener repeatedly. Seven of the larger group came forward. I would estimate that probably five were under twenty-one and two were over. They all seemed familiar with outreach. We didn't recognize any of them from previous outreach up here, though.[37]

We often were asked what our motivations were or which groups we were affiliated with, and we were accused of being with the police or affiliated with religious organizations. The suspicion that outreach workers were acting as narcotics officers hampered our efforts and cut short a number of outreach sessions because of hostility from kids who wanted to use drugs but did not want us to see them. The common tactic of observing young people before approaching them led to this suspicion. One outreach worker exclaimed in frustration during the middle of a street observation, "Could we look more like narcs?" Kids were always watching us watching them.

Outreach counselors tried to ease these tensions by approaching kids well known in the street youth community and asking them to help us in our outreach. A counselor would begin by approaching a regular street kid and then ask her or him to find other young people that she thought needed outreach. Although this tactic limited the outreach workers' contact with criminal activity and the non–street kids present, it also limited our access to the social scene. During the summer, the number of traveler youth began to increase again, owing to the return of warm weather. Over the summer months, our street outreach was divided between the East Village and Union Square neighborhoods. For outreach counselors, this meant having to rapidly alter their outreach tactics and expectations from one group to the next. The outreach continued into the autumn of 2005. By late autumn, because the weather was getting colder, there were fewer kids hanging out in the parks and on the sidewalks. Most of the kids who had arrived during the summer months from other states had already left for southern cities or were trying to return home. Outreach workers were finding mainly local kids, and fewer even of those. Once kids begin hanging out in subway stations and fast-food joints to get out of the cold, they become even harder to find.

Beginning the Second Year of Outreach

By slowly developing contacts with other social service providers, the StandUp for Kids counselors had become aware that a third, large group of homeless and street-involved youth had congregated in the West Village. Most of them were gay and lesbian youth of color from lower-income communities across New York City. Because of some of the difficulties already encountered in conducting outreach in the East Village and Union Square, volunteers were hesitant to take on a third, unknown group. But toward the end of their first year of outreach, StandUp for Kids counselors were asked to help administer a survey of young people hanging out in the West Village and Hudson River Park. During the survey, we counselors talked to many young people and began talking about expanding our outreach efforts to include this third group. Some of the young people that the counselors had contacted in Union Square were already marginally involved with this street youth scene, and the counselors figured they had reached only a segment of the homeless youth population. The problems we already had encountered prompted us to debate how to approach this third group. During the year, counselors had moved from targeting kids who were explicitly presenting themselves as homeless to conducting outreach with young people who were concealing their homeless state in order to survive. Approaching and conducting outreach with a young person who does not want to be seen as "homeless" or who does not identify as a street kid is tricky and can be dangerous for the young person involved.

When I completed my primary fieldwork in 2006, StandUp for Kids was slowly expanding into the West Village. The StandUp for Kids volunteers felt that as an all-purpose outreach group, they should try to contact all segments of the homeless youth population. These efforts continued until 2007 when a loss of volunteers caused the group to suspend their outreach. The burnout rate for volunteer outreach workers runs from six months to a year. The first group of volunteers who began in the summer of 2004 had turned over several times by 2007, with new members who had entered as experienced volunteers became discouraged and left. This is not a problem specific to volunteer outreach, however. Most direct-service social work, like outreach, is low paid and low status, which leads to high burnout rates and the frequent turnover of staff.

Street outreach workers must learn to visually identify and mark their subjects, homeless youth, primarily by how they present themselves in public, that is, how they look and act. Because public-space dynamics are unstable, spotting homeless kids and offering services outside traditional institutions is difficult. Street kids harassed by police and other members of the public are highly mobile and often try to remain invisible in order to blend into public space.[38] The case of StandUp for Kids illustrates the pitfalls of all street outreach. Street outreach workers often try to single out and make visible those young people who are attempting to remain invisible for their own safety and survival in the street community. Timing and location become critical to street outreach interactions. Consequently, conducting outreach in public spaces in the city requires altering one's tactics depending on who is present, often when the outreach already has been initiated. Furthermore, the various strategies that street outreach organizations and street kid communities use feed into the already messy dynamics of public spaces. How street outreach workers adjust their methods of engaging with youth to respond to these dynamics can thus spell the difference between success and failure.

How homeless kids present themselves in public is based on various social factors that change with time and place. A young person who is open to outreach in one instance may have to refuse help at another time, depending on who is present and what is occurring at that moment. Street outreach workers therefore need to be both sophisticated in their methods of identifying homeless youth and sensitive to the ongoing social dynamics that may prevent initiating an outreach session. If the combination of street kids presenting a "not-homeless" appearance and the presence of negative social situations consistently thwarts the efforts of street outreach workers, then social service providers need to reassess the utility of their model of social service provision.

Current models of street outreach are based on finding where street kids hang out, assessing their needs, and then consistently bringing specific services to these locations. The outreach groups with which I had contact varied in how they engaged with young people. How an outreach group initially identifies and seeks out homeless youth is influenced by a range of factors, from stereotypes and urban myths to police logs and social service reports. Once outreach counselors locate young people, how they conduct their outreach depends on many uncontrollable dynamics, including which street kids are present, police activity, the actions of other actors in the street economy, the general public, and other youth. Where street kids hang out and how they present themselves in public determines the type of street outreach to which they are amenable and even whether outreach groups identify them as "homeless" or even "youth." "Spotting" and "marking" homeless youth in order to offer them services outside the traditional institutions is difficult and a questionable approach, due partly to the fluid and unpredictable public-space dynamics and the power imbalances between street kids and street outreach workers. As a result, street outreach is a complicated social interaction in which both street kids and street outreach workers continually adjust and negotiate their performances based on the fluid social dynamics of every public space. In every outreach, street kids teach outreach workers how to do their job better.

Public Space

Policing Street Kids and Outreach

During the midsummer of 2006 as part of a national partnership, StandUp for Kids began a series of volunteer events in New York City for Virgin Mobile employees. Although the StandUp for Kids leadership recognizes the impossibility of recreating a street kid's daily experience, street retreats help break down stereotypes of homelessness. To do this, the participants in the retreat spent twenty-four hours on the street without money, cell phones, or identification. They became tired, stressed, and hungry, but only for a short time, whereas for young homeless people there is no end in sight. As a result, the participants began to understand the formal and informal social regimes that street kids live with everyday, as well as the spaces in which they regularly traveled.

That night, the CEO of Virgin Mobile and eight other employees panhandled in Times Square. For the past fifteen years, Times Square has been the focus of sustained and intensive redevelopment, an effort to reverse decades of disinvestment and rising crime. The area was once known for street kids, sex shops, prostitution, homeless men, and crack users. Today, the redevelopment forces, which include the powerful Forty-second Street Business Improvement District guided by the Disney Corporation, and a sizable increase in the number of both New York police and private security guards have changed the face of Times Square. It is now a tourist- and family-friendly destination in the heart of the new New York City.

Ironically, one of the most stressful activities of the street retreat is panhandling, which street youth do only minimally in New York City because of ticketing and police harassment. Moreover, the city launched a public campaign to discourage people from giving money to panhandlers, with posters in subways and other public places urging the public to donate money to social organizations rather than giving it directly to homeless persons. It also is illegal to "aggressively" solicit money or panhandle near ATMs or mass transit entrances.[1] Aggressive panhandling can be defined as anything from corner-ing someone on the subway for money to simply asking for money. Most pan-handlers therefore rely on cardboard signs or what street youth call "flying a sign" to attract attention. In three hours, the street retreat participants made only $27 from panhandling in Times Square, less than a dollar an hour each, and not enough to buy water, a necessity on a hot midsummer evening.

When the group finished panhandling, it was midnight, but they still had eighteen hours left in their street retreat. Although a police officer had been closely observing their behavior, the passing tourists and visitors had largely ignored their requests for money. Several adult homeless men made them nervous and uncomfortable by asking what they were doing there: they had inadvertently placed themselves in the middle of their turf. Ironically, Virgin Enterprises has a megastore in Times Square, part of the redevelopment surge. In their normal lives, the street retreat participants could easily have used the facilities there, walking past the private security guards without incident. But these men and women had agreed to forgo their real-life resources during the retreat. Because the homeless are regularly dissuaded from using commercial facilities, the participants started walking away from Times Square.

In addition to encountering the hostility, fear, suspicion, and surveillance that street kids are subjected to in public spaces, the participants also were exposed to the spatial regimes that most members of the public navigate yet rarely test in their everyday movements. For example, they were not able to sit and rest on the sidewalk without attracting the police's attention. When I met with them the next morning, they told me they had spent most of the night walking around, stopping only briefly to sleep under a ramp in a West Side skate park. If they had been caught there, they would have been arrested or fined for trespassing on city property after dusk. Both the private park police and the New York Police Department (NYPD) patrol the West Side parks after they close at 1 a.m. While the group was there, they heard some-one climb the outer fence of the park; they had inadvertently followed the same route as the street kids who were sleeping under part of the skate ramp.

When the next morning dawned bright and hot, the street retreat par-ticipants had not made any more money and were facing another scorching day on the streets. I found several of them sleeping on the grass in Tomp-kins Square Park, which also is illegal at that time of day; that area of the park is open to the public for only a few hours in the afternoon. Since its cleanup in the early 1990s, the park has been heavily policed, is cleaned daily, and is closed overnight. Police cruisers often drive along the park's interior sidewalks, rolling to a stop only a few feet away from where youth and adult homeless sleep along the grassy edges. The police regularly "sweep" out these locations, using a quality-of-life initiative that authorizes them to stop and search people in public spaces. In 2007, nearly half a million New Yorkers were stopped and searched by the police, and in 2008, that number rose to more than 530,000.[2] Police officers regularly drive and walk through the park, doling out tickets and warnings and telling street kids to "move on." By keeping them on the move, the police are enacting a subtle form of urban revanchism that robs young people of their right to occupy public spaces.[3]

Zero-tolerance policing and increasingly punitive ordinances have gradually privatized public spaces. This order-maintenance policing targets minor incivilities in order to prevent more serious antisocial practices and social disorder that are thought to lead to criminal activity. Order maintenance is a complex mix of social, moral, legal, political, and economic strategies that encourage the behaviors of some social groups and limit those of others. Because public spaces are material and affective media through which social boundaries and relations evolve, social groups' behaviors, ideologies, and values often conflict in public spaces. Order maintenance has thus fundamentally altered how street youth and other marginalized groups experience public spaces. These new tactics regarding access to many public spaces reflect a wider set of neoliberal policies that privilege the interests of business owners and residents over those of a broader public.[4]

A trend toward neoliberal ideologies in economics has been building in the United States for the past three decades. *Neoliberalism* is "the belief that open, competitive, and unregulated markets, liberated from all forms of state interference, represent the optimal mechanism for economic development."[5] This trend also has steadily privatized and deregulated social services and policing. In New York City, neoliberalism is reflected in the creation of business improvement districts (BIDs) in the 1980s and 1990s, which increasingly took over the burden and expense of policing public spaces and providing homeless outreach services.

Nonetheless, the policing, surveillance, and design of public spaces selectively target and influence public behavior, thereby enabling or limiting various social activities based on the public's perception of social norms. The drive to make public spaces into optimal spaces for capital is being increasingly used to justify harsh policing and zero tolerance of minor disorders linked to the homeless, youth, and minority groups.[6] A neoliberal trend can be seen in the BIDs' privatization of security functions and in the broader push for communities to take responsibility for order maintenance. Among other functions, BIDs levy a separate tax on business owners to provide private/public services such as garbage removal and security and surveillance. In accordance with neoliberal urbanism, the power of the free market to regulate social systems has supplanted state control: "A shift has taken place, with the welfare state stepping back and transferring responsibility onto the private sector and not-for-profit agencies, the community and the citizen."[7] A critical outcome for policing has been the geographically uneven application of a "clean streets" order maintenance policy. Neighborhoods with active BIDs, like Times Square and the West Village and the area around Grand Central Terminal, initiated crackdowns on panhandling, loitering, street vending, and other activities of the homeless.[8] The greater regulation and privatization of public spaces thus structure the experiences of both street youth and outreach workers. The kids "moved on" from the Times Square area merely go to neighborhoods that are less heavily policed. Because the implementation and maintenance of quality-of-life initiatives are by no means uniform across New York City, zero-tolerance policing has created a fluid landscape of surveillance and enforcement that street youth and street outreach workers must navigate.

Policing Disorderly Publics

Quality-of-life initiatives are based on social norm theories stemming from order maintenance and the "broken windows" ideology. The broken windows hypothesis was formulated by two criminologists, James Q. Wilson and George Kelling,[9] and has its roots in theories of community stewardship of public spaces. Wilson and Kelling theorized that if communities took responsibility for and actively engaged in maintaining order, it would naturally increase community surveillance (or eyes on the street) and control disorderly behaviors. Although they did not claim that this process would increase the "public-ness" of public spaces, they did support the norm that orderly and safe spaces would encourage people to use them more and care for them better, thereby perpetuating a cycle of community stewardship.

Wilson and Kelling's early work on community stewardship identified the perception of crime and the importance of communication between citizens and police as critical to the order maintenance of public spaces. By deterring small crimes such as litter, noise, graffiti, and public drunkenness, Wilson and Kelling convinced policymakers that the joint efforts of community and police would discourage larger crimes. Criminals would see that people were in control of their neighborhood and accordingly would move on to less-visible or less-controlled locations to commit crimes. The underlying assumption is that illegal activities are performed by people outside the community and are detrimental to its success or survival. Highly structured illegal activities like organized crime are not considered alternative forms of stewardship. This theory also acts on the deterministic assumption that honest and orderly are linked social concepts set in opposition to dishonest and disorderly[10] and that furthermore, these social attributes are embedded in individual subjects. In other words, when "good" citizens control their neighborhoods, "bad" citizens move out because the environment does not support illegal activities.[11]

In New York City, the "broken windows" first targeted were graffiti and fare evasion in the subway system. In 1990, William Bratton, the chief of New York City's Transit Police and the man responsible for safety in New York City's public transportation system, initiated a series of crackdowns on petty crimes in the city's subways.[12] According to Bratton, muggings, litter, and vandalism in the mass transit system created a perception of danger and fear for riders: a classic "broken windows" rationale. At that time, graffiti-covered subway cars were an iconic image representing New York as a rough, unforgiving city.[13] Gang signs and the omnipresent homeless were reminders of the physical and social disinvestment that many New York neighborhoods suffered in the 1970s and 1980s. Unlike these outlying neighborhoods, the subway and its riders traveled through the heart of the more affluent mid- and downtown Manhattan landscape. By the 1990s, visible markers of economic and social distress such as the homeless were a glaring contrast to the wealth, tourism, and mass consumerism of downtown Manhattan and gentrified enclaves such as the West Village and SoHo.

The crackdown in the subways then was used as a new approach to preventing bigger crimes. Drawing on the work of academic criminologists, Bratton (who became the police commissioner in 1993) and Mayor Rudolph Giuliani began an order maintenance program that aggressively ticketed misdemeanors—particularly turnstile jumping (fare evasion) and panhandling.[14] It now was illegal to sleep, beg, or eat in the subways. People stopped for relatively minor crimes were arrested and spent anywhere from one to four days in jail, waiting for New York's sluggish justice system to either charge them or dismiss their case.[15]

The mass transit police began stopping fare evaders and the homeless, fingerprinting them and checking for outstanding warrants. Between 1994 and 1998, these new measures resulted in 40,000 additional misdemeanor arrests in New York City, despite no significant increase in misdemeanor complaints. New York City also added 12,000 more police officers to its force, bringing the total to nearly 40,000.[16] Crime in the subways dropped precipitously, reinforcing the idea that signs of disorder and serious crime were linked.[17] Mayor Giuliani ran for reelection on a tough-on-crime platform that promised to clean up New York City. His "quality-of-life" initiative focused on order maintenance in all the city's public spaces, which he promised to reclaim for "average" New Yorkers. What Giuliani meant by "average" is part of the social discourses of behavioral norms and moral order that are mapped bodily onto social subjects.

Social Norm Theory

New York's quality-of-life ordinances can be traced to social norm theories made popular by the "new progressives," or the New Chicago School of Urban Criminology.[18] Social norm theory proposes that through an intersection of law and social values (norms), society can achieve public order.[19] This theory presupposes that human actors will make rational decisions based on the context and available information. People's behavior may therefore be regulated and modified by altering the social meaning of particular behaviors. The primary goal of policing, then, is to maintain order, and order itself is usually understood to be morally "good."[20] There are several good examples that speak to how youth on the streets are perceived by society as moral signifiers of disorder, and how kids are dealt with through socially normative policies and policing efforts. Forms of urban revanchism are founded on moral claims of restoring public order by attacking or driving out "disorder," which often takes the form of a teenager.

In the 1960s, a moral panic developed over the growing number of missing and runaway children in the United States, especially after several well-publicized kidnappings. Towns began using youth curfews as a way of steering young people into the supposedly safe space of homes and off the streets at night. In 1969, a public service campaign begun by WNYW-TV in New York City ran the message: "It's 10 p.m.—do you know where your children are?" Other television stations throughout the country adopted this slogan as well. Its impact was immediate and twofold. It reminded parents that there might be a curfew in effect in their town, and it played on their fears that they did not know what their children were doing and the dangers they might be facing. The message served to discipline parents and children alike. Children who were out after ten o'clock at night were morally coded as endangered or out of control and thus clearly the product of careless parents or "bad" family environments.

Social norm theory explains how youth curfews alter the social meaning of young people out at night in the context and interpretation of their nocturnal behaviors. In the past, young people's hanging out with friends at night was considered (a slightly annoying) rite of passage. Consider George Lucas's iconic film about American youth, *American Graffiti*. The protagonists spend their last night before adulthood cruising the nocturnal landscapes of late 1960s California. The night was an endless series of youthful adventures. But over time, pastimes such as cruising were reinterpreted, and the kids themselves became agents of nighttime disorder.[21] Young peoples' nocturnal "disorderly" behaviors were thus interpreted as potential precursors of gang activity, vandalism, drug use, promiscuity, and violence. As a result, since the 1970s, youth curfews and anticruising laws have been strengthened,[22] and kids have been increasingly constructed as disruptions to, rather than active members of, communities.

There is a powerful ambiguity in discourses of "community." Community is often constructed as an ideal form that excludes problematic members such as youth. Antiurbanism and revanchist policies are often cloaked in the moral language of family values, security, and a community that excludes the homeless and young people. The broken windows ideology relies on a "politics of fear" that builds moral panic, creating anxiety about boundaries of community and threats of outsiders. By classifying small acts of disorder as gateways to larger crimes, they transform what once was considered annoying behavior into threatening or even dangerous behavior and its perpetrators into potentially hard-core criminals.[23] These potential criminals are then defined as "outsiders" or external to the community, an important spatial logic used for excluding people from spaces. The broken windows hypothesis encourages communities to assume responsibility for preventing crime in their public spaces, rather than relying on police to step in once a crime has been committed. On one hand, community policing can encourage the formation of neighborhood watch groups that bring communities together—the type of "eyes on the street" that Jane Jacobs described in her work on traditional city neighborhoods.[24] On the other hand, community policing can also lead to increased territoriality, xenophobia, and vigilantism.

Zero Tolerance, Community Policing, and Order Maintenance

Policing strategies in the United States have changed fundamentally, with zero-tolerance policing tactics gaining in popularity.[25] In the wake of the civil unrest, rising crime, and racial tensions in several major U.S. cities in the mid-1960s, both community groups and police organizations began to call for public/private partnerships in the management and security of public spaces. Local communities began to take an active role in policing policy, at the heart of which is reducing the community's fear of crime by means of joint problem solving. Rather than waiting for crime to happen, community policing focuses on a partnership between the police and residents to identify problem areas, whether a local drug house or noisy teenagers, and prevent crime. The social imaginary behind community policing relies on a romantic nostalgia for cohesive, homogeneous neighborhoods and the local "beat cop"— walking the streets, knowing everyone, and keeping the peace[26]—an "Officer Krupke"[27] effect. Community policing discourses rest on imaginaries of communities coming together to work for the common good. In practice, however, what and who constitutes the "common" and the "good" are boundaries that diverse social actors struggle with in their everyday lives and behaviors.

Community policing is both a philosophy and a loose set of tactics and structures for bringing together communities and police to maintain the social order;[28] that is, the driving concept behind policing is order maintenance.[29] The experience of order varies by neighborhood, community, and spatial/temporal/social context. The communities, and not just the police, are responsible for defining "order." The police enforce laws against what the larger community ostensibly has already identified as problem behaviors, spatial or temporal occurrences, or individuals. A common example is the ordinance against public drinking and open containers. In many communities, the public-drinking ordinance is heavily enforced against youth and the homeless but not a family picnic or professional event.[30] Enforcement also has changed over time, so that open container violations that were often overlooked in the 1980s were suddenly enforced in the 1990s.[31] The police's responses also differ depending who called the police, who is involved, where and when the activity is occurring, which police are responding, and whether any of the participants are known to the police. In other words, police discretion is a powerful and ambiguous social tool that enables shifting geographies of enforcement, public behaviors, and, ultimately, access to public spaces.

In practice, community policing creates social boundaries between "legitimate" community members and "others." In these discourses, understandings of the public good and expectations of public/private boundaries reflect the social position of relatively small, yet powerful social groups that benefit from the privatization of public space. What constitutes a "community" is rarely addressed in the policing literature.[32] In community-policing discourses, the interests of landowners and business leaders are often substituted for broader public opinion.

For example, in many New York neighborhoods, old brownstone and tenement buildings are entered from a "stoop," or a short, broad staircase leading to an elevated front door. Stoops have long been interstitial sites of public/private socialization. Residents sit on their stoops, talk to their neighbors, and engage in street life—but only if they own or live in that building. Because stoops are privately owned spaces, police frequently chase street kids and even outreach workers away from them. Nonetheless, the "publicness" of the stoop has been long held as the space in which community comes together, albeit a community restricted to those who own or control that space. Ironically, a recent battle over the public/private divide in Brooklyn neighborhoods centered on the venerable stoop: a Brooklyn resident was cited for public drinking on his stoop in 2008 and brought suit against the city. A recent article pointed out that even though the Brooklyn borough president was caught drinking on his stoop, he was not ticketed.[33] The city claims, however, that the stoop is public enough to fall into the area regulated by the open container laws, whereas city residents claim stoops as private spaces akin to suburban decks or porches.

The community, the public, local authority, and public/private partnerships are dynamic social relations that have complicated and politicized community policing. The profiling and systematic harassment of marginalized social groups in many cities across the United States is the result of public pressure to cleanse urban public spaces and gentrifying neighborhoods of the perceived polluting presence of groups that fall outside socially constructed, normative communities. The social norm theories informing "broken windows" conceptions, order maintenance strategies, and community policing efforts are, by definition, normative, morally coded, and exclusionary. Social norms serve to organize and maintain boundaries of inclusion and exclusion, limiting and shaping the access of social subjects constructed and placed outside fictive communities. Spaces become restrictive and privatized, and social subjects are organized into those whose "quality of life" is threatened. Mainstream subjectivity and behaviors are protected by spatial regulations applying to those whose behaviors conflict with societal norms.

Current zero-tolerance policing relies on the surveillance and harassment of "undesirables" to maintain a neighborhood's certain look and feel. That is, what is often more important than an actual reduction in crime is a perception of order.[34] Therefore, in order to maintain the "feel" of orderliness, communities across the United States are increasing the number of public-space ordinances that are strictly enforced against such minor offenses as panhandling, loitering, open (alcoholic) containers, noise, curfews, and obstruction of public sidewalks. These ordinances punish the visible signs of broader social problems—such as homelessness, poverty, and drug addiction—that are often associated with criminal activity and social disorder. Critics claim that public-space ordinances are selectively enforced against the homeless, minorities, and youth, especially in the form of stop-and-search policing tactics.[35]

Policing Moral Geographies

Debates over morality, community, and rights to public spaces have monopolized the research on the quality of life and the policing of public spaces. Much of the work on the privatization of public space in particular has been characterized as a "literature of loss" focused on the "end of public space."[36] These discourses concentrate on the loss of access to public spaces by marginalized communities such as youth, ethnic minorities, and the homeless. The popular media, however, have touted numerous accounts of the "success" of privatization techniques, that parks are safe, clean, and frequently used by a wide variety of people who previously were afraid to stray beyond the sidewalks. Newspaper headlines in the 1990s cheered the reclaiming of space for everyday New Yorkers. The author of one *New York Times* article urging the continued cleanup of public transportation contended that "subways are not for sleeping. Transit police have yet to get demonstrably serious about enforcing rules against sleeping on subway cars and in stations. Prostrate forms on the benches take seats and erode the comforting sense of control the M.T.A. has reestablished by effacing graffiti." The public was well aware that the quality-of-life crackdown was as much about a perception of civility as it was about crime itself. Much of the debate surrounding homelessness purported to help the homeless, but only as part of a larger public good. If the city could find " a humane way to move the homeless out of the Port Authority Bus Terminal, Grand Central Terminal and Penn Station," then "helping those homeless people would be worthy; so would reclaiming public space for hundreds of thousands of commuters."[37] Social scientists have argued that a host of antihomeless measures and outcomes—among them zero-tolerance policing and the privatization of public space—have ended up denying marginalized groups equal access to the city's spaces.[38] In popular rhetoric, however, this urban revanchism is deemed to be in the best interests of homeless and street kids, an argument remarkably similar to social reformers' spatial-moral arguments more than a century earlier that 200,000 street and orphaned youth should be forcibly removed from New York City on "orphan trains."

Again, the social bounding and construction of moral communities fuel these debates. The two main arguments that complicate the social regulation of public spaces are the concept of public space as an ideal form and the shifting geography of public access. The ways in which we experience public spaces—both the limits and the access—are part of the structure that constrains and enables our opportunities and our actions in society. We experience public space through the design, control, uses, surveillance, and boundary making of a variety of actors and institutions. Privatization is one mechanism affecting the quality of access to decision making in urban society, and the social regulation of public spaces is critical to who has a right to a voice both in and concerning today's public spaces.

Despite nearly twenty years of steadily decreasing crime, in 2006 more than 700,000 quality-of-life summons were issued in New York City, an increase of 52 percent from 2002.[39] By 2008, the New York police had stopped and frisked more than half a million New Yorkers, 80 percent of whom were black or Latino, even though the actual number of summons and arrests was the same for all racial categories.[40] Racial and class profiling directly affect homeless youth in their impact on the implementation of quality-of-life ordinances. In the summer of 2005, a West Village–based youth advocacy group conducted a small survey of primarily African American and Latino kids hanging out in and around Hudson River Park, asking them about their interactions with local police. More than two dozen young people filled out response forms detailing their recent interactions with the NYPD and private security guards. Their response was overwhelmingly negative. Of those reporting, nearly two-thirds had been stopped by the police while in a public space. In more than 40 percent of these incidents, the young people were not told why they were being stopped. Although the majority of youth in the survey reported feeling harassed or threatened by the police, they did not report this to an adult. When asked what the officers said to them, most of the kids remembered some form of being told to "move on." One young man stated that he "came out of the store, and police said, 'Excuse me, gentlemen, get off the corner.'" Another youth commented that "I was walking down the street, and he told me if he catch me out here again, he would lock me up." Young people read their own understandings into these interactions: "My friend was asked to move while waiting for me outside Washington Mutual [a bank]. He was approached because they thought he might mug the people inside."[41]

Based on the negative responses by young people in earlier street surveys and the escalating tensions between youth and local residents in the West Village, a second youth organization conducted focus groups with kids in the same West Side park in late 2005.[42] The kids in these groups insisted that the harassment by the police and residents had as much or more to do with class and race issues as with age or sexual orientation. One young woman mentioned that a local resident had told them that "Harlem kids" were taking over the neighborhoods and should go home. Although a few young people occupying the West Village actually are from Harlem, these generalizations were interpreted as meaning that the problematic youth were low-income African Americans.

In addition, young people reported that some residents had complained to them about other youth, implying that they all knew one another or were from the same place. Residents complained that the kids look tougher, more "gangster," which only confirms to the kids that this is really a class and race issue. Young people often complain that they are targeted for noisy behavior and that the noise of white, more affluent bar patrons or traffic is overlooked: "They blame kids for all the noise, yet there is more car noise than talking noise." Other young people stated that residents misinterpret kids having fun (vogueing, showing off) as engaging in violent or erratic behavior.[43] One participant mentioned that when a female cop was being rude to him, he said, "Don't talk to me like that—you're a public servant." The police officer responded, "I get paid to talk to you like that." Encounters like these are repeated to other kids and become a form of local youth "knowledge." All the young people who participated in the focus groups believed that rude behavior from police was not just overlooked; it was encouraged. They felt, too, that the local police had been given a mandate to drive them out of the neighborhood. The following is an excerpt from the final focus group report addressing the youths' typical responses to the question about their recent problems with the police:

- There is an overall, in-your-face, lack of respect. The kids feel dehumanized.
- Police make kids move on when there is a group on a corner or blocking a sidewalk, yet when sports fans spill out of bars during a game and block the same sidewalk, the police do not say anything.
- Police tell only kids of color to move on, not white bar patrons.
- Police stop all the trans-women walking down side streets because they assume all trans-women are sex workers.
- One youth participant saw six police officers holding one guy down and said that excessive displays of force were common and made kids feel even more defensive.
- Kids over twenty-one are pulled out of bars and questioned about their age and what they are doing in the neighborhood.
- Kids feel that the police will arrest them for everything or anything.
- The police give us dirty looks, and the kids feel like people are telling them to "go home," even if they do not say it out loud.

The negative tone of these surveys and focus groups was not a surprise to social workers attempting to mitigate the tensions between street youth and local residents. In summarizing these results, their hope was that local officials would begin to see the extent of the youths' frustration over the atmosphere of hostility that had built up in the neighborhood.

The police often threaten kids with arrest but do not tell them what the charge would be. Most kids assume that it is illegal to "loiter," although that is not a formal charge. Groups of young people are often charged with blocking the sidewalk, noise, or disorderly conduct, all of which are relatively subjective charges that are hard for kids to challenge. In any case, most kids will not challenge a police officer or security person telling them to move along, as they do not want to attract more attention.

The apparent success of New York City's quality-of-life initiative has served to spread order maintenance policing and the accompanying privatization processes to cities around the world. Rudy Giuliani's consulting firm has implemented a series of recommendations in Mexico City for policing tactics that give police more discretion to stop, search, and arrest people for minor crimes. Whereas in New York, people arrested for misdemeanors might spend a night in jail, Mexico City's notoriously inefficient criminal justice system can result in people's spending three to six months in jail for similar crimes.[44] Former police chief William Bratton used the same tactics against gang violence and delinquent youth as the chief of the Los Angeles Police Department until he retired from that job in January 2010.

Street youths' spatial behaviors have been steadily changing over the last decade because of changes in public-space regulation in the United States. Pressure from gentrification forces and business interests has led city governments to adopt policing tactics that sweep undesirable populations from downtowns and tourist sites. Police are quick to ticket groups like the homeless for small infractions in order to push them out of public spaces and the public view. Such tactics have dramatically affected the geography of street kids in urban areas. One street outreach worker admitted feeling more frustrated with the police when he saw his efforts to engage young people being hindered:

> The Police are everywhere there are unattended youth after hours. They are on corners in cherry-picker security outposts, cruising in cars, marked and unmarked. They have finally begun to patrol on foot, but to a man they have no respect for the people they are paid to serve. At least after dark on the streets. For this reason, the only youth on the streets after dark

tend to be defiant. Often this means there are no unaccompanied youth on the streets after dark. [However], some neighborhoods are bastions of defiance.[45]

Most street kids simply move in order to avoid engaging with the police. Consequently, as young people become more mobile in an effort to avoid harassment and arrest, it becomes increasingly difficult for street outreach workers to locate them. Because street outreach is organized around the concept of "bridging," it is difficult to maintain a bridge whose foundations are continuously fluctuating. Ultimately, the breakdown of street outreach as a bridge to off-street social services may be hurting street youths' chances of receiving the help they need to get off the street.

Street Kids and Policing

In the 1990s there was a surge of public fear of "lawless" young people, egged on by media representations of "besieged" neighborhoods and allusions to a "tsunami" of youth crime. In turn, this public fear was used to justify cities' increasingly harsh zero-tolerance policies toward youth in both public spaces and schools.[46] Homeless young people across the United States and Canada report being frequently ticketed for public-space violations, searches, and threats from police.[47] Also in the 1990s, New York City stepped up its purge of young people from Times Square. Policing strategies are directed toward driving street youth to less visible street activities and dangerous living situations.[48] As one outreach worker remarked, "I think they are really trying to do community policing. But it does drive the youth indoors." For kids who do not have regular access to a home, indoors can mean abandoned buildings, subway cars, or other places where they can get out of sight, but they become more difficult for outreach workers to find when they are ensconced in progressively more hidden and out-of-the-way locations.

In addition, the crackdown on minor crimes such as turnstile jumping and trespassing has led to more street kids being arrested and incarcerated. A study of Minnesota homeless youth found that 34 percent had spent more than a week in jail.[49] In New York City, 76 percent of street kids were detained by police, and a third were incarcerated for more than a year.[50] Time spent in jail because of unpaid tickets and misdemeanor warrants, the disruption of traditional hangout sites such as Times Square and the East and West Villages, and the movement of street kids both around and out of public spaces undermine these youths' ability to seek out and receive public aid. Social workers and outreach personnel are frequently frustrated that their youth clients were either being jailed or were fleeing warrants. Both jail time and the "clearing out" of street kids disrupt counseling, drug treatment, and relationship building that are the keystones of street outreach work.

Although the American Civil Liberties Union has challenged many of these laws, the only result of the lawsuits has been many cities' rewording and implementation of even more specific ordinances. For example, when laws outlawing panhandling were challenged in a number of cities, local governments then passed antiaggressive panhandling ordinances. In New York City, it now is illegal to approach anyone after dark or in a verbally aggressive manner to solicit money or to ask for money within fifty feet of an ATM or a transit stop. Although some of the new regulations are specific, most are left to the interpretation of the responding officer.

All policing involves some discretion by the individual officer, even when the officers are following a strict enforcement mandate. Even though enforcing the law requires numerous judgment calls, police discretion is highly problematic in that it places decision making in a gray area between the law and the demands of local residents. Complicating matters even more, policing data record only when the police arrest or ticket an individual or formally file a report of action. When a police officer deals with individuals in a manner other than through formal legal tools, it is called *noninvocation discretion*.[51] Although a substantial amount of policing is "on the record," telling a young person to move off or be ticketed is a good example of noninvocation discretion. There is no record of these encounters, and noninvocation policing tends to be shaped by the wishes of local communities but is interpreted by individual police officers. As policing experts have stated, "By virtue of their ability to choose which laws to enforce, when, and against whom, the police effectively act as policy-makers. It is the police, not the legislature, that decides which behaviors are to be controlled by the criminal law and which behaviors can be tolerated."[52] Studies have indicated that police are generally more likely to use noninvocation policing tactics with juveniles.[53] Everyday interactions between police and street kids are made legally invisible. Nonarrest order maintenance policing strategies may seem like a positive development for street kids trying to avoid an arrest record. Yet because there is no record at all, young people and youth advocates have few legal ways of combating the harassment of street youth in public spaces. Police can invoke their authority and establish a socially normalized form of order that excludes street kids from public spaces in such a way that both the regulation and the regulated subjects are made invisible. Young people protesting police demands to clear out can be searched, ticketed, or arrested. As one kid stated in response to advice about advocating for legal rights at a counseling session run by a drop-in center, "They'll arrest you anyway."[54] This kind of attention is the last thing a street kid wants.

Policing, Public-Space Ordinances, and Street Outreach

Contemporary policing tactics complicate street outreach as they increasingly push street kids out of public spaces to places that outreach workers cannot easily access, such as abandoned buildings, nightclubs, and commercial establishments. Other street kids try to "hide in plain sight" by not attracting the attention of police or private security. As a street outreach worker explained,

> When we were looking for kids around the major Path/Train stations, like Penn Station and Grand Central, that wasn't very successful. The kids move around a lot inside those spaces so that they won't be found. We know that they're in there, but we don't know where to find them. And the kids that are there are good at it, otherwise they would have been harassed or kicked out by security. We know they're there, though, because the kids at the [drop-in center] talk about being at places like Penn Station.[55]

Increasingly, young people successfully living on the streets do so only by making themselves hard to find.

Order maintenance policing also actually makes some forms of outreach illegal, thereby exposing outreach workers to ticketing or arrest. For instance, Las Vegas, San Francisco, and Atlanta have comprehensive bans on feeding the homeless in public parks. Ordinances like bans on public feeding often are rooted in negative public perceptions of social aid. Communities believe that acts like feeding the homeless attract them to certain locations and enable them to stay there, thus violating social norms of public and private behavior. Negative reactions to outreach practices can lead to hostility between residents and youth workers. But in other communities, outreach workers have also encountered the opposite reaction:

> When we're up in places like Inwood, which are underserved and sort of forgotten sometimes—people often don't even know that Inwood is in Manhattan—the parents will wave us down and will often point out where the kids are hanging out. They seem happy to see us. Working-poor communities are more receptive.[56]

This may be because in some communities, outreach can be consistent with order maintenance. Outreach workers may be trying to mediate or defuse street youths' offensive public behavior and so may be viewed as a benign form of community policing when compared with the police's interactions with youth.

Regulating the Right to the City

Public spaces have never been open and accessible to everyone in society; rather, policing and social norms have functioned together to shift geographies of access and rights to particular spaces and subjectivities. Over time, women, children, and minorities all have struggled to gain the right to access, use, and be visible in the public. The "end of public space" argument assumes that there is a pregiven public space with fixed qualities socially linked to an ideal "public." Instead, however, public spaces are socially produced, through struggle, by diverse social agents.[57] In this way, public spaces become arenas for members of society to claim their rights. According to this view, public space is a process, a nexus of power relations, not a fixed state. Public space may not "end," but it can shift in regard to power relations.

The social regulation of public space disempowers some members of society by denying them equitable access while at the same time it empowers other groups to claim more access than they might previously have held. What is rarely addressed is how various public spaces are struggled over and function in relation to one another through social regimes of regulation and control: a geography of access. Not every public space is policed in the same manner or to the same extent. Youth, however, are extremely sensitive and observant when it comes to police. As one outreach worker stated, "The police don't need to always physically remove young people—just sitting there is off-putting and intimidating and young people will move off." When kids move, they often do not have enough energy or resources to move very far. Moreover, whereas quality-of-life ordinances may be heavily enforced in one park, they may be ignored in a neighboring space. Youth begin a game of circling blocks to avoid police.

How is the topography of access and rights being reshaped by order maintenance policing tactics and social regulation? Several urban geographers have addressed public space using Henri Lefebvre's notion of an *oeuvre*: the city as a work in which all citizens have a right to participate. Don Mitchell[58] stresses that participation is conceived as a right to inhabit the city and have a voice in decision-making processes. Fear of disorder and violence has served to limit this right through mechanisms such as privatization and surveillance. Traditionally, the dominant classes in society have appropriated the oeuvre of cities, usually to the exclusion of the less powerful. In cities, the "right to inhabit" regarding the poor, marginalized, or young has always been tenuous.

Different groups' access to public spaces is based on socially defined norms of behavior and rights. Street kids' access to public space is temporally conditional as well as spatially restricted; they can pass through public spaces, but they cannot linger. These experiences are often marked by struggles over access to the public realm and the right to public space. The actions and perceptions of social groups, organizations, and individuals determine how spaces are used for inclusion and exclusion, dissent and agreement. From the struggle over the shape, meaning, and access to public spaces come ways of inhabiting the city; that is, the opportunities, restrictions, and behaviors that determine how people use, and produce through use, both public spaces and a sense of the public as a cohesive group. Out of these struggles come new and innovative ways of inhabiting the city, because just as social trends are experienced through spaces, they also can be contested and transgressed in spaces. The current policing of public spaces is a reflection of an overall trend in society toward greater regulation. How people inhabit the city directly intersects the spatial restrictions through socially normative regulations. Social regulations are complex tools of control as well as a terrain on which control can be contested. Rather than conclusive "winners" and "losers" over the right to public space, then, there is a constant give and pull of access, restriction, transgression, and resistance.

A shift in policing tactics and the social regulation of both public spaces and public subjects has increasingly altered the spatial behaviors of street kids. They have responded to policing tactics and increased social surveillance by becoming more mobile. Indeed, mobility may be their only way of resisting the zero-tolerance policing and increasingly harsh revanchist policies that are driving them out of public spaces. Revanchism serves to drive "disorder" to the periphery, and zero-tolerance policing drives out street kids, but with no set destination.

Running off the Map

Mobility, Street Kids, and Street Outreach

On a warm spring evening in New York City, small groups of young people stroll around a West Side park and the adjoining neighborhood. They chat animatedly, gesturing wildly and laughing loudly. Young people run up to welcome friends and shout greetings across the narrow streets at other young people passing by. The general mood is one of excitement: young people out in the city, socializing. Groups of kids zip in and out of coffee shops, pizza joints, and corner stores. To a casual observer, this scene would seem like a slice of relatively normal urban life. Yet in the past few years, residents and city officials have constructed the movements of young people through the West Village neighborhood as a social problem, and youth often are described as noisy and disorderly. Most of these young people are black or Hispanic and from the outlying boroughs of the city, thus visibly out of place in the upscale, mostly white, and gentrified West Village. Most of them are seeking spaces where it is acceptable to be a gay youth of color, and many are fleeing abusive domestic situations or have been kicked out by their families. As I reported in chapter 2, gay and lesbian youth comprise 30 to 40 percent of the homeless youth population in New York City, and most of them end up in the West Village at some point: "They go from the pier [in Hudson River Park] to the McDonalds to the Starbucks and then back to the pier. Then they get into cars with johns.[1] They stay at a friend's house. They ride the trains. But physically, they move in public spaces a lot."[2] Ali Forney was one of these kids, as was Blacc. Social service providers see the movements of young people in the West Village in wider urban contexts of marginalization and exploitation, rights and acceptable public behaviors, belonging and communities.

West Village residents and business organizations have consistently and successfully lobbied city government for more police in the West Village, where policing often takes the form of informal warnings to "move on" or be ticketed for blocking the sidewalks and making noise. Usually a specific offense is not even mentioned because when the police say "move," the kids move. Although these policing tactics specifically target young people, calls by local residents for young people to just "go home" reflect the general ignorance concerning them and the geography of youth homelessness. Because the street kids occupying the West Village (and many neighborhoods like it in the city) have no home to go to, threats and surveillance by the police, neighborhood watch groups, and private citizens end up encouraging young people to "stay" on the move. Street youth are increasingly fixed in patterns of mobility in their everyday lives, and this mobility functions as a reaction to public and social regulations that operate in response to their seeming immobility. The principal organizing components in both street youths' lives and street outreach workers' efforts are systems of mobility and immobility, which operate as a complex choreography of voluntary and involuntary movements.

Those working with street kids have tried to adapt to their increased mobility. Social service programs like street outreach rely on some measure of consistency and stability to attract young people to services and resources. Beyond this, social workers may also be morally or ideologically invested in "grounding" mobile street kids; helping young people "off" the streets is a spatial metaphor that encompasses both movement and place. Ideological understandings of mobility and place underlie both the construction of social service models and the ways in which social workers speak about and engage with youth on the streets. As a result, theorizing practices of mobility and immobility can lead to a deeper understanding of street youths' survival and street outreach strategies.

In the first half of this chapter, I discuss the current social constructions of movement and mobility. Mobility is both romanticized and stigmatized, so there is no level and spatially abstract playing field in which social actors trace their movements. Instead, street kids and street outreach workers are embedded in constantly changing terrains in which mobility and immobility are powerful structuring and structural components.

In the second half of the chapter I describe three key themes drawn from my fieldwork regarding mobility, immobility, street youth, and street outreach. The first theme addresses mobile lives, or the practical, tangible movement of street kids in and between cities and towns. My research found that their everyday movements are influenced by society's social geographies and regulatory regimes as well as the individual choices made by the young people. What does the "average" day of a street kid look like? How do young people discuss their own mobility? How do kids use mobility strategically? How do social workers understand the concept of mobility for street youth and their own work?

The second theme that I address is the emplacement of street youth, or how they "touch down" in a system of fluidity and mobility. Young people play strategically with the meanings of mobility in order to survive on the street, in part because physically they cannot constantly keep moving. With this in mind, street outreach workers try out different ways to connect to and stabilize mobile young people, those who may not want to leave or cannot see their way out of their street experiences of "life at 90 miles an hour."[3] Street outreach workers believe that the constant movement and crisis in which the average street youth exists must be stopped in order for him or her to move off the streets.

My final theme is the metaphor of outreach as a bridge that spans sites and unites subjects of mobility and immobility. The social meanings we attach to mobility and place give them power, so that mobility shapes how we experience places, events, and people just as much as place shapes our "being in the world." Mobility, too, affects the social experience of being street kids and street outreach workers inhabiting public spaces.

Movement and Mobility

Mobility is a spatial, geographic practice encompassing migrations, immigrations, transportations, and circulations.[4] Mobility marks out territories on every scale; places are made and experienced through interlocking systems of mobility and immobility. Tourists practice mobility by visiting places, as do students moving to and from school, skateboarders occupying parks, stockholders moving capital, skinheads relocating to rural Pennsylvania, and street kids traveling through truck stops looking for rides and engaging in sex work. Mobility has a vast array of forms, conceptions, and figures throughout human geography, and moral understandings of mobility are part of our cultures and everyday actions. Only recently have critical human geographers renewed their interest in theorizing this important underlying concept.

In contemporary social theory, *mobility* is generally defined as movement infused with meaning, which, in Western society, can have either positive or negative connotations depending on who is moving, for what reason, and in what context. Just as places are spaces imbued with social power, relationships, and significance, mobilities are enabled or constrained by the social organizations of power in which individuals are situated. Much of human social organization is based on assumptions of sedentarism, the idea that people settle in particular places that then become stable and meaningful through intimate, long-term interactions.[5] According to this conception, we know the world through places and learn to value them as "fields of care" or moral commitments to places. Places are not just spaces imbued with meanings; more than that, they are imbued with meanings that we are personally invested in maintaining. Because emotional investments in place are often naturalized through daily practices in cultures and communities, place politics and identity politics are commonly interwoven. People "dwell" in places, determining how they experience "being in the world."[6] In addition to being moral-spatial concepts, places can be idealized, becoming essentialist and potentially exclusionary.

Mobility gains much of its meaning through its construction in opposition to understandings of immobility (sedentarism) and vice versa. In this paradigm, mobility is opposed to stability, for movement creates distance, change, placelessness, and instability.[7] In a moral-spatial construction, social and physical mobility are often set in opposition to the positive values linked to a place-based society. For example, social groups that are labeled as nomads or wanderers produce negative conceptions of mobility in sedentarist societies.[8] Here, mobility does not just create unstable social structures; it also creates unstable moral subjects. Accordingly, it is assumed that a tramp is always a degenerate drunk, a homeless man is mentally ill, and a street kid is a delinquent. In this manner, "others" (a subjective position) become "outsiders" (a spatial-social position). Mobile subjects are constructed as morally or physically threatening to place-based communities. Although critical social theorists have addressed the social stigmatization of mobile populations,[9] not until recently have critiques of the ideological nature of mobility merged with interests in modernity, technology, transportation, and human migration to form a loose "mobility turn" in the social sciences.[10]

Critical geographers are interested in understanding how place as a site of "authentic," rooted identity is given the moral high ground over mobility and mobile identities[11] and what this binary means for human action and social organizations of power. What happens when the "roots" of places are more important than the "routes" of people?[12] Mobility is often conceived as a problematic state that causes placelessness.[13] But even when mobility is celebrated as nonplaces in a postmodern world, it often is generalized as the mobility of elites and romanticized.[14] Some critical geographers argue that a postmodern celebration of mobility that deterritorializes identities may obscure a politics of mobility. A discourse of hypermobility and global connectivity thus can serve to obscure the social relations and spatial ideologies that produce variations of mobility and immobility within a global system. For instance, discourses of globalization and "time-space" compression may flatten out differences, such as who has access to the "road." While some social groups increase their mobility, others may be progressively demobilized by globalization.[15]

Even in increasingly connected, mobile, and networked societies, places may still provide important sites for the location of identity.[16] The idea that all human existence is lived locally and in place and that place is therefore the basis of all human experience and identity is still powerful, especially during secular violence, civil wars, and land and boundary disputes across the globe. The power of international social discourses such as the "grassroots" speaks to the naturalization of place-based political struggles across cultures.[17] According to Sarah Dempsey, the formulations of place-based identities are not limited to local, place-based actors. Rather, the ontological normalization of place-based identities, morals, and values obscures their contested and ongoing production and local differences. Ideological and idealized conceptions of place also tend to simplify how places are experienced on a variety of scales and through numerous facets of identity. Experiences in places are thus part of broader, complex power structures mediated through multiple axes of identity, such as gender, race, age, and sexuality.

Another idea is that place is an embodied relationship with the world and is experienced through movement and mobility, so that places exist through the performance of bodies.[18] Geographers have addressed this new turn toward an interrelation of place and mobility through studies of tourism, migration, and disability and through the creation of a new academic journal, *Mobilities*.[19] In some respects, mobility work might represent a return to a phenomenological focus. Because human geography is thought of as "being in the world," it cannot be reduced to just the social, the natural, or the cultural. Mobilities therefore, create geographies in which places, people, and phenomena bring these relations together and are shaped by them in turn. To understand how mobility comes to bear on place and vice versa, it is useful to look at how mobility has been constructed historically.

Historical Mobilities

Western societies' understanding of mobility can be traced back to the social and cultural landscapes of medieval Europe, where, until well into the Industrial Revolution, the vast majority of the population was agrarian. Political power was centered on regional landholders and the Catholic Church. Individuals were usually identified by where they were born, since in most cases, this was where they would spend their entire lives. Medieval settlements were inward looking, and towns were collectively responsible for crimes committed within their boundaries. Those individuals not included in the collective community were deemed to threaten the security of the place-based society. As a result, many towns barred strangers from entering, and other towns locked their gates at sunset.[20] Strangers could not receive confession or be buried outside their home parish. The concept of the "outsider" was thus not a vague division but a concrete, located subjectivity structured by strict social regulations. At the same time, however—in the thirteenth and fourteenth centuries—large numbers of people willingly undertook long and often dangerous pilgrimages, which were the only socially condoned form of travel for the majority of the lay population. Indeed, traveling outside these limited social formations risked a denial of one's placed identity and therefore one's personhood.

Throughout history, the social meaning of mobility has been tied to the social meaning of place in a number of ways. To divest oneself of one's only indicator of social value—one's literal place in society—it was necessary first to secure a new and accepted identity or to risk becoming an outsider or stranger. Places represented order, authority, and an established social hierarchy that were directly tied to the social and moral hierarchies of the established church. In other words, an individual's place was divinely ordained. While traveling, people were disconnected from their homes and therefore their place in society, and so roles could be confused, control might be sacrificed, and moral anarchy could result. For example, during times of socioeconomic change in England—when the fear of disorder was great—the first vagrancy laws came into effect.[21] The end of the feudal system across Europe (and the subsequent freeing of serfs from landholdings) foreshadowed a rapid rise in vagabondage in the sixteenth century[22] and the further criminalization of mobile subjects. Beginning in the 1870s in the United States, this took the form of "tramp scares."

Mobility and Otherness: The Tramp

Like earlier vagrancy panics in England, the tramp scares in the United States can be understood in the context of the political economy. A series of economic depressions in the late 1800s, coupled with a rise in immigration in the United States, led to increased numbers of unattached men traveling across the country, mostly in search of seasonal work. During this time, the newly built railroad network allowed for cheaper, safer, and more frequent travel for the population in general, and the rail system opened small towns and communities across the country to greater contact with other communities, cities, and, ultimately, strangers. In his book *The Tramp in America,*[23] Tim Cresswell argues that the figure of the tramp was "discovered" by social reformers in the 1870s. Rising fears of social unrest and the displacement of large numbers of people during and after the Civil War led to a series of moral panics centering on unemployed and itinerant men. At the same time, a series of bountiful agricultural seasons in the far West encouraged men to seek seasonal work as fruit and vegetable pickers.[24]

Several different social identifiers were lumped into the figures of the tramp, the hobo, and other labels for itinerant men (some of which survive today in the discourses of skid-row homeless men). Men who did not physically travel far from certain cities were labeled *bums* or *beggars*, while men who did travel (and often worked) were categorized as *tramps, hobos, pickers,* or *drifters.*[25] The figure of the tramp was separate from the social construction of unemployed families, displaced by the same series of economic depressions. For example, the Great Depression and the mechanization of the agricultural sector in the 1930s displaced nearly 100,000 midwestern farmers, who migrated west to California and became known as *Okies* (although only some of them were from Oklahoma). While certainly discriminated against because of their poverty in their new home, these people were called *migrants* rather than *tramps.* That is, their mobility was understood to be both physically and socially linear (from point A to point B) and thus was coded differently from the mobility of the tramp figure. Paradoxically, at the same time that tramps were feared and vilified, a social romance grew up around the figure of the masculine rootless adventurer as part of the mythology of the expanding American West. The traveling cowboy in search of work was an acceptable form of unemployed mobility. The cowboy figure also was not vilified for his mobility because conceptually he did not exist in either a placeless void or out of place. Instead, his "place" was the vast landscape of the American West. Unlike the figure of the tramp, who either "had no place" or was "out of place," the cowboy occupied an expansive place physically and in our collective social imagination. The manner in which mobility, place, and identity intersect in social subjects therefore is important because it affects how society organizes itself around ideas of spatial morality and immorality. While paradoxical on the surface, the differing conceptions of the tramp and the wandering cowboy reflect a deep engagement in the social production of mobility.

Mobility as a Social Problem

One important effect of the American cultural fear and fascination with mobility is how mobility is used strategically to erase or punish social actors. In Edward Everett Hale's precautionary short story, "A Man without a Country,"[26] the narrator recounts the fate of a young military officer who renounced his country. His punishment was to be imprisoned on a series of ships at sea so as never to hear of or see his homeland again. In the story, his name was not recorded in the ships' logs, and the public did not know about his punishment. He was viewed as an object of pity, an outcast among the ships' crews: "No mess [dining hall] liked to have him permanently because his presence cut off all talk of home or of the prospect of return, of politics or letters, of peace or of war, cut off more than half the talk the men liked to have at sea."[27] Over the course of the narrative, the imprisoned man becomes quiet, growing discouraged as he is disconnected from the lives and events occurring on land. He becomes "lost": "Later in life, when I thought I had some influence in Washington, I moved heaven and earth to have him discharged. But it was like getting a ghost out of prison. They pretended there was no such man, and never was such a man."[28] Hale's "A Man without a Country" was required reading when I was in grammar school. On the surface, it is a fable for citizenship, loyalty, and patriotism (and the harsh consequences of disavowing allegiance to one's country). But the story itself is built on an older fear of having no place. The land in the form of America represents meaning, value, life, and beneficial changes in the form of progress, whereas the ocean stands for loss, conflict, and placelessness.

In sum, while the mobilities in the nineteenth and twentieth centuries that led to the domination of the western United States were lauded, this mobility was nevertheless grounded in an ideal of place, images, and constructions of what it meant to settle a new country. In Hale's story, the sea was fought over but could not be settled or placed; it became a mobile space of exile. In both "A Man without a Country" and in the figure of the tramp, mobility is a form of exile from society, a casting out into a void. Mobility represents the absence of place and its accompanying sense of self and morality.

Some examples of mobile relationships to places are coded differently. For instance, nomadic peoples wander through territories along seasonal routes that are tied to economic, social, and cultural systems.[29] In this sense, the territories are relational and the practice of mobility is also the materialization of social relations. Contemporary studies of nomadic peoples have found that far from being "nonterritorial" or placeless, nomadic peoples have complex internal logics that structure their movements. Mobile practices create territories as a series of peripatetic nested scales from the individual's space, to the home space, to the community space, to the regional/seasonal space. In history, nomadic groups have been both vilified and romanticized by sedentary societies, which have rarely understood the everyday workings of nomadic cultures, instead creating a sense of the mobile "other," mysterious and feared.

In Western civilization, the excitement or romanticization of travel is understood differently from the fear of losing one's home or place in the world. It is when fears of mobility coalesce into moral panics that certain groups are stigmatized for their mobility or are even forced into mobile patterns to begin with. When sedentary societies code mobility as a threat to the established patterns and rules—the opposite of social order—a type of "sedentary metaphysics" is created that sets mobility in opposition to place: "place, home and roots are profoundly moral concepts in the human lexicon."[30] When this occurs, certain types of mobility and mobile subjects are constructed as morally out of place and thus degenerate. When mobility is regarded as a social problem, then mobile subjects are understood to be the appropriate site of social interventions. Likewise, kids and social workers play strategically with the spatiality of youth homelessness in different ways through mobility narratives.

Mobile Lives

Street kids are quite reticent about what they do all day, for good reason. Social stigmas and legal issues force them into a kind of silence concerning their daily movements and activities.[31] As a result, street outreach workers can spend months working with individual kids before they start talking about their daily activities. They often feel that revealing their daily activities will turn adults away from them, that they will not be accepted. Street kids also feel threatened when adults ask them what they do all day, because the question comes too close to the common assumption that street youth are lazy or "do nothings" or that there are stigmas and shame associated with many street survival strategies such as sex work. Street youth already confront these labels in the comments of passersby, in the media, and in some institutional settings. They also are wary of revealing their involvement in illegal activities.

Outreach workers also dislike the question, "What is the average day of a street kid like?" but for different reasons. As one worker explained, "I'm fighting with the concept of 'average' in this context."[32] Outreach workers know that there are many forms of youth homelessness and many variations in street youths' behavior. Yet it is knowledge about street youths' daily, weekly, and yearly patterns of movement that structure outreach efforts. Outreach workers must be able to find street kids before any outreach is possible. Through small interactions and questions, most outreach workers have assembled a detailed picture of the "average" movements of a street kid, whose motility is as much temporally structured as spatially defined:

> Most kids have to leave their shelters by 9 a.m. If they are sleeping on the street, they've been waked up by police or foot traffic by 7–8 a.m. They will often try to find some public bathroom. Their street profession structures the rest of their day. If they are spanging, they have to find a good location to set up and start working. They spend time meeting up and networking with other street-involved kids. If they are connected to adults, it's usually as part of their trade. Hard-core street kid culture tends to be fairly separate from homeless adult communities. They have to kill time until evening when other types of street work start up (sex work, drug trade, theft). There is a feeling of "hurry up and wait"—long periods of boredom interspersed with short bursts of frantic, often stressful activity.[33]

Most street youth move each day from sleeping places (shelters, friends homes, parks, etc.) to where they might make money (downtown streets, tourism areas) to where they might receive services or go to school (often in different parts of the city from where they sleep or make money). Kids might also be hanging out in places where they will not be harassed: friendly coffee shops, bookstores, libraries, and out-of-the-way locations in public spaces. These trends are well documented in cities across the United States: youth use the same strategies in Denver or Phoenix to find places to rest or socialize as they do in New York City.[34] Street kids also move to find friends, avoid enemies, and evade arrest or harassment by police.

> They start early—the shelters close or they get rudely awakened in the parks. Then they have to make an income—they travel into the city to make money. Kids doing prostitution spend the day hanging out and the night working. It depends. That's what they train us to look for, anyway. It fits the categories. But some kids might spend their whole day doing something different. I met a kid that designs computer games. You have kids who stay in school. . . . Some kids' days are organized through social services, the system, or through their street families. There are different frames.[35]
> . . . there is nowhere for them to really go, and in the morning there is nothing to do either. Although some of the kids have jobs, a lot of them

don't. Or some might still go to school, but again a lot of them don't. I mean, there has always been service hopping . . . I'm not sure if it is more or less, but it probably is more because they are not able to hang out on the street as much.[36]

In general, street youth speak of a "hurry up and wait" lifestyle that is punctuated by periods of extreme crisis and stress. Points of crisis (from violence, drug deals, police interactions, or something else) structure the daily movements that are limited by street youths' lack of access to many spaces and resources such as bathrooms, beds, or just a place out of the rain. It is the repetitiveness of these patterns that lead to a sensation of the "endless day." With nowhere to go, street kids wander.

In places like New York City with extremely cold winters, there also is some seasonal variation in street kids' movements, both within the city and between cities.

> The number of kids that we see in a given outreach is quite seasonal, as expected with the winters in New York. Finding young people in private spaces during the winter poses more of a challenge than finding them out in public during the summer. Even during the peak outreach times during warmer weather, it can be very hit or miss—young people are often pulled into entertainment venues that disrupt the regular pattern of where and when they hang out. We have learned to find kids in private spaces such as libraries, movie theaters, drop-in centers, and Internet cafés. There is an Internet café at 42nd Street that is particularly popular. Because the owner lets kids hang out even when they are not spending money . . . he is in some ways running his own informal social service.[37]

In my two years of outreach in the city, street youth from other cities usually started to show up in March (when it still is quite cold in New York) and would arrive in a continuous stream until October. Street kids from outside New York would often be harassed by police and, in a short time, would receive several tickets for sleeping in parks, open containers, and other small infractions of the public-space ordinances. It was unusual to run into the same out-of-town young people more than once or twice before he or she would move on to another city. In several instances, however, the same kids were seen around the same time the following year.

Outreach workers also have observed changes in street kids' daily and yearly patterns.

Well, that's where the whole political Giuliani thing impacted. The kids used to come in and just sleep in Midtown, on the streets or in the train yards or wherever. But with that whole Midtown, Disneyland, sweep, the kids are being driven back to their own communities. They'll come in for assistance or just to get out of the area, or they've negotiated something with their parents where they can sleep there but they can't stay at home while the parents are at work. So they'll leave in the morning and they'll come into the city and stop by [the drop-in centers] and spend the day downtown. And then as the night gets late, they'll either go back up or they'll hook up with a date if they're hustling. Or they'll get into some activity down here.[38]

During my fieldwork from 2004 to 2006, social workers became increasingly concerned that street youth were returning to unsafe homes and neighborhoods in order to avoid being harassed in downtown areas. This pattern was brought up in numerous meetings of different service providers, along with changes in how long young people were using emergency services without accessing long-term care. The persistent use of crisis services often is a reflection of highly mobile, unstable homeless youth population.

Part of the decrease [in the number of kids being seen] is because kids are staying for shorter periods of time in one place. This change is attributable to increased police harassment and ticketing. Whereas kids used to hang out for the entire summer and access services, they now stay for a few days to a few weeks, then move on to Boston or Philadelphia, only to hit New York again over the course of the summer. Most kids travel south or west for the winter. This is a much faster cycle of travel than before. It's increasingly difficult to provide consistent services for this group.[39]

In addition to street youths' patterns of dispersal and instability, some workers saw points of concentration as other young people found fewer options for hangout sites.

Union Square kids seem more dispersed than in previous years while at the same time a larger variety of kids are using the Square. Kids who used to segment into different public spaces in Lower Manhattan are being found more often up at Union Square. There is also an increased presence of drug dealing, gangs, and police at the Square.[40]

Those youth who attempted to remain in place were exposed to increased tensions over territory from different social actors, which contributed to violence, stress, and further instability.

Narratives of Mobility and Immobility

Young street people often use structural stories to interpret their mobility. *Structural stories* are

> the arguments people commonly use to legitimize their actions and decisions. The individual views and expresses structural stories as universal truths, agreed upon by all. A structural story is used to explain the way we act and the choices we make when exercising our daily routines. It is a guide to certain actions that, at the same time, emancipate us from responsibility.[41]

Young people often interpret their movements as seeking freedom or adventure, as in the American social mythology of the independent traveler or youth seeking his identity. One kid described this to me as doing the "Jack Kerouac" thing, in reference to the famous countercultural road-trip memoir *On the Road*.[42] This does not mean that street kids are "fooling themselves" when they interpret potentially involuntary movements as freedom seeking or a personal choice. Progressive social service providers often reinterpret and place value on street youths' coping skills such as mobility; they discuss the independence, motivation, and ingenuity that young people develop when living a mobile existence on the streets. I have found three kinds of mobility narratives in my outreach notes, personal experiences, and interviews with outreach workers. These are the stories that street kids tell about their own mobility. What do these stories say about their relationship with mobility? How youth speak about mobility is critical to how they think strategically about the social organization of their everyday movements.

The "Moving On" Narrative

When street outreach workers engage kids, a common conversation they have with them is about "moving on." Moving on usually refers to their movement to another town, city or state, although sometimes the kids talk about going back to their old neighborhoods, families, or homes. Usually, the aim of these conversations is the young person's convincing the outreach worker that he or she is getting off the street on which the outreach workers found the youth, literally and/or figuratively. The following are excerpts from my outreach notes:

> We talked to one of our regular kids for a while today at the park. He said that he was going to Detroit this winter to finish a vocational degree. We all joked that if he was trying to get away from the New York winter, Detroit didn't seem like the warmer option. Two other kids were hanging out with him and said that they had just arrived from Michigan.[43]
>
> Just after the start of outreach, we see two white traveler kids hanging out in the park with their backpacks and a dog. The young woman says that she is from Chicago originally and that they have only been in New York a few weeks. They are sleeping in another nearby park, but the police have been waking them up early in the morning. They have both heard of squats out in Brooklyn, but aren't staying out there. The young woman says that they are thinking of heading to Florida next. The young man says that he is from Southern California and has been hopping freight trains for a while. His favorite place is Vancouver because there is an alternative drop-in center that will pick up and drop off kids at the rail yard.[44]

Many outreach workers assume that young people are using the discourse of moving on as a defensive mechanism, especially if they do not know the outreach workers well. When young people are approached by authority figures, such as police or social workers, they often preemptively engage them with an expectation that they are out of place and/or not welcome in a public space, by saying in one form or another that they are "just leaving."

> I think one way that homeless young people are similar is that they know how to market themselves to their environment. They know how to sell themselves. Whether it's a smooth "I'm not threatening" sort of demeanor or whether it's more "I've got what you want" or whatever. They learn quickly how to give people what they want or to tell people what they want.[45]

Where, how, and when street youth use talk of "moving on" is both spatially and socially important. Moving on displays a variety of coping skills, resistance, and other identity-based movement actions. Related to talk of "moving on" are narratives of being new to the city by having "just arrived."

The "Just Arrived" Narrative

The "just arrived" narrative was another way that street youth spatially and temporally bounded their engagement with the places in which the outreach workers found them. The theme of having just arrived lent itself to assumptions of helplessness (they did not know where services were located or how to access them) or ignorance (they were unaware of public-space ordinances or other local laws). Young people who said that they had just arrived often received more attention, care, and advice from outreach workers than did those youth who claimed to have been in the city or on the streets for a longer period of time.

> After walking up to the park, we sat down on a bench near some chess tables. A while later, a young guy came up and asked us for the time. In return, we asked him if he knew any under-21 street kids, explaining that we were a street outreach group and had outreach bags with us (he had been hanging out in a part of the park where we had found street youth in the past). He said that he was 20 and would like an outreach bag. He told us that he was from Indonesia originally and had been in New York for a few months (he had a standard American accent). He said that he was finding places to stay but wouldn't give us any details. He had gotten all of his clothes at a nearby youth drop-in center and looked like any other hipster 20-year-old in the East Village or Brooklyn. He was skinny, wore clothes in muted colors, lots of layers, a corduroy jacket, dark pants, and leather shoes. His hair was clean, and he was healthy looking. I wouldn't have spotted him. He said that he was heading south soon, to look for work, and then he left to go and talk to some older homeless men.[46]

As can be seen in these examples, the "moving on" narrative and the "just arrived" narrative are often used simultaneously. The "just arrived" narrative signals impermanence: if a young person had just arrived, then he had yet to "do harm" and could leave again just as easily. These narratives positioned street youth as mobile subjects with no claims to place or rights to those places. By claiming mobility (and putting a positive spin on mobile experiences such as traveling), street kids put up barriers between themselves and sited, immobile, institutional aid. It was extremely difficult to engage highly mobile young people in conversations about social service programs that lasted months, if not years, when they did not expect to be around for longer than a few days. In many instances, the sensation of crisis that daily movement produced in young people permanently located in the city had the same effect. They would often talk about "going home," only to return in crisis to the streets a short time later. These patterns of intra- and extra-local mobility solidified the effects of moving on and just arriving in a way that "fixed" street youth into patterns of movement. Street kids stay on the move mentally, physically, and socially, making constant mobility itself a kind of immobility.

Immobility Narratives: Getting off the Streets

Some young people use immobility as a way to describe their situation, insisting that they never leave particular places, patterns, and activities. For example, Blacc discussed at length how getting out of the city might break his pattern of homelessness (see chapter 3). That is, he saw homelessness as something that he could leave behind by physically removing himself from the environment in which he lived on the streets. Jobs and other opportunities were things that young people often imagined to exist "elsewhere." In 2005, after Hurricane Katrina, young people often spoke about heading to New Orleans to get jobs rebuilding houses.

> He said that he was saving money to head south—he figured that there would be plenty of manual labor cleaning up after the hurricane that hit New Orleans. We warned him that there were still more storms coming and that he might want to wait a few weeks. He said that he wasn't planning on leaving for a few weeks anyway.[47]

Other youth speak of "getting off the streets" or performing a kind of controlled mobility in order to achieve immobility.

For street kids to leave the street, they often must move physically to a new location in order to break their ties to the street culture. Because group ownership is part of the code of survival, it is nearly impossible for newly housed kids not to help their friends by letting them stay in their apartments. But in turn, this often leads to a kid's being kicked out of his or her housing program.[48] Kids who are highly mobile, moving from city to city, also must decide where to leave the pattern of mobility. This usually means leaving the "circuit" and choosing a place to put down roots and work at getting off the street.[49] Outreach workers use the interplay of mobility and immobility in trying to find outreach tactics that fit and fix young people momentarily in place on the streets.

Emplaced Lives

> It's like they ran away but wanted to be found by someone who cares about them.
>
> —Outreach director, e-mail correspondence, May 2, 2007

Emplacement is the "act of putting into a certain position," or the process that encompasses a fixed locating of people, objects, or activities. I would argue that street kids use their location and mobility strategically as a survival tool and are placed into this position through the social organization and disciplining of their everyday actions. Street youth are not just located on the streets; they are emplaced there through their position in a society that simultaneously attempts to limit homeless persons' access to spaces and drives homeless behaviors out of sight. Outreach workers also use mobility and immobility strategically to "emplace" street youth.

> Absolute acceptance is at the center of outreach. Handing out stuff or maintaining connections to kids is what we do, but it is more important that we are actually available and open to anything that they say or need. It's hard to explain to someone who grew up in a regular family how much this means. Helping them move on with their lives is important, but not pushing them, accepting them for where they are right now, is the most important part. Creating that space for acceptance is so much more . . . it's creating boundaries, a place to move on from.[50]

Part of this process is to meet young people's immediate crisis needs so that they can begin to process and reflect on their current location. The space of outreach tries to "fix" a young person in place—if only momentarily—in order to connect with that youth.

Touching Down: Outreach Models and Mobility

The two basic models of outreach interaction are mobile and stationary. Outreach teams can focus on a series of mobile intersections with street youth as they move from place to place, or they can try to create a temporary fixed space on the streets where kids can find them at a set time and place.

In mobile intersections, outreach teams aligning with the current public-space environment that pushes street kids to move frequently between hangout spots, neighborhoods, and even cities. This model assumes that outreach workers are very good at finding young people's routes and can predict and engage a subject who already is in motion and may need to stay that way in order to avoid unwanted attention. Outreach workers often describe this as "trolling" or "fishing" for street kids:

> More word of mouth . . . a friend would bring someone over to us. Or tell their friends that we would be out here at a certain time. Because we had a pattern; where it was the same route everyday. When we did outreach it was always the same time and places. So we could catch kids . . . it was like a net.[51]

This process is often made easier in combination with other factors such as kids remaining stationary: "There are a lot of situational factors that make for a successful outreach: warm weather, small groups of kids that are already sitting down, when you have something good to offer them."[52] Stationary youth, however, are often engaged in some aspect of the street economy, be it panhandling or drug dealing. Furthermore, when youth do remain stationary, they attract the attention of police, shop owners, and the general public. Often the outreach needs to be conducted on the fly, with a minimum of attention being drawn to the young person. This can be extremely difficult for outreach groups that are well marked as street outreach, through either brightly colored and labeled T-shirts or a van with a large outreach logo on the side.

> When I was doing outreach, you really learned how to blend. So that you didn't stand out. You weren't then identified . . . you wanted to keep it secret. If you were on a crowded street, you'd tell a kid "come walk with me" and go around the corner where it was more private. So it wasn't like "here is this person talking to a young person, what's going on?" We'd approach a young person in Times Square and if they were there with their parents . . . we'd just say that we were working with young people. We'd spin it. I think the public sees street outreach as useful, as long as it's not too official . . . because then it turns into NIMBY [not in my back yard]. . . . They want to solve the issue, but they don't want it where they can see it. It turns into this harsh attitude of "just arrest them."[53]

However, well-marked groups can often create a clearly bounded "safe space" on the streets, in part because their visibility as street outreach gives them an air of authority. One outreach worker said that he always made his presence known in some way if police approached kids during an outreach session.

> I am so amazed at how smart and calm some of my clients are. Police were everywhere and they were on foot. I saw supervisors checking on foot patrol officers. I followed two cops to talk to [a young person] because he was tweaking and dancing in the street. . . . I always follow cop action because I want them to know there's a witness to their behavior. . . . I am committed to letting them know they are not free to do whatever they want. And I can be calm when they are freaking out [the police].[54]

So while having a social worker present can mitigate some tensions between street kids and police, in other instances, being "marked" as street outreach makes both social workers and youth feel exposed: "We have IDs in our pockets. The coordinator is obsessed with being sure we're labeled. I think it might be easier for us if we stay a bit on the DL [down low]." Nearly all professional outreach workers carry work IDs with them, but when they are on foot, most can easily blend into the street scene in urban neighborhoods. An exception would be white outreach workers looking for youth in the public spaces around predominantly African American public housing projects.

Being poorly marked or not identifiable as street outreach can lead to other problems. An outreach van that is not marked can be mistaken for a commercial van or someone "cruising" for either drugs or sex workers. Outreach teams have gotten into dangerous situations when not easily identified as outreach:

> We were passing a [housing project] when a group of guys flagged us down. My partner, sensing a chance to connect with some young people, turned the van around as if to stop and speak with them. They obviously thought we were a dollar van. This is because the grant we won didn't come with a budget for a vehicle. We were using a van that had been in the program for years, a fifteen-passenger shortbus, black, with tinted windows. I call it the Death Star. By the time my partner completed the U-turn, three guys were blocking the van from going any further down the block. Maybe fifteen other guys were at the side of the van, asking us to take them to a party on 152nd Street. We had also forgotten to lock the doors of the van, so the guys opened some of them. Once they realized we weren't a dollar van, they wanted to find out how much stuff they could get out of us. They started looking around the van for what was in it. More than three arms

were waving in the passenger window as I tried to calmly give away condom packages and de-escalate the crowd. I reached behind me and managed to get the back door closed . . . my partner was shouting at the guys in front of the van to move away so she "could pull over." She was bluffing, see. I was fixing to lose my composure just as she was able to pull away, leaving the group of kids in our dust. About an hour and a half later, our heart rates returned to baseline.[55]

Outreach workers also have been kicked out of public spaces when they were mistaken for sex workers soliciting clients. Indeed, unmarked outreach can be misinterpreted in the street environment as a variety of practices.

In the stationary model of outreach, young people approach street outreach workers who have established a regular outreach location. This operational format can make it easier for young people to find outreach workers, but it also can visibly unmask street kids as homeless to the rest of the public. Groups that perform outreach in street clothes also can create temporary safe spaces on the street that are less visible to the general public, but they often have a harder time defining and defending the boundaries of their space, which are constantly shifting. Finding young people in private spaces during the winter poses more of a challenge than finding them out in public during the summer. Even during the peak outreach times in warmer weather, it can be very sporadic, as young people are frequently pulled into entertainment venues that disrupt the regular pattern of where and when they hang out.

Although outreach can vary in how workers are marked as outreach, how they mobilize outreach in urban spaces, whether they approach young people or young people come up to them, the basic premise that street kids must mentally and emotionally "come to them" is the same in all cases. To return to our "bridge" metaphor for a moment, outreach workers create and maintain opportunities for street youth to access social services. The first step in this process is creating a firm foundation for the end of the bridge that connects to the street and young people. How and where opportunities are operating affects young people's ability to access and use outreach. Ultimately, though, it is still the young person who must see, understand, and decide to use the opportunity to receive aid. The process of grounding outreach in spaces and behaviors that are changing is tied to how outreach workers try to emplace young people. Again, the emplacement of mobile youth is a necessary step toward moving them out of mobility patterns and off the streets. Outreach workers usually call this practice "stabilizing" youth, but the general public often negatively describes it as "enabling" street kids.

Outreaching in Other Spaces

Negative perceptions of outreach as enabling and the increasing harassment of both street outreach workers and street kids have led some groups to experiment with alternative sites for outreach. Some outreach workers are connecting to young people through websites and in off-street locations. Tracking young people through their personal web pages, where they post personal thoughts, stories, and poetry is particularly useful. Little work has been done on how outreach workers use the Internet as a form of both virtual connectedness and surveillance. "I can instant-message him on MySpace, and I know his girlfriend, too. . . . I keep in touch with a few of them [through the Internet]. I usually respond if I see some suicidal or depressive thoughts. I just say a hello to them. Usually they respond."[56] Although the Internet obviously removes the outreach worker from the immediate site of street youths' lives, it is another way of connecting to those who are hard to find. Outreach teams also are experimenting with a variety of semipublic venues for outreach:

> The outreach team is working on a campaign to use public libraries for programs that would be both about and for runaway/homeless youth. It is difficult to get libraries to stay open after hours for these types of programs, however. We have targeted libraries because young people already congregate there in order to use the free computers. The goal is to create a sense of community in a space where young people already feel safe. The libraries would provide a good space to do indoor programming during the winter months as well.[57]

In addition to libraries, outreach groups frequently attend special music events, parades, or other festivals that might attract street youth. Targeting events that pull in young people to a centralized location for a period of time helps outreach groups concentrate their resources.

Bridging Mobility and Emplacement

> We're more like a post-it board . . . displaying information. A bridge implies that there is a way off the streets. The streets stay with kids. Outreach is more about being a facilitator. Mentally getting a kid off the streets . . . you have to let them know that they have absolute acceptance from you, week after week. In two years, I've reached that relationship with one kid. There is no way to quantify that.
>
> —Outreach worker, e-mail correspondence, May 6, 2007

Current trends in the policing of public space in the form of tickets for blocking sidewalks, making noise, and engaging in panhandling, as well as police sweeps of popular hangouts, are driving street kids to even more mobility. Mobility undermines street outreach workers' attempts to offer homeless youth services in a number of ways, from the outright inability to find kids to the difficulty of finding the same kid over and over. Young people cannot obtain basic services, make appointments with clinics, or complete counseling or therapy programs when they are moving from place to place. More important, young people who are regularly on the move have difficulty forming strong emotional ties to people or places, and outreach workers typically depend on these situated emotional linkages to connect to and stabilize them. Moreover, kids who speak of always "moving on" are less likely to begin relationships with social service workers or programs if they do not expect to be around. "Siting" street youth is thus integral to the process of outreach itself.

Outreach acts as a bridge between mobility and emplacement, but not in the way conceived by the street outreach literature or social service philosophies. Rather than functioning as a link between social services and the street, the temporary space of outreach acts as the still point in the stream where outreach workers connect to and stabilize youth. The outreach relationship is a bridge for young people to cross from a state of crisis to a state of stability, which is necessary for them in order to move off the streets and out of homelessness. But acting as a bridge is a hard position for outreach workers. The instability in street youths' lives and their state of mobility often destroys these relationships just as they are forming. Furthermore, outreach workers dwell on their perceived failures; they are continually looking for those kids who might be just around another corner. In some sense, outreach workers are "haunted" by street youth, wondering what happened to each kid to whom they almost connected. Outreach workers thus experience the mobility of street kids through their presence and in their absence.

Most of the kids stayed in cheap hotels or with friends. A few slept on the streets or in squats. I remember one girl in particular who was passed out in a squat and was terribly bitten up by spiders. Squats were in old warehouses. I took her to a hospital. I had to half carry her in . . . I never found out what happened to her.[58]

There was a really messed-up guy who was very upset about his life. His child was staying with his aunt, his wife/girlfriend had left him, and he was feeling very hopeless. He really was crying for help, and we listened to him, but all that time I knew that it was unlikely that we would run into him again.[59]

Outreach workers realize that the moment of outreach is crucial and yet uncontrollable: "You cannot step into the same river twice."

Street outreach workers believe that the enactment of new public-space ordinances is increasing the mobility of homeless youth. Moreover, this mobility is leading to the further erasure and marginalization of street kids from public spaces and the public's perception while at the same time making it difficult for young people to access the limited social services available to help them leave the street. Young people who are highly mobile cannot be regularly found by street outreach counselors, nor can they consistently access social service programs such as job training or drug counseling that require them to be in one place for an extended period of time. Street outreach is meant to act as a bridge between kids living in the streets and social services housed in private institutions, yet street outreach counselors cannot find street kids when they are regularly cleared out of parks and other public spaces. Street outreach workers have reported mounting frustration with police sweeps that clear out prime outreach locations, often minutes before the outreach begins. Once the youth are scattered around a neighborhood or retreat into less visible and often more dangerous locations, outreach is impossible.

The practice of outreach is causing social workers to rethink the relationship among street youths' mobility, place, identity, and survival. Outreach workers serving as a bridge is a powerful spatial and moral metaphor for how we conceive of and work with homeless youth. But my work revealed that outreach does not act as an effective bridge between the street and services so much as a temporary bridge for young people between mobility and stability. Outreach workers try to create space on the streets to stabilize young people so that they can begin to mentally and emotionally move out of a state of crisis: "Street outreach and drop-in centers are all about creating a safe space for homeless kids, even just for a few hours."[60] Conversely, sometimes "street outreach is even less effective in stabilizing the kids because you only see them shortly. I think it's about providing a temporary safe space and giving out information in case they need to be on the street for a while."[61] In order to move youth off the streets, we, as a society, must enable them to be on the streets. We must stabilize young people in place socially so that they can take that next crucial step forward. Paradoxically, street outreach workers try to legitimize street kids' place on the streets in order for them to alter their own social existence. In this way, street youth are socially constructed as both *on* the street and *of* the street.

Conclusion

Where Does the "Move Along" Dance Take Us?

Every contact is banked up in my head like a litany of the saints.
—Outreach worker describing the kids he remembers

In 1998, the *Village Voice*, a New York City–based, alternative weekly newspaper, ran an article entitled "Nowhere to Go: New York Is Hell If You're 18 and Homeless."[1] The article centered on an account of city council members riding along in a street outreach van through Times Square. They watched as an outreach worker handed out condoms and informational fliers to kids who "flocked to his window." They were reportedly amazed that these kids looked like any other New York teenagers. One city council member remarked, "What's shocking is not that there's this group of young people but that we're ignoring them." A decade later, street kids are caught in a vise of attention and inattention, physical mobility and social isolation. Police and private security forces move street youth out of public view; kids respond by scattering across the cities' public spaces. As the broader society continues to ignore the plight of homeless youth, the policies regulating public spaces push the experiences of street kids even further from our view and collective social conscience. When street kids are "moved on," it is easier to ignore them and deny them social aid. To repeat what the city councilman pointed out, what is "shocking" is not that youth homelessness exists but that our policies seem to perpetuate it. We cannot change the status quo until everyday people "see" youth homelessness as a real and immediate problem.

A critical step toward changing our vision of youth homelessness is to address our public-space policies. If we are to begin acknowledging street kids as legitimate public actors, we also must address the inadequacy of current policing methods, such as zero-tolerance policing and quality-of-life initiatives. Our collective ignorance of street kids' experiences is not an excuse, as it arises from our active acceptance of current policies that displace youth and subject them to permanent mobility. At the intersection of this process, street outreach workers try to create spaces of advocacy for young people, which can function as physical and emotional havens for young people trying to find their feet on the chaotic and shifting terrain of adults' demands and regulations. Since the intensification of quality-of-life policing in the late 1990s, we have done more than "ignore" street kids: cities across the United States have pursued policies that exacerbate the problems of homeless youth, driving them away from social services and access to social aid. As a result, social workers have only a limited ability to engage with and advocate for young people, and youth have only a limited ability to advocate for themselves. Public-space policies push homeless kids closer to the fringes of society, penalizing and sanctioning them to even darker regions of social exclusion. Social exclusions have a concrete geography in large cities, and street outreach work in New York City is a good example of the geographical aspects of our collective sociospatial marginalization of street kids.

This autumn, I went on a walk through my familiar outreach paths. Starting in the East Village, I wound my way through Tompkins Square Park. The gutter punk kids who had flocked to the park all summer were nowhere to be seen now that the cooler weather had arrived and the warmer weather in the South was beckoning. Traversing the length of St. Mark's Place and cutting up to Union Square, I noticed plenty of college students and young professionals scurrying along the sidewalks, but no obvious signs of squatter kids or traveling homeless youth. Most of them already were heading to cities in Florida, Texas, and California. As I walked along, I remembered a young couple and their dog that I met earlier in the summer. They had been spanging for bus tickets to North Carolina and were trying to get a service-dog license that would allow them to take their dog with them. I had called the agency that distributed service-animal licenses for them but could not reach anyone. I wondered if they had been able to navigate through the city's licensing bureaucracy or if they had ended up hitchhiking their way south.

Upon arriving at Union Square, I found thousands of people enjoying a warm fall evening. The back platform, which had previously functioned as the primary outreach site for StandUp for Kids, had been ripped up and surrounded by chain-link construction fencing. Smooth new paving stones had replaced the platform and picnic tables, in preparation for a new café and bar. Ironically, on one of my first outreaches in 2004, several street kids mentioned that the back platform at the Square would be reconstructed. In that year, they had already found themselves fenced out of a popular public space in the West Village, fondly referred to as the "Benches." Outreach workers knew that the Benches were a good place to find younger street kids and new runaways. The year before that, youth had been kicked off the West Side piers to make way for the construction of Hudson River Park. Kids showed no surprise that the city was continuing its reconstruction, targeting areas popular as youth hangouts. At the back of Union Square, park employees had warned the kids to clear out nearly four years before the construction started. The groups of kids who used the old concrete platform to meet up, deal drugs, take naps, and practice skateboard maneuvers are scattered around the area, though harder to see now in the larger crowds of young people. Across from the Square, the building alcove of the record store, where kids hung out when it rained, also is gone, replaced by a wall of bright blue construction plywood covers. These changes are not unexpected, however, as New York City has been on an development spree for several years, shutting off and reinventing the uses of public spaces to improve their look and access for middle-class uses. The cleanup of major public sites such as Times Square and Bryant Park made headlines in the 1980s and 1990s. Although smaller projects like the alterations at Union Square rarely make newspaper headlines, they have profoundly affected street kids and street outreach workers. Before each new wave of construction, the street kids are told to clear out, usually by police mandated to clean up the area of users seen as undesirable.

The shifting regulation of public spaces and public subjects through policing tactics increasingly alter street youths' spatial behaviors. Kids who are frequently told to move along will find other, less visible spaces to occupy. Some, like Ali Forney, head back to neighborhoods that they had previously fled, reencountering the people who had abused them and spaces they know are not safe. Others, like Blacc, continue to struggle to stay out of sight, find work, and get off the streets. Public-space regulations have devastating effects on young people as well as the social service agencies attempting to aid them. As I have argued throughout this book, street youth have been forced into a state of fixed mobility. Mobile youth do not occupy an abstract void; they exhaustively traverse real urban territories, wandering in and out of parks and McDonalds, down empty side streets, and hanging out under building alcoves, only to be told by a bored security guard to keep moving. Mobility is physically and emotionally exhausting, and it has tangible and detrimental effects. It is no wonder, then, that the street youth whom outreach workers encounter often exhibit the same posttraumatic stress disorder as do children in war zones.

How Effective Are the Current City-Run Outreach Models?

Contemporary outreach efforts have been hindered by a number of social trends, among them the alteration of public spaces, the implementation of zero-tolerance policing through quality-of-life ordinances, and the neoliberalization of both public policing and social services. Outreach groups struggle under the weight of these trends. Small nonprofits compete for dwindling funds with more and more regulatory strings attached. One outreach worker expressed his frustration over the limits imposed by street quotas and the vast geographic area that his group needed to cover every night in the city:

> Outreach under the grant we received is really a token effort by an agency with very little power. I went out with Citywide Harm Reduction one night. They know the neighborhood where they work. They only work in the South Bronx. That anchors them in one place and allows them to be specialists in the needs of their clients.

Even observing another outreach group's work is a rare chance to share ideas and information, as the neoliberalization of outreach services has set up confidentiality and funding boundaries that discourage cooperation among different groups. Outreach workers go out in isolation, not knowing where they will find youth or even the same young person more than once. Outreach workers tell street kids that they will be back to help them but do not know if their funding will last through the month. They also do not know whether the young person they worked with ever can find other social services after the outreach is over. The constant mobility of youth attempting to stay out of sight, dodging police attention and ticketing, and blending into New York City's vast terrain of public spaces only exacerbates these issues. In this environment, outreach workers have trouble creating and maintaining the "safe spaces" that are basic to the street outreach model of engaging and bridging youth from the streets to sited social services.

Despite the roadblocks to performing meaningful, effective outreach, the reaching-out-to-the-streets model of social service provision still retains a powerful enticement for people committed to engaging street kids. I spoke to a young, formerly homeless women who was starting an outreach group in the city. She was familiar with the constant mobility of being young and homeless, as she had "couch-surfed" between the ages of eighteen to twenty-four. She emphasized the importance to her of finding a place to be still, to reoccupy her own body and identity after years of physical abuse and emotional turmoil:

Every once in a while, I'll get a good spot and be able to stay there for a while. But it's a life in movement. It's a very difficult thing. It does something to your mind—not having a foundation. I think a lot of homeless people are constantly on that search for home. I know that I am.[2]

When I asked what motivated her to begin an outreach group, her answer revealed a dual understanding of mobility and invisibility in her desire to create a space for street youth that was tangible and "present":

I just saw a lot of stuff that needed to be addressed. I was very inspired in that moment to do something more tangible. I needed to do something right there in the moment that was important and helpful. I think that there are a lot of organizations doing a lot of things but sometimes we overlook the smallest . . . more personal interactions between people. . . . The tiniest conversations always made a big change in me. I feel like having a presence. . . . I think one of the most important things is to just be there. I just left this situation myself but I can offer a lot. I can offer myself . . . someone who is familiar with this thing. . . . I want to be a presence. I don't think there's enough of that. Homeless kids . . . are really good at hiding the fact that they're homeless.

Creating presence on the streets is an enormous challenge in today's public spaces. This young woman plans to offer sandwiches, information, free yoga, and an open ear as a way of starting that process. The spaces she chooses for outreach, how that space is policed, and how young people navigate that space all are critical to her success. Outreach is about more than "reaching out"; it is about creating a space in time for young people to reach in. Young people who are being watched by police often move along long before being issued a ticket. Just walking up to an outreach worker is itself an enormous act of trust, especially from a kid who has consistently been abused and who constantly feels watched. One young person expressed this constant surveillance as an unspoken message that he was not welcome: "They give us dirty looks—kids feel like people are saying 'go home' even if it is not vocalized."[3]

The social and physical position of outreach work is both difficult to pin down and highly important. Street outreach tries to create a space in young people's own territories where adults can engage with them, to fix them in place. Even though outreach depends on flexibility and movement, these factors also work against it. An outreach worker observed that during outreach, "things change with every step. Walking it another way or direction will change everything." How can outreach workers build a bridge between youth on the streets and social services when the terrain on which the bridge rests does not stay still?

Where Does the "Move Along" Dance Take Us?

As I have argued, the social and physical placement and displacement of street youth is important to how the social services for them are mobilized and structured. Street outreach models are based on an ideology that places homeless youth not just outside the home but also in a socially constructed space called the "street." This powerful public/private binary logic has been used to structure the provision of services for street kids out in public spaces in the form of street outreach. Yet clearly the majority of homeless youth are no longer easily identified on the street itself. The days of street arabs and guttersnipes are, fortunately, gone, but homeless young people having to engage in the street economy remain. Increased police surveillance has pushed the street economy into a wide variety of locations that are not in the public eye or on a public sidewalk. Revanchist policing policies have driven most street kids into states of perpetual motion and invisibility. In New York City today, sex work is arranged on the Internet, in nightclubs, in adult video stores, and only rarely in dark alleys. Drug deals are more likely to be carried out in apartments, hallways, and the relative privacy of public bathrooms than in a public park. Street kids who engage in spanging are still located on the street, but city crackdowns on aggressive panhandling (the definition of which is left to the subjective interpretation of each police officer), have discouraged many homeless youth from this public, visibly homeless activity. What do these changes mean for the study of "street" kids and "street" outreach? One outreach worker grimly assessed street youths' chances of getting help when they need it:

> Those who aren't lucky enough to receive the help they need toward independence are tomorrow's wards of the State. Runaway and homeless teens are as often the ones who got away, the kids who escape [abuse]. . . . But only when they get the support they need from the system, mutual aid, or luck.[4]

Reaching out to young people relies too much on "luck" and chance. Street outreach workers are well aware of the difficulties of finding young people who have retreated from the street into less visible and less accessible places or who are trying to be invisible while still under the public gaze. Dual outcomes of mobility and invisibility by vulnerable and marginalized populations such as street kids thus complicate outreach, operationally, ethically, and conceptually.

Street Outreach as a Creative Spatial Solution

Current models of street outreach have outreach workers chasing after street kids, but they feel as though they are chasing ghosts, that the kids are just around the next corner. Social workers are haunted by the young people they find and lose in the shifting fabric of life in the city. If street outreach is to be the creative spatial fix imagined by social workers, policymakers, and academics, then we need a better conception of the geographies of street youth and the types of spaces made possible by outreach in today's public spaces. Current conditions require that outreach be geographically strategic. Similarly, youth workers on the ground need to be able to make critical spatial decisions. One outreach worker described the perfect model of outreach: "Ideally, the City would create neighborhood teams for each neighborhood, the more homelessness and violent the neighborhood, the larger and more diverse the team. Neighborhoods would then be able to rely on a team of specialists in that geographic area."[5] In contrast, most outreach workers currently cover large, diverse areas of the city with little training or support by the community.[6]

Street quotas accounting for large numbers of kids are forcing outreach teams into even wider areas of mobility, rather than encouraging them to stay in one place and establish an outreach site that young people can find. Two decades ago, an outreach team might focus on only those young people along Christopher Street in the West Village. These workers would have known that kids hung out around a local pizza joint, and they also would have known the owner of the pizza joint, the drug dealers, the pimps, and the beat of the local police officers. All these people probably would have known the outreach workers as well and where and when they would appear in the neighborhood. Nowadays, however, outreach workers rarely find young people consistently in the same locations. Instead, they seek kids on a hundred different streets and do not know the local shop owners or the local police. Outreach thus ends up being an educated guessing game: looking for kids in ever widening circles out from where they used to congregate. Because every neighborhood has its own street economies and local actors, outreach workers usually know less about them, resulting in confusion dangerous for both social workers and homeless youth.

If we want street outreach to be successful, it needs to be spatially and socially transformative. Street kids are socially and, increasingly, spatially isolated in U.S. cities. Engaging youth on the streets and drawing them out physically, socially, and emotionally from that isolated borderland is difficult to do and to maintain, as outreach work is often sidetracked or reduced to providing basic resources:

> I think that a lot of outreach services are limited to giving food or infor-
> mation. I view it more as an opportunity for transformation (not just for
> youth, but also for their environments, which include people who abuse
> them). I think there is room to approach it from a very creative standpoint.[7]

Accordingly, the act of simply finding the young people has become the goal, rather than creating responsive outreach spaces once the youth are engaged. The concept of building transformative spaces for outreach is one way of addressing the marginality that street kids confront in their everyday lives. A youth service director explained that a primary goal of transformative outreach centers on "replacing traditional 'reaching out' activities with establishing temporary spaces (emotionally speaking) on the street where people can come in and take a break from their identity. I think it is a very transformative and healing way of doing outreach."[8] Outreach spaces could offer a place to create new relationships and social networks that young people cannot find in the street environment. Young people must begin making broader social connections as a way of exiting street life, and social workers, academics, and policymakers must resolve a number of conceptual and material problems to produce more effective street outreach and aid to street youth in today's public spaces.

Implications for Outreach Workers

Traditional models of street outreach would benefit from becoming more spatially aware. In the past, social workers could safely assume that street kids would congregate in visible and known locations, enabling street outreach workers to easily identify and "reach out" to them. But this is no longer true in an environment of punitive policing and public surveillance. Simply chasing street kids into ever widening ranges of mobility is particularly ineffective in cities like New York. There are simply too many streets, parks, subways, buildings, hallways, and McDonalds for kids to disappear in as they evade the attention of authority. Outreach workers would benefit from identifying where in this system they could intercept the mobile paths of street kids and create safe and consistent places where kids may find them. If this place turns out to be a subway platform or a street corner, it needs to be a space where youth are already congregating during the day and where they can safely take a break from their street life. This is an enormous challenge. It will require that outreach workers go out, day after day, and establish their own territory on the streets that other actors in public spaces can identify and respect. Issues of safety and visibility are complex, which outreach workers and street kids must negotiate in order for these spaces to have transformative effects.

Implications for Policymakers

The policy changes that would make the most difference to street youth would address the root causes of their homelessness. Reforming the broken foster care system and school programs to give youth the help they need before becoming homeless would drastically reduce the number who eventually run away or are kicked out of their homes. Because larger institutional and structural changes are slow to develop, a series of smaller policy changes could greatly improve the way we work with homeless youth in public spaces.

The first step is recognizing that our policing policies are hindering the work of social services and may even be keeping kids on the streets. We cannot make better policies until we understand how our current public-space policies affect the everyday lives of real kids in real places. If street kids need to be able to occupy public spaces in order to halt a ceaseless pattern of mobility and outreach workers need to be able to engage with them in those spaces consistently over time, how can we make that happen? One way would be to readdress the utility of park and other public-space curfews. Parks that are open late at night are congregating points for young people where social workers could find the time, and especially the quiet, away from the general public to work with them. Once the parks close at 1 a.m. in New York City, young people scatter throughout the city streets, and outreach workers are left circling the blocks, searching for kids in a hundred shifting locations.

A second tangible point of entry into street youths' mobility patterns is sites of public transportation. For example, New York City is currently pursuing policies meant to clean up its subway systems by discouraging any homeless activity in its stations. Mass Transit Association (MTA) "outreach" teams have gained a poor reputation for harassing and moving street youth and adult homeless out of these spaces. But the indoor spaces of the public transportation system could provide a safe place for young people during the night and over the winters. If they were able to use subway platforms as places of refuge, social workers could engage them there. Street outreach workers already try to find kids in New York's labyrinthine subway system in the winter, but when youth must play a game of cat and mouse with the MTA police, they also become hard for social workers to find. Of course, at the end of the day, gains in street outreach efforts will pay off only if street kids have services to access. That is, the outreach "bridge" needs to lead somewhere other than the street.

Implications for Academics

Academics need to consider two issues when working with marginalized youth populations and the equally marginalized youthwork profession. A significant body of work by feminist and critical scholars addresses the ethics of praxis in research. Although we all strive to be ethical and productive in our work with marginalized populations, ethics and the products of our research are part of a wider social world that is not fully under our control. For many people, working with street kids is a lifelong commitment, and they expect no less of academics seeking to enter this world. The level of commitment necessary to work with homeless youth far exceeds what is expected of most doctoral candidates or even professorial research and service requirements. When an abused young person opens up to an adult, be it an outreach worker or a researcher, that relationship needs to be committed.

A long-term, stable commitment is equally important to academics' volunteer work for social organizations as part of their praxis. By becoming an experienced outreach worker during two years in the field, I accumulated vital "street knowledge" concerning where and how to engage homeless kids. But when I left the field, I was in danger of compounding the same weakness that most outreach groups suffer. When senior counselors leave, they take all their knowledge with them. By writing this book, therefore, I hope to describe to a broader audience the problems that street kids and outreach workers face when confronting today's public-space regimes, and more important, I hope to pass on to others some of what I learned during my time as an outreach worker.

Critical Endings

> I believe that we can get the public to "see" the plight of street youth as long as we don't exploit them in the process. Too many programs tend to go down that road of showing the face of the homeless young person. And it ends up following them throughout their lives.
>
> —Former outreach worker

In the small college town in Pennsylvania where I grew up, I cannot remember any young people "running away" or being homeless. In retrospect, though, I realize that we did not talk about youth homelessness in those terms. Kids moved in with grandparents or other relatives for a while. Others stayed with friends. Older kids dropped out of school and got jobs, trying to make it on their own. One girl whom I knew stayed with a teacher when her own family life became too scary. Kids who had problems at home spent more time cutting school, thus making their eventual disappearance from our social scene unremarkable. After my research, however, I now remember these young people very differently; that is, they have become visible to me in a different way. I wonder where these kids went and how they survived. I wonder what was going on in their lives that caused them to slowly fade away from friends, teachers, and other people who might have helped them. And I wonder why so few people (adults or youth) commented at the time on their absence.

I realize that my own youthful obliviousness to what was going on with some of my former classmates is indicative of a broader social pattern. I recognize that just as street youths' and street outreach workers' experiences with social norms and regulations are profoundly shaped by the environments in which they interact, my previous understanding of youth homelessness was situated in a social frame that marginalized and eradicated any evidence of this phenomenon. Young people rarely display their own homelessness, for it is a highly stigmatized status. Studies of street kids have linked youth to feelings of loneliness, depression, and suicide.[9] Although kids will go out of their way to avoid looking homeless, they still suffer the mental anguish of homelessness and the stigma of that label. Current social norms and practices only reinforce this invisibility by organizing street kids into highly mobile lifestyles.

One of my goals throughout this project has been to understand how the strategies of street outreach practices intersect with the survival strategies of street kids in increasingly regulated public spaces. Critical ethnography informed by a feminist geography ethos has given me a framework in which to situate my research. This approach encourages researchers to go beyond observation and actively engage with the processes, actors, and settings that comprise the wider social practice. From this perspective, then, I could not merely talk to outreach workers and young people. Instead, to fully understand how public spaces and social regulations affect their practices and relationships, I needed to become an outreach worker and work with street youth. My understanding of what it means to be an ethical, active, and productive researcher has thus been challenged. Grappling with the intersections of research practice and outreach practice has forced me to address the contradictions, limitations, assumptions, expectations, and power relations of social science research processes, including my own work.

Outreach workers are like ethnographers in that they seek out a site and a group of people whom they get to know very well over a long period of time. They try to become part of those people's lives. The formation of outreach knowledge and the street is more organic than structured. We inhabit places because we have invested them with meaning. Socially situated understandings of our environment determine our inhabitation, how we "dwell," and how we relate to others (both people and things) within these meaningful spaces. In outreach, that positioning carries great responsibility. Rather than using knowledge to construct a larger product outside the research environment, outreach workers immediately reapply the information that they gather. That knowledge structures the ongoing process of data acquisition and applications. It is applied ethnography and, for me, organized my engagement with critical praxis. As a researcher and an outreach worker, I folded my intellectual knowledge of outreach, youth, and public spaces back into the process itself. My hope is that my work will help outreach workers as much as academics and policymakers. Activist research has a powerful and unpredictable weight. Praxis is not easily set down once taken up in the field, by people who continue to work, strive, and suffer in their everyday lives.

Appendix A

Research in the Streets (in Retrospect)

My research was marked by several methodological and ethical challenges. Studying mobile street kids and outreach workers in public spaces made it difficult to find a place for my research and presented many practical issues related to data collection and my activist identity. Indeed, the problem of "fixing" mobile practices in place is fundamental to the relationship among street outreach, street youth, and social regulation. By attempting to "fix" these issues long enough to complete a comprehensive ethnographic study, I encountered a number of conflicts between the abstract goals of qualitative research and the realities of street outreach.

My use of critical ethnographic methods profoundly shaped my understanding of the interactions between outreach workers and street youth. Using such methods to study youth and social services is controversial and includes ethical concerns related to the researcher's positionality, reflexivity, and power.[1] At the same time, critical ethnographic methods are concerned with understanding how academic research participates in social change.[2] I encountered each of these methodological dilemmas in my own attempts to do ethically informed, activist fieldwork.

Part 1: Problems Conducting Research "on the Streets"

Social scientists first must select an ethnographic methodology for research with marginalized groups.[3] The use of ethnographic methods to study young people in social service work is part of the academic debates concerning the limitations and critiques of traditional ethnographic methods.[4]

The category "homeless kids" is inherently ambiguous. In practice, outreach workers must regularly decide whether the kids they encounter qualify as "homeless," an ambiguous judgment that also determined the boundaries of my own fieldwork practices. During my time in the field, I often had difficulty classifying a young person as homeless and quickly learned that many young people hesitate to confide their living situation to an adult. I also learned that contrary to the popular media, most homeless youth disguise any visual markers of homelessness; indeed, their very survival may depend on their hiding their homeless state.[5] But over the long term, maintaining their invisibility only increases their vulnerability, thereby perpetuating the cycle of homelessness. This intersection of invisibility and vulnerability not only complicates situated, ethnographic research praxis but also marginalizes young people living on the streets.

During my fieldwork, I also encountered difficulties deciding whether the various people I encountered qualified as "kids." As a social construction, the category of youth varies with the cultural context and setting. Each of the outreach groups with which I worked negotiated this tension by creating a standard age range for its youth clients, but I quickly learned that any such standards had to allow many exceptions. Kids living on the street age rapidly. As a result, outreach workers and researchers can easily overlook those who appear older. Ambiguities related to age are further complicated when kids change their appearance to look younger, either to accommodate sex work or to better appeal to public sympathy. In the first few months of outreach, nearly a dozen teenage-looking people told me that they were "twenty-four." I later found out that police would often ask young people under the age of twenty-four for identification, thereby giving younger street kids an incentive to lie about their age to strangers. Although most street outreach workers understand the stereotypes that obscure youth homelessness, these are still often the only visual indicators that they have to quickly identify a street kid. Thus, outreach and research with street kids are a guessing game as to whether an individual is either "street" or "kid," in part because the categories themselves are socially constructed and highly unstable. Decisions have to be made on a case-by-case basis, on the fly.

Determining the boundaries of the population that I would include in my study was frustrating. While the young people that I engaged through street outreach with were roughly twelve to twenty-four years old, were males and females, came from different ethnicities and races, and were experiencing some form of homelessness, I could never be sure this was true for each kid. I also had trouble discerning whether these boundaries were reflective of the larger population of street youth. For example, should I include a thirty-year-old active member of a street youth community? How about a youth who sleeps at home but is close friends with youth living on the street? These dilemmas related to classification become more complex when researchers play the role of scholar/activist/social worker. While I was standing on a street corner staring at a group of kids, it was agonizing to realize that my "work" of establishing who was or was not homeless could have very real and lasting consequences for them. Would a kid be harmed because I, as a participating social worker, did not recognize his or her need? Outreach workers ask themselves these questions on every outreach. For them, it is an extremely tricky process, especially when outreach materials and resources are in short supply. In the end, it is difficult to decide who is or is not a street kid. As both an outreach worker and a researcher, I could simply listen to each kid as an individual and follow the guidelines of the outreach groups.

Because of social service providers' many definitions of youth homelessness and street kids, deciding which outreach groups to include in my study was difficult as well. No two groups have the same guidelines for those with whom they would do outreach and for what they considered to be "outreach." In the end, I included only those groups whose specific mission was to work with young people, on a regular basis, on the streets. I omitted those groups that conducted "event" outreach for specific programs or searched for young people through the Internet, in jails, or at music shows, as they were outside the scope of my research questions about the structuring context of urban public spaces and order maintenance policing. In addition, I did not include some adult outreach groups that aid young people (especially those over eighteen) because their adult-specific guidelines for identifying homelessness captured only a small portion of the street youth population.

I also chose not to interview police, residents, or business owners. Although some outreach groups have minimal contact with police and local business owners, most are careful to limit any interactions (especially contact that street kids might observe or misconstrue as "informing"). Street youth generally have adversarial relationships with police and local businesses and so may shun outreach workers who become associated with either. Furthermore, some outreach groups themselves are in conflict with members of the community who view outreach as enabling or attracting street kids to their neighborhoods. Outreach workers have been ticketed by the police, harassed by resident groups, and even arrested while hanging out with street youth. While I could have sought out police and local business owners for interviews, I felt that my intimate involvement with street outreach groups would color my perceptions of these other social actors. Moreover, a few formal interviews with police or business groups would not be comparable to the wealth of field notes and participant observation with street outreach and street kids. Nonetheless, police, residents, and shop owners were present at every community board meeting, and their views have been well documented in newspaper accounts of street kids. In addition, they were present in public spaces and therefore are incorporated into my observation notes. In the end, I felt that there were more than enough questions concerning street youth and street outreach to occupy one researcher. Even so, I want to emphasize that many voices and views are missing that still deserve careful attention. For example, an ethnographic study of police interactions with street youth would make a challenging topic for future research.

Part 2: Critical Ethnographic Methods

To uncover how interactions between street youth and street outreach are framed by the ever changing dynamics of public spaces and public agents, I used a critical ethnographic methodology. Ethnography is a contextual, generative, inductive, and holistic approach to research that, rather than testing a hypothesis or theory, tries to achieve a depth of understanding by studying a "whole way of life."[6] Traditional ethnographies are long-term studies of cultural or social groups focusing on ordinary, everyday actions, with the goal of "render[ing] the familiar strange in order to expose the common-sense understandings and practical reasoning that sustain local social orderings."[7] This goal is generally achieved by ethnographers living with, observing, and participating in the daily lives of those whom they are studying. Likewise, a critical ethnographic approach allowed me to investigate the small, everyday interactions comprising street outreach, a social service performed under the public gaze.

Among the critiques and debates accompanying critical ethnographic methods (and, indeed, a variety of current research models often used in geography and other social sciences) are concerns about the researcher's positionality and reflexivity, power and ethics in research through nonexploitative data collection, and insiders' and outsiders' relations and processes. I encountered each of these issues in relation to my work as an observant participant in the street youth / street outreach scene. Critical ethnographies seek to understand how the practices of research are brought to bear on social issues, that is, how researchers act as agents of change.

In the past, geographers have addressed spatial-social research questions using a variety of ethnographic methodologies incorporating different political and paradigmatic stances. Traditionally, ethnography has been made up of a set of qualitative methods developed by anthropologists to study the everyday behaviors, customs, and traditions of non-Western cultures. Accounts of exotic-seeming "others" were produced by scholars moving to isolated locations and submerging themselves in the (foreign) languages, value systems, and environments of small groups of people. The ethnographers then described and interpreted the relationship between social practices and spatial organization.[8] These studies involved long periods of fieldwork during which the ethnographer, as an outsider, slowly became acclimated, in some cases gaining temporary or contingent insider status. If we accept on face value the accounts of early ethnographic methods, texts, and accounts, we will see the clear boundaries between the researchers' "real" life and their fieldwork experiences, that is, between their personal relationships and their research subjects. When sociologists began using ethnographic methods for domestic studies, the problems with ethnographic boundaries and practices were brought home, quite literally.

Domestic ethnographies were initiated in the 1920s by the Chicago School of Urban Sociology.[9] These studies mirrored research conducted outside the United States, in that the objects of study were usually isolated or marginalized groups of people and were socially constructed as the "other" in both the domestic context and in relation to the researcher's social position. Although the Chicago School included more female academics than did other disciplines at that time, its ethnographers were usually educated white men. Their accounts of skid-row denizens, dive bars, hobos, train hopping, and the gritty underside of industrializing America reflected a romantic notion of the intrepid researcher-as-explorer scouting out a dangerous and exciting terrain, even if that terrain were only next door or down the block. This method of data collection required extensive periods of time to gain access to informants and their social settings, as well as to establish the familiarity necessary to interpret these settings. In other words, a lot of unscientific-seeming "hanging out" was required. Positivistic practitioners in the social sciences were highly skeptical of the ethnographic approach to studying social systems. Critiques included the biased and often unsupported nature of ethnographers' representations (ethnographers rarely reveal their raw data, such as field notes, informal conversations, and jottings) and the inability to generalize statistically from unique and highly descriptive accounts. Ethnographers thus began using a variety of data forms and sources (observations, archival data, photography, mapping, surveys, interviews) in order to enrich and situate the validity of their interpretations. Ethnography slowly emerged as a major methodological tool kit for exploring the relationships between moral/social order and spatial patterns.[10] More recently, ethnographic methods have been the subject of feminist and postmodernist critiques, further complicating academic understandings of power, ethics, positionality, and performance in the social construction of knowledge.[11]

Critically informed ethnographies focus on the issues of power and oppression that have not been addressed and reproduced using traditional ethnographic methods.[12] Traditional ethnography makes authoritative claims in representing cultures and social groups through the researcher's interpretations and appeals to authority through such concepts as the researcher gaze (observation/witnessing) and the researcher voice (constructing narratives that give voice to others). Contemporary critical and feminist ethnographies, however, increasingly focus on the ability of research to uncover injustice and function as a form of activism, rather than on the purely descriptive power of older ethnographic projects.[13] Critical ethnographers do not try to alter traditional ethnography's tools but instead adopt a critical lens to approach the data and the research process. As Jim Thomas[14] argues, ethnographic data can be a powerful force for social change and mark a departure from traditional ethnographic approaches, as "conventional ethnographers study culture for the purpose of describing it; critical ethnographers do so to change it." Feminist ethnographic practices, in particular, try to create an inclusive research experience that uses collaborative data collection and analysis techniques with research respondents.[15] Thus, the research process itself serves as a medium for empowerment through a dialectical relationship between critical social theory and ethnographic practices, that is, a critical reflexive praxis.

Both academics and professionals have been working with young people for critical reflexive praxis in research with children.[16] Because adults have traditionally controlled the production of knowledge about and for children, feminist geographers have raised concerns about power and the research process in regard to children and youth and have argued that any work with children must question the relevance of adult-defined social categories.[17] Adult researchers try to create a rapport with their young subjects that is often marked by respect, caring, and mentoring but can often lead to failure or misinterpretation. Working with young people carries a great responsibility, as it entails a powerful relationship. Mentoring a young person often injects a measure of guidance and assimilation into the researcher's standards and ethics. For example, what do researchers do when the children that they are studying follow alternative logics of justice and ethics? Social power imbalances between adults and children are large, and the intermediary position of youth both reifies and challenges this social binary, especially in regard to the extended period of youth frequently encountered in Western societies.

Fieldwork: Reflexively Recording the Field

At the heart of ethnography lies fieldwork, which "demands the full-time involvement of a researcher over a lengthy period of time . . . and consists mostly of ongoing interaction with the human targets of study on their home ground."[18] Fieldworkers write extensive descriptions of their experiences in the field, noting what they saw and heard and describing their experiences and impressions of social actions. Field experiences and field notes are the building blocks of ethnographic accounts and are what give ethnographies their narrative structure. While much time is spent on the actual process of writing field notes, the notes themselves are rarely presented in their original form.[19] While I certainly have field notes that will never see the light of day, the outreach workers with whom I worked not only saw but also helped me compile much of my outreach data. My outreach notes contain far more of the thoughts and opinions of outreach workers than they would have if I had used other methods, such as interviewing. Just as ethnography seeks to be a holistic approach to social inquiry, my field notes turned out to be a holistic, cooperative affair typical of feminist approaches to "know with" your research respondents.[20]

Many of my written accounts begin with group observations about an outreach attempt and include contributions by my fellow outreach workers. By sharing the raw data of ethnography with my research participants, I attempted to break down the traditional social boundaries of the relationship between the researcher and the researched. It can be exceedingly disconcerting for researchers to show their own subjectivity to their research subjects, and in my study of street kids and outreach workers, I rarely had the opportunity to share my ideas or field notes with street youth. The young people with whom I worked over the two years of my fieldwork were generally in a state of crisis, and most of my interactions with them centered on finding resources, making referrals, or just listening to them. In quieter moments, I was able to explain my research to a few young people with whom I had more contact. But the vast majority of street kids whom I encountered during outreach were highly transient. It was exciting—and rare—to find the same kid more than once or even to hear about a kid that I had encountered months earlier. With street outreach workers, it was exactly the opposite. I not only was able to share and build my research along with other counselors, but I also was often able to send interviews and field notes directly to a respondent to ask for further input. Through this process, some of these interviews evolved into written records of several months' worth of conversations.

Ethnographers often question the right time to "let respondents in." In other words, when should the researchers' own thoughts and ideas be shared with those whom they are studying? As ethnographers, we hope that our respondents will be as open as possible with us, yet we often feel exposed or defensive when this relationship moves in the other direction. Feminist scholars have addressed these power dynamics in a number of ways, such as by involving the participants in the data collection and analysis.[21] In my case, however, the outreach in which I participated was a highly collaborative process from the start. Participating often meant being an outreach worker first and a researcher second. For this reason, my role tended to be closer to that of an "observant participant" than a "participant observer."[22] During each outreach, I had to balance research and outreach goals in the moment. For example, even if I were having an interesting conversation with a street kid, if one of the other outreach workers was having problems with the outreach, we both would break off the outreach. Outreach is never done individually, and outreach workers often have a code phrase for breaking off an outreach. This is for safety reasons—one worker might notice activity by a drug dealer or pimp that another outreach work might miss but that would necessitate breaking off the contact. In addition, outreach often must be stopped without explaining why in front of the youth being served. Outreach workers practice in pairs for both their own protection and that of the kids they contact.

As my study progressed, I began to realize that a central challenge was figuring out how to conduct fieldwork with fieldworkers. In some ways, this made my project quite easy, as outreach workers were carrying out the very same practices required for my own study of street youth. Like participant observers, outreach workers also must learn to "read" the street. For instance, scholars conducting research on AIDs outreach have similarly noted that street outreach workers observe a kind of natural ethnography through the practice of their work.[23] They spend long periods of time observing street youth and the public, looking for patterns of behavior. The questions that outreach workers asked kids were those that I also was interested in asking, such as, Where are you from? Where are you going? How are you surviving? How do people treat you on the streets? How do the police treat you? How'd you get that black eye? Being an outreach worker did make some questions easier to ask. Moreover, I was able to ask them with other people, who also were nervous, making mistakes, laughing at themselves, becoming frustrated, and constantly starting over. While many ethnographers feel isolated and alone in the fieldwork experience, I had the equivalent of a dozen research associates actively involved in a similar process.

Ethics and Nonexploitative Data Collection

Beyond the problems with identifying street kids and working with street outreach, I also had difficulty collecting basic data. By focusing on outreach workers and their interactions with young people, I limited my research setting to those young people found out on the streets. During an average outreach, the majority of street kids we found were tired, ill, drunk, high, or all of the above. It was rare to encounter a kid who was not mentally "altered," be it chemically, psychologically, or emotionally. There was no easy solution to this situation in terms of outreach or research. If a kid were judged by outreach workers to be too "out of it," we would stop the outreach and walk away (unless it was judged that he or she needed immediate medical attention). In most cases, the outreach had to be short and to the point in order for the young person to receive the maximum amount of aid in the brief time that we had his or her attention. This problem is frustrating for outreach workers, but over time we get used to it. As a researcher, though, this caused me endless hours of angst. I got better at spotting the kids who were more lucid and open to receiving outreach. I also felt that it would be unethical to repeat many of the stories that youth told me, even when I had asked and received their permission to include them in my study, because I could never be sure how altered their mental state was at the time. In many cases, however, the outreach encounter was too brief even to broach the subject of my research. During outreach, you may have a young person's attention for only a couple of moments. They often are in crisis, and every second is critical.

Street kids may tell outreach workers or researchers interesting stories, but the meanings of these stories, why or what they expect from the telling, and how we should interpret them is a tricky subject. My difficulties with obtaining an ethical consent from street youth made me increasingly critical of and troubled by other studies of street kids that I was reading. In a number of studies of street youth, researchers use existing outreach structures or forms of surveying to gather data on street youth. Most studies ask for written or verbal consent from young people and then ask them fairly invasive questions about their lives. In addition, most of the data seem to be collected at night when there are more street kids out on the street but also when they are the least sober. Where were these researchers and outreach workers finding hundreds of sober, awake, calm street kids at midnight? How were they following up with young people who are mobile, socially invisible, and nearly impossible for professional social workers to track down? How were they able to help young people deal with the emotions and traumas that talking about their street experiences evokes, sometimes days or weeks later? In research with vulnerable populations, social scientists are often put in situations normally held by professional counselors or social workers. How do we perform these roles in our research practices? Participation is productive, but productive of what and for whom? As my research progressed, I began to question the ethics of asking young people to talk about their experiences when we as adults are not open to them, as academics we may not have the skills to help them navigate painful emotional issues, and as researchers (or even as outreach workers) we may not be able to find them again to help them deal with the issues that arise from talking about painful experiences. For young people, taking part in social research can open a Pandora's box of unresolved mental and emotional problems.

I never found a good answer to these questions for myself as a researcher or an outreach counselor. I consoled myself that much of time I was following the lead of other youth workers and conforming to the rules set by each organization in regard to data collection. The outreach groups with which I worked had strict ethical guidelines in place that restricted practicing outreach with youth who were too drunk or high. All the organizations have confidentiality rules that far exceed those required by most academic ethic committees. As I pointed out in chapter 7, street kids "haunt" outreach workers and public spaces, and these unanswered questions should haunt the pages of any account of street kids' lives.

Insiders and Outsiders

The goal of ethnography is to obtain a view of the lives and motivations of a studied group. In traditional ethnography, the lines between outsider researchers and insider natives are clearly drawn and generally preestablished. Not until the inception of critical theories were the power relations built into binaries such as insider/outsider challenged. Critical ethnographies highlight, among other issues, how insider/outsider binaries frame what constitutes "indigenous" knowledge that can serve to obscure power relations that may be mutable and experiential: "The bipolar construction of insider/outsider . . . sets up a false separation that neglects the interactive processes through which 'insiderness' and 'outsiderness' are constructed."[24] In my fieldwork, I had to cope with my position as both a researcher and an outreach worker dealing with street youth in a street environment. Concepts of insider and outsider did not begin to approach the complexity of participation and social position here. In outreach, the lines between insiders and outsiders were constantly shifting in accordance with the intersections of experiences, other counselors, street kids, and street contexts. Often, outreach workers perform as intentional outsiders in settings in which they are assumed to be only marginal insiders. But this description fails to encompass peer outreach subjectivities and outreach experiences by adult workers who once were street kids themselves.

A strict conceptual division between insider and outsider narrows the discussion of street outreach and simultaneously organizes, disciplines, and diminishes the bonds that outreach workers and street youth build with each other. Yet the bridge-building metaphor commonly used to describe street outreach flows seamlessly into spatial conceptions of street youths' identities as outsiders of society. Outsiderness mobilizes and demobilizes social power, in performance and discourse, access and social position. Outsiderness is fundamental to a wider geographical romance of freedom, antiestablishment behaviors, and independence from social norms that lock street kids out on the streets. Perhaps by understanding how street outreach workers and street kids practice and construct insider/outsider relations, we can begin to understand how these binaries themselves organize social-spatial relations.

Part 3: Praxis in Fieldwork

In the end, my position as an outreach counselor/researcher changed frequently during my extended fieldwork experiences. It is hard to say what kind of insider/outsider I became or even what my social position constituted in an ongoing process. All outreach counselors go through individual reflexive processes—shaped by their histories, experiences, interpretations, and identities—and are not isolated from the group's experiences and positions. For example, one of my outreach partners struggled during and after each outreach to mesh our outreach experiences with his past experiences of homelessness and abuse. His struggle is reflected in my interpretations of the outreaches that I went on with him, as it influenced how we acted as an outreach team, as social performers, and as individual agents. For instance, while we did outreach several times around a park where gay youth picked up sex work, it was emotionally painful for him and brought up some of the stress of his teenage years. After a while, we steered our outreach path to areas where there was a greater mix of youth and activities. I participated in his social positioning as much as he influenced how I read an outreach scene or interacted with a young person. The dynamic of each outreach varied with who was present and what was going on at the time.

Over time, my fieldwork became increasingly collaborative with other outreach workers. Because the practices of ethnography and outreach overlapped extensively, my and my fellow outreach workers' field notes resembled a collaborative ethnography in which several researchers observe and analyze the same social setting.[25] Proponents of collaborative ethnography point to the strength of many views' providing a richer description of social practices. Collaboration also emphasizes the varying histories and views that each "researcher" brings to his or her understanding of what goes on in the field. In my study, collaboration with outreach workers who had experienced homelessness themselves often provided a level of insight that I could not have achieved by myself and affected how I perceived the social world of street youth and the relative value of adult interventions.

Academic descriptions of ethnographic fieldwork have much in common with street outreach methods. For instance, outreach workers also spend long amounts of time in the field (on the street) becoming familiar with the daily experiences of street kids on their home turf. Locating the "street" in street outreach turned out to be a continuing process for all the outreach counselors in my study. Rather than attempting to narrowly define the "site" of my fieldwork, as my study progressed I began to realize that "siting" street youth was integral to the process of outreach itself. That is, street outreach is structurally organized to find street kids on the streets, thereby opening up a number of issues regarding the social construction and operation of geographic subjectivities. The production of a field site by outreach workers or ethnographers is a critical praxis, created by ideologically informed practices that locate the field. For outreach workers, this happens in thousands of small, everyday conversations and decisions about where to find young people and sites to conduct outreach that is based on ideological assumptions of the street, homelessness, youth, public and private spaces, and their social regulation.

Ethnographers are expected to enter and exit the field as though the "field" were a separate, controlled space set aside from everyday life. Yet when in the field, their expected focus is on the everyday lives of others. This paradox is always present in the practice of street outreach. Outreach workers and ethnographers alike struggle with the complicated maneuvering of a "field" that is always present. How is the field a continuation of everyday life? The distinction lies in the fieldworker's motility. According to traditional ethnography, fieldworkers have the ability to move, to leave the field, that their subject may not have. Street outreach workers can leave the public spaces in which they find kids, but invariably they will find themselves back in those same spaces as part of their everyday lives. In what ways can we leave the field behind us? If we could physically remove ourselves from study sites, what about from social, mental, or emotional fields? We can leave the field and go home, but we often cannot get the field out of our minds and hearts. Outreach work embodies these tensions.

Arguably, we researchers continue to dwell in the field through our practices and the products of our work. Heidegger speaks of the phenomenon of "dwelling," described as an "openness to being."[26] In critical ethnographic fieldwork, fieldworkers seek openness as well, which reaches far beyond narrow conceptions of the field. Fieldwork often evolves by not actively seeking out and controlling the boundaries of the study, study site, study subjects, or the researchers' own positionality. Instead, boundary maintenance and creation inform and shape research over time.

Appendix B

Data Collection Methods

Working with young people who have been profoundly abused is very difficult. Part of the difficulty in working with street youth is maintaining healthy boundaries. In both ethnography and street outreach, boundary making and maintenance are important organizers of everyday interactions, structuring the mode and manner of ethnographic information that I was able to collect and how I organized it. I collected a wide variety of textual, visual, and experiential data by observation of public spaces, participant observation of street outreach groups, interviewing, involvement in public meetings, and secondary archival sources such as third-party surveys and focus groups.

Observation

I conducted public-space observations in three locations before beginning my work as a street outreach counselor. For four months, I observed and recorded publicly visible activities in Washington Square Park, Union Square, and Hudson River Park. All these public spaces are located in the lower portion of Manhattan and are within walking distance (about twenty minutes) of one another. All three are popular public places with a wide range of social groups using them throughout the day and evening. All three locations have curfews in effect from roughly midnight or 1 a.m. until 6 a.m. Each space is near public transportation (buses and subways), and each has a history of being frequented by homeless individuals and youth. I observed each space for an hour at a time, three times a week, and I handwrote my observations in field notebooks and later transcribed them.[1] Toward the end of this observation period, I began conducting outreach that encompassed these three public spaces as well as Tompkins Square Park and the East Village. My descriptions of public activity changed after my training as an outreach worker, as outreach work training entails learning to read and observe public actors in a highly specialized manner. At that point, I shifted my focus to describing out-reach spaces and interactions as a participant observer and outreach worker.

Participant Observation

"Hanging out" is a power-laden social act made up of complex social perfor-mances. For many ethnographers, being able to hang out with their subjects without feeling intrusive can be a long and delicate process. Because few peo-ple spend their days just sitting around, most researchers must learn to work or socialize in accordance with their research setting. My research setting was somewhat different in that hanging out is what outreach workers do most of the time on the job. In this sense, my participant observation was not out of place in the context of outreach work. While I was learning to inhabit my research setting and become an outreach worker, so were most of the people in my study. As I described in chapters 4 and 5, outreach work is low-status, often stressful and underpaid, social work, with a high rate of turnover for both professional outreach organizations and volunteer groups. As a result, outreaches were often carried out by novice workers still learning the routines. Learning to read the street environment—even in areas that outreach workers frequent—is dif-ficult. Time spent hanging out on outreach was invaluable for finding out what motivated outreach workers, both the volunteers and the professionals. This was also the time when I could examine my own motivations as an activist researcher and to regularly assess (often with other outreach workers) how the situated processes of fieldwork had reformulated my research goals.

In all, I conducted participant observation with four outreach groups from 2004 to 2007. I collected my primary data from the summer of 2004 to the summer of 2006, but I returned several times while writing up the results of my primary fieldwork in late 2006 and early 2007, as well as various times in 2010 to collect additional material. As I described in chapter 5, I usually produced my field notes in collaboration with other outreach workers after each outreach, and we often discussed them before the next outreach.

Interviews

In addition to extensive participant observation and conversations with street kids and outreach workers in the research setting, I also conducted semistructured interviews with twenty current and former outreach workers (thirteen men and seven women) and three former street youth (two men and one woman). Several of the outreach workers had also been street kids and talked about outreach in reference to their homeless experiences. The street youth that I interviewed formally were either in training or were interested in training to be outreach workers. The interviewees came from nine different organizations in New York City, and many had worked as outreach providers in other states besides New York. Several of them were thus able to compare New York City outreach with that of other locations and to explain how outreach differed among organizations and over time. My interviewees' experiences covered a wide spectrum of outreach provision, locations, and time periods. In all, their outreach experiences encompassed nearly twenty years of outreach in New York City. I solicited my interviews using a structured snowball method,[2] from drop-in centers, clinics, and advocacy and volunteer groups. At various meetings of homeless youth service providers and public forums concerning youth issues, I introduced myself and my project to groups working with street youth and asked them for interviews. At each interview, I also asked for an introduction to another potential interviewee.

Using a feminist ethnographic ethic,[3] my interviews largely followed the interviewee's comments and interests in the topic of street outreach. Each interview was loosely structured by a few general questions concerning practice: How did you begin/come to be doing outreach? What is a typical outreach like? What would you consider to be a "good" outreach? What is a "poor" outreach? What do you see as the main difficulties of outreach? What are the strengths of outreach? What are your strategies for improving outreach? With a few exceptions, I did *not* record the interviews. Outreach workers are extremely conscious of the confidentiality of their work, and taping tended to produce stilted conversations. But I did take detailed notes during each interview, transcribed them, and sent them back to the interviewee for further comments. In most cases, the interviewees added significantly to the original interview. In this way, the interviews became ongoing conversations. I conducted the interviews in drop-in centers, coffee shops, bars, on the streets, and in apartments. The interviewees were not paid.

Blacc's Interview

My interview with Blacc forms the heart of chapter 3. The opportunity to meet with him arose from an invitation I received to write a profile of a homeless youth for a book. Even though I had talked with Blacc many times before this interview, the youth profile project offered a chance to sit down with him and discuss his life in a highly structured manner. Our interview was conducted with the goal of obtaining a temporal narrative of his homeless experiences, from the first time he was thrown out of his home to the present. This inter-view was conducted in a private office at a drop-in center with a social worker present. The social worker was Blacc's main case manager, and both he and I had requested that she be present, due to the likelihood that painful issues might arise from the interview. The interview was tape-recorded and lasted for about two hours. Afterward, I transcribed the interview, and both Blacc and the social worker were given a chance to review it. Blacc requested that several points be clarified, and he reviewed the final narrative but declined to com-ment on it. His refusal may have been due to the residential instability that he experienced around the time that I finished writing his narrative profile.

"Blacc" is a street name, and he felt that one reason for recording his story was to describe, honestly, the reality of being a street youth and to "reclaim" these experiences. Many of his experiences were negative, and they shape who he is today. In the fall of 2006, Blacc was arrested and ejected from his shelter program. He also cut ties with the drop-in center where I met him. I reestablished contact with Blacc in 2009. He was working and living in New York City and had become the father of a young son. He contributed a few more details to his profile at that time and was able to reflect more fully on his homeless experiences.

Public Meetings

During my fieldwork, I attended monthly meetings held by a coalition of youth and family service groups dealing with homeless youth clients. Each meeting included updates by organizations, a series of pressing topics con-cerning service provision, and a general discussion/debate that was prese-lected and varied in each meeting. These debates centered on broad policy issues and usually solicited heated and extensive conversations. Five to fif-teen representatives from runaway and homeless youth (RHY) organizations attended these two-hour meetings. At times, I volunteered to take the meet-ing's minutes as a service to the group.

I also attended four public Community Board 2 meetings concerning the policing and social regulation of street youth in the West Village and an adjoining park, as well as the conduct of street youth, park police, the NYPD, and local residents. The central issue was the imposition of a curfew on the park. At these meetings, I took extensive notes and photographs. I transcribed the notes, which then informed some of my later interview ques-tions. My attendance at these meetings also led to my participation in a city-funded survey of young people using Hudson River Park.

Secondary and Archival Data

In addition to preexisting surveys, public reports, and media coverage of street kids, I participated in surveying more than two hundred young people in the West Village area in conjunction with a local drop-in center. I was able to have a minor involvement in the construction of the survey itself and was asked to summarize the results for the funding organization. This survey allowed me to speak to a number of youth outside the format of outreach and gave me a more detailed understanding of street kids in the West Village in particular. The survey questions ranged from public activities to identity and demographic data.

I also participated in the initial organizing meetings for the 2007 Homeless Youth Count in New York City. This count took place in 2007 and was the first homeless youth count conducted in New York City in thirty years. In my own review, I found research surveys to have limited value because of their structural constraints, such as their limited interaction time with young people. However, my involvement in the production of these two surveys greatly enhanced my understanding of certain structural aspects of street youth, street life, and public aid. Because of funding and accountability pressures, these surveys heavily emphasized quantitative indicators of homelessness. As a result, the survey questions often generalized or obscured the youths' homeless experiences and denaturalized the voice and language in which they described their own condition. However, surveys do speak to how social service providers frame youths' problems and are powerful means by which the general public is made aware of street kids. Accordingly, the knowledge produced through surveys has far-reaching consequences for funding social service programs.

Data Organization and Analysis

Ethnographic analysis strives to represent social orderings through the researcher's interpretations, sometimes by constructing "narratives" from the stories, everyday incidents, and interactions encountered in the field.[4] Researchers produce narratives, which interpret and explain the stories and descriptions that people use to convey their experiences and to participate in everyday life.[5] In this way, I collected textual data and images that I then organized into broad narrative themes based on context, content, and participatory experiences. I interpreted these themes in relation to secondary data and archival materials to form structural narratives. Researchers use narratives to construct social science frameworks that show how groups of people understand society and subsequently act in it. The form of the narratives varies according to the content and origin of the data.[6] Narrative analysis is an induction-based approach to knowledge creation, whose goal is to identify and understand the social frameworks underlying the stories that people tell about themselves. Moving from individual stories to broader concepts is the goal of narrative analysis.[7] Some narratives were highly descriptive, whereas others were more interpretive. In a few instances, I attempted to incorporate an "impressionist" style in order to ground my ethnographic interpretations in my own experiences and subjectivity.

Impressionist Tales

Some ethnographers experiment with "impressionistic tales," which seek to draw the audience into the experiences of fieldwork through first-person accounts of events in the field. Thematic analysis then flows out of a linked series of descriptive events told through first-person narratives.[8] Impressionistic descriptions do not attempt to be overtly interpretive. Rather, they balance the description of the process, action, and emotions in collecting data in the field with a narrative openness allowing readers to make their own assessments.[9]

In interpreting the difficulties of conducting outreach with young people, I tried to use an impressionistic style in part because street outreach and youth homelessness are experiential and difficult to describe adequately. In this sense, impressionistic narratives seek to "show, not tell." In the areas where I constructed impressionist descriptions, I shared my early- and later-stage thematic accounts with several outreach workers in order to assess the validity of my ethnographic interpretations.

Notes

PREFACE

1. National Law Center on Homelessness and Poverty 2004
2. Director, Ali Forney Center, personal correspondence, August 15, 2008
3. Director, Ali Forney Center, personal correspondence, August 15, 2008
4. Harcourt 2001; McArdle and Erzen 2001; Vitale 2008
5. Harcourt 2001; Mitchell 1997; Mitchell and Staeheli 2006
6. Director, Ali Forney Center, personal correspondence, August 15, 2008
7. The term *revanchism* comes from a French term coined in the 1870s that reflects the political will to reclaim space and that stems from the root word for *revenge*. It was first used to describe the taking back of territory by the middle class from forces of disorder associated with the working classes in the rapidly industrializing city of Paris. The modern-day term combines the idea of "reaction" and "revenge" in the punitive retaking of the city from the poor by the middle class. Neil Smith revived the term in his work on gentrification (1996) in New York City in the late 1980s and 1990s to describe the taking back of low-income neighborhoods by economic elites. The term encompasses both the taking back of space and the consequent banishment and/or curtailing of a right to space. The scholarship on revanchism focuses on the structural processes of sociospatial injustice and rights to the city. Geographers discuss revanchist urban policy using examples of zero-tolerance policing, gentrification, and the privatization of public spaces. Contemporary street kids intersect with revanchist urban processes through their marginalized status in the public and public spaces.
8. Carter 1999; Rosenberg 1998

CHAPTER 1

1. Chauncey 1994
2. The Door 2005
3. Mananzala 2005
4. www.hudsonriverpark.org/construction/pier57_dev.asp (accessed March 1, 2010)
5. Community Board, 2nd meeting, December 6, 2005
6. Former director, Homeless Youth Services, Safe Space, August 15, 2008
7. Director, Ali Forney Center, personal correspondence, August 15, 2008
8. Accessed August 1, 2006
9. Deleuze 1992; Foucault 1984; Lefebvre 1991; Thrift 2000, 2003

10. Cresswell 2006; Sheller and Urry 2006

11. Best 2007; Bondi 2005; Davidson and Bondi 2004; England 1994; Lawson 2007; Skelton and Valentine 1998

12. For a complete description of data and methods, see appendices A and B.

13. Clatts et al. 1999; Ennew and Swart-Kruger 2003; Finkelstein 2005

14. In academic literature, also referred to as *street-involved youth* and *homeless kids*. The contemporary terms *street kid, street-involved youth, runaway, throwaway,* and *homeless youth,* as well as the older, no-longer-used names such as *street arab, guttersnipe,* and *urchin,* have evolved as part of the diversified literature on youth homelessness. The nomenclature of youth homelessness often speaks more to the social discourses on youth than to the realities of young people's lives. These terms also indicate a stability of young people's living situations that in reality are highly mutable. Young people may evolve from being "homeless" to "street involved" to being self-defined as a "street kids" or may be considered all three simultaneously by themselves or by social workers. Social service providers generally use these terms interchangeably.

15. Gwadz et al. 2005; Karabanow 2004

16. Clatts et al. 1999; Sedlak et al. 2002; Witkin et al. 2005

17. Cwayna 1993

18. Karabanow 2002, 2004; Molnar 1991

19. For example, see Artenstein 1990; Clatts et al. 1999; Finkelstein 2005; Karabanow 2004.

20. Ringwalt, Greene, and Robertson 1998

21. Kidd 2007; Molnar et al. 1998

22. Baron 2003

23. Annie E. Casey Foundation 2004

24. Cwayna 1993; Greene, Ennett, and Ringwalt 1998; Hagan and McCarthy 1998; Karabanow 2004; Mallet et al. 2004

25. *Survival sex* refers to trading sex for basic survival necessities such as food, shelter, and clothing, as well as money. Many youth engage in sexual relationships as a way of surviving while homeless. Social workers have tried to substitute the term *survival sex* for prostitution in order to reframe social understandings of youth sex work away from stereotypes of adult female sex workers. The majority of young people engaging in sex work whom I encountered as an outreach worker were young men.

26. Greene, Ennett, and Ringwalt 1998; Whitbeck et al. 2001

27. Gwadz et al. 2005

28. Lankenau 1999; O'Grady and Greene 2003

29. Gwadz et al. 2005. Clinical depression is defined as a major depressive disorder with both biological and environmental causes. It is characterized by low mood, loss of self-esteem, and a variety of physical symptoms that adversely affect sleeping and eating habits. A major outcome of clinical depression is an increased risk of suicide.

30. Kidd 2004, 2007

31. Roy et al. 2009. Many social workers consider drug overdoses to be another form of suicide, although an unknown number of overdoses are accidental or due to tainted drugs.

32. Rotherman-Borus et al. 2003

33. Pain and Francis 2004

34. Bolas 2007

35. Gwadz et al. 2005

36. Bolas 2005

37. Roy et al. 2009; Slesnick et al. 2008

38. www.empirestatecoalition.org 2005

39. Christian 2005

40. Despite its origins in gang work, in the past twenty years street outreach has evolved to work with street and homeless youth primarily through federal funding for HIV prevention.

41. Thompson 1999

42. Outreach trainer, August 2004

43. Abel-Peterson and Hooks-Wayman 2006

44. Roy et al. 2009

45. Only two of the eight outreach groups accessed youth in neighborhoods outside Manhattan, partly because of the expense of obtaining transportation (an outreach van) and partly because of the concentration of street youth in Manhattan.

46. Bolas 2005

47. Gwadz et al. 2005

48. Runaway and Homeless Youth Management Information System 2003

49. Bolas 2005

50. Director, Ali Forney Center, personal correspondence, August 15, 2008

51. http://www.raconline.org/funding/funding_details.php?funding_id=1151 (accessed March 19, 2010)

52. Outreach worker, February 21, 2006

53. Former outreach worker, August 15, 2008

54. Abel-Peterson and Hooks-Wayman 2006

55. Collins and Blomley 2003; Harter et al. 2005; Hunter 2003; Lankenau 1999; O'Grady and Greene 2003; Robinson 2000

56. Beckett and Herbert 2009; Mitchell 1997

57. Mitchell 1997

58. Beazely 2000a, 2000b; Karabanow 2004; Lee 2000; Lule 1998; Robinson 2000; Swanson 2005

59. Wyn and White 1997

60. Valentine 2004, 95

61. Swanson 2005

62. Karabanow 2004; StreetWork, personal correspondence 2005, New York City

63. Finkelstein 2005; Karabanow 2004

64. Gwadz et al. 2005

65. Hagan and McCarthy 1998, 40

66. Formerly homeless youth, September 18, 2009

67. Hagan and McCarthy 1998; Lewnes 2002

68. Best 2007; Matthews and Limb 1999; Valentine 2004; Vissing 2007

69. Cloke, Johnsen, and May 2007, 1089

70. Statistics on the numbers of homeless and runaway youth are difficult to obtain owing to the lifestyle of this population. Street kids are hard to identify and, therefore, to count. Federal approximations are provided by the Office of Juvenile Justice and Delinquency Prevention through its National Incidence Studies of Missing, Abducted, Runaway and Thrownaway Children (NISMART) report, available at http://www.ncjrs.gov/html/ojjdp/nismart/04/.

CHAPTER 2

1. Accessed November 29, 2006
2. *Kids* 1995
3. Accessed November 30, 2006
4. Cresswell 2006
5. Ruddick 1996; Skelton and Valentine 1998
6. Cresswell 1996
7. Driver 1988; Jackson 1984
8. Erikson 1950, 1968.
9. Driver 1988
10. Park and Burgess 1984; Thrasher 1927
11. Cohen 1955
12. Adler and Adler 1998
13. For reviews of the social construction of childhood, see Mintz 2004; Savage 2007; Sibley 1991; Valentine and Skelton 1998
14. *New York Times*, November 8, 1860
15. Homberger 1994
16. Riis 1971
17. Miller 2008
18. Inciardi, Horowitz, and Pottieger 1993, 12
19. Driver 1988
20. Chapin 1857, 19
21. Driver 1988, 279
22. Anderson 1987
23. Wines 1880, as quoted in Platt 1977, vi
24. Mintz 2004
25. Mintz 2004, 136
26. Mintz 2004, 142
27. Mintz 2004, 159
28. Mintz 2004, 161
29. Cressey 1932; Donovan 1920; Gubrium 2007
30. *New York Times*, November 20 1870; May 21, 1883; March 27, 1869
31. Brace 1869
32. Brace 1872, reprinted in Jackson and Dunbar 2002, 293
33. O'Connor 2001
34. Ward 1971, 117
35. Thrasher 1927
36. Walters 1978
37. Anbinder 2001; Platt 1977
38. Mintz 2004, 157
39. Riis 1971
40. *New York Times*, March 27, 1869
41. *New York Times*, May 1, 1871
42. *New York Times*, March 8, 1854
43. *New York Times*, May 1, 1871

44. Mintz 2004; O'Connor 2001; Platt 1977
45. O'Connor 2001
46. Platt 1977
47. Baldwin 2002
48. Ruddick 1996
49. Anbinder 2001
50. Platt 1977, 4
51. Walters 1978
52. Riis 1971, 145
53. Foucault 1984
54. Deleuze 1992
55. Cresswell 1996, 8
56. Cresswell 1996, 27
57. Bourdieu 1977, 78
58. Becker 1963; Cohen 1955; O'Connor 2001; Platt 1977
59. Cresswell 1996, 25
60. Becker 1963
61. Riis 1971, 153
62. Riis 1971, 153
63. Aitken 1998
64. Anbinder 2001; Mintz 2004
65. Becker 1963; Cohen 1955
66. Bennett and Kahn-Harris 2004; Hebdige 1979
67. Erikson 1950, 1968
68. Erikson 1968; Finkelstein 2005
69. Brotherton and Barrios 2004; Modan 2007; Venkatesh 2008
70. Hall and Jefferson 1976; Hebdige 1979
71. Bunge 1971
72. Hart 1979; Katz 2004; Lynch 1977; Matthews 1992; Ward 1978
73. Bennett and Kahn-Harris; Hall and Jefferson 1976; Hebdige 1979; Redhead, Wynne, and O'Connor 1997
74. Hall and Jefferson 1976
75. Willis 1977
76. Cohen 1955; Huff 1990
77. Corsaro 2005; Jenks 2005; Savage 2007; Valentine and Skelton 1998
78. Ambrosino 1971, 5
79. Staller 2003
80. Ambrosino 1971
81. Staller 2003
82. Wosh 2005
83. Staller 2003
84. Wosh 2005
85. Wosh 2005
86. Madison 1979; Staller 2003
87. Staller 2003
88. Greller 1975

89. Greller 1975, 81

90. Greller 1975, 224

91. Madison 1979

92. Cole 1970

93. Brotherton and Barrios 2004; Inciardi, Horowitz, and Pottieger 1993

94. Wacquant 2008, 2009; Wilson 1987, 1993. The term *underclass* itself has fallen prey to ideological debates over individual pathologies and environmental structures and has been widely replaced by many social scientists with the term *ghettoized poverty*.

95. Lister 1996a and 1996b

96. Barnes 2000, 748

97. Hagan and McCarthy 1998; Karabanow 2002, 2004

98. Best 2007; Macek 2006; Valentine 2004

99. Clatts et al. 1999; Gwadz et al. 2005; Hagan and McCarthy 1998; Karabanow 2004; Mallet et al. 2004

100. Finkelstein 2005, Lewnes 2001; Ruddick 1996

101. Aitken 1998; Beazley 2000a, 2000b

102. Hickler and Auerswald 2009

103. For an excellent study of homeless youth and their relationship to social stigma, see Kidd 2007.

104. For a thorough review of this work, see Best 2007.

105. Adler and Adler 1998

106. Valentine 1996, 2004

107. Travelou 2003; Valentine 2004

108. Lau 1995, 170

109. For memoirs of being young street kids in Seattle, see Early 2008; or in Vancouver, see Lau 1995. An international example of street kid memoir is Judy Westwater's *Street Kid* (2006), about a childhood on the streets of South Africa. For a memoir of a GLBTQ youth in New York City, see Wojnarowicz 1991.

110. Current ideologies shaping Western perceptions of childhood led to the conferring of a special status, rights, and value on childhood, which was codified by the United Nations Convention on the Rights of the Child (UNCRC) in 1989. The UNCRC supports the idea of a universal childhood, but with greater cultural sensitivity to an international diversity of children. The convention has drawn attention to the disparity of children's experiences of a safe and valued childhood in contexts of severe poverty, war, and social unrest. International studies on street kids have followed a similar trajectory.

111. Beazley 2000a; Swanson 2005

112. Rosenthal and Rotheram-Borus 2005

113. Beazley 2000a

114. Bourdieu 1977

115. Ennew and Swart-Kruger 2003, 2

116. Finkelstein 2005

117. Valentine 1996

118. *Eugene Register-Guard*, July 22, 1985

119. Flash mobs first began as public performance pieces, organized over the Internet and involving predominantly young, educated, white professionals in their twenties and thirties. Some of the original flash mobs organized people to "freeze" in Grand Central Station

or involved large numbers of people pillow fighting, dancing, or snowball fighting. These mobs have been held in cities all over the world. The intent is to show that members of the public can momentarily take over and rewrite the use of public space. Recent flash mobs in Philadelphia were organized through social networking sites like Twitter and involved much larger numbers of African American teenagers doing a group sprint down major commercial streets or through malls. Some violence and vandalism have been reported.

120. http://www.nytimes.com/2010/03/25/us/25mobs.html?sudsredirect=true (accessed March 27, 2010)

121. In the case of Hurricane Katrina, there were a number of allegations that curfews and bridge blockades were illegal and targeted low-income and African American victims of the disaster.

122. Ennew and Swart-Kruger 2003; Hagan and McCarthy 1998

123. Hagan and McCarthy 1998; Miles and Okamoto 2008. The majority of young people involved in these studies are recruited through established social service centers, that is, private spaces that are off the street. Which kids access these spaces and how they interact once there is fundamentally different from the context of public space.

124. Accountability is a problem affecting a broad range of nonprofits. For a critical discussion of neoliberalism and nonprofit accountability, see Dempsey 2007.

125. Finkelstein 2005

126. Clatts et al. 1999; Gwadz et al. 2005; Yoder, Whitbeck, and Hoyt 2001

127. Finkelstein 2005; Flynn 2003; Lewnes 2001; Wright 2008

128. Ennew and Swart-Kruger 2003, 6

129. Accessed September 12, 2009

CHAPTER 3

1. For example, see Flynn 2003; Stateman 2003.

2. Bolas 2005

3. Robertson 1991

4. Bolas 2005

5. I have encountered street youth who became homeless when they were younger than twelve, but they were a rarity. Nationally, the average age of runaways is fifteen and has been since the 1960s when young people running away from home was first identified as a social phenomenon. The other common age to begin youth homelessness is eighteen, the age when young people leave foster care. Street outreach workers often use these two benchmark ages plus the length of time that a youth reports being on the streets to approximate an age range. For instance, if a young person has been homeless for three years, an outreach worker might guess him or her to be between the ages of eighteen and twenty-one.

6. For example, see Clatts 1999; Cwayna 1993; Hagan and McCarthy 1998; Karabanow 2002, 2004; Kryder-Coe, Salamon, and Molnar 1991.

7. Cook 1991

8. NAEH 2006

9. Hagan and McCarthy 1998; Karabanow 2002

10. Hagan and McCarthy 1998, 158

11. Hopper 2003; Spradley 1970

12. Robertson 1991

13. When I first asked Blacc if he would consent to be interviewed for my research, I thought that I knew a fair amount about him. I had met Blacc several months earlier when I trained him to be a peer outreach counselor for a drop-in center. The interview itself was conducted at the drop-in center with a social worker who had known Blacc for about a year. During this interview, Blacc told us details about his life on the streets that the even the social worker had not known before. The process of working with Blacc and writing a detailed profile of his homeless experiences reminded me to not presume that I "know" street youth. Over long periods of research, assumptions inevitably build up, muting important questions. I have generalized details concerning Blacc's hangouts and have left out certain details and locations pertaining to illegal activities. I discuss issues of ethics, methods, and confidentiality with street youth and street outreach in appendix A.

14. Street names are important acts of agency for street youth. By choosing a street name, young persons create a street identity that is separate from the identity they left behind when they became homeless. Street kids often return to their legal name or choose a third name once they leave the streets, so as to mark another change in their status. Most street outreach workers and many drop-in centers ask a young person only for his or her street name, important in that it signifies a willingness to meet a young person where he or she currently is in life.

15. Hagan and McCarthy 1998; Karabanow 2002

16. Hagan and McCarthy 1998

17. Slesnick et al. 2008

18. Outreach workers often hear young people say that they would not consider going to a shelter because they did not want to leave the relative safety of their street family. Street youth who travel with dogs have also said that they stay on the streets because no shelter will allow them to keep their dogs with them.

19. Bolas 2006

20. Bolas 2006

21. E-mail correspondence, 2006

22. Gwadz et al. 2005

23. Gwadz et al. 2005; Hagan and McCarthy 1998

24. One of the more popular shelters—the Ali Forney Center—has a waiting list of more than one hundred young people for its twelve beds. In the two years (2004–2006) that I conducted outreach, I met only a few young people who had obtained shelter outside Covenant House.

25. Six young people could be sheltered without the hosting organization going through the exhaustive and expensive process of gaining a shelter license from the city or fighting a zoning battle with local community boards. The dual obstacles of licensing and permissions by local government have prevented new shelters being set up in neighborhoods where street youth congregate (Empire State Coalition meeting notes 2005).

26. E-mail correspondence, December 4, 2006

CHAPTER 4

1. Administration of Children and Family Services 2007. Since 1996, federal street outreach programs to youth have been administered by the U.S. Department of Health and Human Services (Public Law 103–322) through their Family and Youth Services Bureau (FYSB), and they currently are regulated in accord with the Runaway, Homeless and Missing Children Protection Act of 2003.

2. Accessed January 7, 2007

3. For example, see Hagan and McCarthy 1998; Webber 1991.

4. Clatts et al. 1999; Ennew and Swart-Kruger 2003; Finkelstein 2005

5. Ennew and Swart-Kruger 2003, 11

6. Abel-Peterson and Hooks-Wayman 2006; Thompson 1999

7. 1970

8. Clatts et al. 1999, 152

9. Baizerman 1999; Thompson 1999

10. Thompson 1999

11. Thompson 1999

12. Cohen 1955

13. Thompson 1999

14. New York City Youth Board, as quoted in Thompson 1999, 15

15. Bernstein 1964

16. 1999

17. Outreach director, April 29, 2007

18. Most social service providers who work with GLBTQ youth use a series of short-hand titles to distinguish young people's sexual/gender identities. For example, a "trans" youth refers to a transgender young person.

19. Outreach worker, February 28, 2006

20. Outreach supervisor, February 28, 2006

21. Abel-Peterson and Hooks-Wayman 2006; Thompson 1999

22. Thompson 1999, 33

23. This movement has been spearheaded by the United Nation's Convention on the Rights of the Child, which explicitly states that children have a right to voice in decisions that affect their lives and well-being.

24. Bolas 2009

25. Job advertisement, peer outreach worker 2005

26. New York City's business improvement districts (BIDs) employ homeless men to "outreach" to other homeless men, with mixed results. At one point, allegations that outreach workers were systematically harassing the homeless and physically threatening them came to light. See Vitale 2008.

27. Outreach worker, February 28, 2006

28. Outreach worker, February 28, 2006

29. Job advertisement, peer outreach worker 2005

30. A verse at the end of one popular song focuses on reaching out to "outcasts" and "strangers"—representing the marginalized of society—as a central tenet of Christian faith: "Let us build a house where hands will reach beyond the wood and stone / to heal and strengthen, serve and teach, and live the Word they've known. / Here the outcast and the stranger bear the image of God's face; / let us bring an end to fear and danger: / All are welcome, all are welcome, all are welcome in this place" (Haugen 1977).

31. Cloke, Johnsen, and May 2007

32. Cloke, Johnsen, and May 2007, 1094

33. Outreach workers, May 10, 2005; September 12, 2005

34. Outreach worker, February 22, 2006

35. Outreach worker, April 18, 2006

36. Gregson and Rose 2003; Thrift 2000

37. Latham and Conradson 2003

38. Latham and Conradson 2003

39. Conquergood 1991

40. Latham and Conradson 2003

41. Cresswell 2006; Gregson and Rose 2003; Johnson 2003; Latham and Conradson 2003; Mahtani 2002; Modan 2007

42. Conquergood 1991

43. Gregson and Rose 2003

44. I do not believe that any one theory of performance fully explains street outreach practices. However, performance theories allow me to broadly conceptualize and denaturalize different aspects of the outreach process as a powerfully complex sociospatial practice.

45. Goffman 1959

46. Broadhead and Fox 1990

47. The act of passing an object such as drugs in the action of a handshake is in itself a performance that takes into account a public gaze.

48. Outreach worker, February 16, 2006

49. Gregson and Rose 2003, 434

50. Butler 1990; Gregson and Rose 2003

51. Gregson and Rose 2003, 433

52. Gregson and Rose 2003

53. Irigaray 1985; Riviere 1986

54. Harter et al. 2005

55. Latham and Conradson 2003, 1904

56. Gregson and Rose 2003, 434

57. Lefebvre 1991

58. Tonkiss 2005

59. 1986

60. National Coalition for the Homeless 2009

61. Outreach worker, February 28, 2006

62. Outreach worker, April 18, 2006

63. Bolas 2010

64. Outreach worker, February 28, 2006

65. Outreach worker, February 28, 2006

66. Outreach supervisor, February 28, 2006

67. Outreach worker, February 22, 2006

68. Baizerman 1999, xvi

69. Heatherington, as quoted by Thrift 2000, 556

CHAPTER 5

1. As a young researcher, I was grounded in feminist methodology, combined with a practical interest in social justice issues. Feminist methodology begins with the understanding that power relations are materialized in discourses, representations, and actions. What we say, how we describe and display knowledge, and how we act out these epistemologies shape and are shaped by our own position in social systems and social relations. From this

perspective, researchers do not exist outside the research produced. Philosophies of feminist activism seek to drive social change on multiple scales and venues.

2. National Center on Family Homelessness 2009

3. Bolas 2007

4. Bosman 2010

5. Finkelstein 2005

6. Accessed August 5, 2009

7. Because the public spaces discussed in this research have been studied and cited as street youth locations in a wide variety of publications—academic, popular, and civic—I have not altered their names (e.g., see Lewnes 2001). However, I do not describe individual street kids in exact detail or the locations and times of particular gathering or outreach points.

8. Smith 1996; Vitale 2008

9. The traveler or traveling-kid subcultures referred to by outreach workers have no relation to Gypsy/Romany groups. Some young people still jump freight trains in the traditional manner of historic tramp/hobo groups, but most hitchhike or save up money for buses.

10. The street-kid term for asking for spare change or panhandling.

11. Cotter 2005; Stateman 2003

12. Karabanow 2004; Yoder, Whitbeck, and Hoyt 2001

13. Harter et. al 2005

14. The Door 2005

15. Bolas 2005

16. Christian 2005; Mananzala 2005

17. Christian 2005

18. Accessed November 25, 2006

19. Popa 2005

20. http://www.nyc.gov/html/dycd/html/runaway/street_outreach.shtml (accessed August 22, 2009)

21. Clatts et al. 1999; Cwayna 1993; Karabanow 2004

22. Popa 2005, 3

23. Popa 2005, 3

24. www.cccnewyork.org/ . . . /09AdoptedBudgetSummaryFinal091008.pdf

25. E-mail correspondence, August 20, 2009

26. Accessed August 1, 2006

27. We rarely found the kids that other street kids would direct us to because street kids must frequently "move on," owing to police pressure. But on later outreaches, we often would find the young person who fit previous descriptions. We were told on several occasions of a young pregnant woman panhandling in the Union Square area and did eventually find and do outreach with her for a number of months before she disappeared.

28. Outreach notes, April 22, 2005

29. Outreach notes, August 27, 2005

30. Single-room occupancy hotel, a common interim shelter for homeless people that rents small rooms by the week. Residents share bathroom and cooking facilities.

31. Several street kids died from tainted heroin in late 2005. Outreach workers were asked by social service agencies to spread the information about tainted heroin to the street youth population.

32. A typical street kid scam was to pick up dropped receipts for books, find that same book at the store, and try to return it for cash. Ben was doing this three or four times a day and was caught. It was during this time that he was participating in methadone treatments and was caught with heroin while holding a friend's backpack.

33. Outreach notes, June 2005

34. Outreach notes, August 11, 2005. StandUp for Kids volunteers had a policy of moving away if kids were doing visibly illegal activities. This was for the volunteers' safety, as police would often mistake outreach volunteers for street kids.

35. I'm including this level of detail from the outreach logs because this particular street-kid hangout no longer exists. In 2008 and 2009, the back platform area of Union Square was closed for renovation and street youth have relocated elsewhere.

36. Outreach memo, August 1, 2005

37. Outreach notes, August 27, 2005

38. Harter et al. 2005; Ruddick 1996

CHAPTER 6

1. Mitchell 2003; Vitale 2008

2. Center for Constitutional Rights 2009

3. Smith 1996

4. For a survey of how neoliberalism has altered urban structures and policies, see Brenner and Theodore 2002.

5. Brenner and Theodore 2002, 2

6. Stenson and Sullivan 2001

7. McLaughlin and Murji 2001, 107

8. Vitale 2008

9. 1982

10. Harcourt 2001

11. Kelling and Coles 1996

12. Harcourt 2001; Joanes 2000; Kelling and Coles 1996; Silverman 2001

13. Cresswell 1996

14. McArdle and Erzen 2001

15. Murphy 2006

16. Harcourt 2001

17. Kelling and Coles 1996; Silverman 2001. For critiques of this theory, see Harcourt 2001; Herbert 2005, 2006; Karmen 2000; Vitale 2008.

18. Harcourt 2001

19. Harcourt 2001

20. Langworthy and Travis 1999; Miller and Hess 2005

21. Best 2007; Chatterton and Hollands 2003

22. Best 2007; Collins and Kearns 2001; Matthews, Limb, and Taylor 1999

23. Herbert 2006

24. Jacobs 1961

25. Vitale 2008

26. Herbert 2006

27. Officer Krupke was the neighborhood cop in *West Side Story*, who knew everyone and everything going on in his beat.

28. Miller and Hess 2005

29. Langworthy and Travis 1999

30. Langworthy and Travis 1999

31. Vitale 2008

32. Harcourt 2001; Langworthy and Travis 1999; for an exception, see Herbert 2006.

33. Carlson 2009a and 2009b

34. Vitale 2008

35. Mitchell 2003

36. Davis 1990; Kilian 1998; Sorkin 1992

37. *New York Times*, April 11, 1990

38. Mitchell 1997, 2003, 2005; Staeheli and Mitchell 2008

39. Murphy 2006

40. Center for Constitutional Rights 2009

41. Mananzala 2005

42. I was asked to co-conduct two of the five focus groups run by The Door as part of a larger survey of street youth in the West Village. The following examples are from my notes.

43. The Door 2005

44. Guthrie 2003

45. Outreach worker, September 12, 2009

46. Macek 2006

47. Karabanow 2004; StreetWork, personal correspondence, 2005, New York City

48. Finkelstein 2005; Karabanow 2004

49. NAEH 2006; Wilder Research Center 2003

50. Gwadz et al. 2005

51. Goldstein 1960; Langworthy and Travis 1999

52. Langworthy and Travis 1999, 348

53. Moore and Stephens 1991; Novak 1999

54. Youth participant, legal counseling session, New York City

55. Outreach worker, February 28, 2006

56. Outreach worker, February 28, 2006

57. Mitchell 2003

58. 2003

CHAPTER 7

1. A "john" is a street term for a sex worker's client.

2. Outreach director, May 2, 2007

3. Outreach worker, May 6, 2007

4. Ogden 2000

5. Cresswell 2004; Relph 1976; Tuan 1974

6. Sheller and Urry 2006

7. Relph 1976

8. Cresswell 2006

9. Cresswell 2006; Sibley 1995

10. Sheller and Urry 2006

11. Cresswell 2004; Sibley 1995

12. Cresswell 2002

13. Relph 1976

14. Auge 1995; Cresswell 2006; Massey 1994

15. Cresswell 2002, 2004; Massey 1994

16. Cresswell 2002, 2006; Massey 1994

17. Dempsey 2007

18. Cresswell 2006

19. Cresswell 2006; Sheller and Urry 2006

20. Sumption 1975

21. Cresswell 2004

22. Cresswell 2006

23. 2001

24. Cresswell 2001

25. Spradley 1970

26. 1917

27. Hale 1917, 21

28. Hale 1917, 68

29. Delaney 2005

30. Cresswell 2001, 16

31. Although in my work, I found outreach workers discussing stigma with young people fairly regularly, very little academic work has been done on how street kids internalize social stigma into their behavior. One exception is the work by Kidd (2004, 2007), which addresses depression and suicidality in street kids in New York City and Toronto.

32. Outreach worker, May 6, 2007

33. Outreach worker, May 11, 2005

34. Hagan and McCarthy 1998; Miles and Okamoto 2008; Outreach interviews, Denver and Boulder, 2004 and 2005.

35. Outreach worker, May 6, 2007

36. Outreach worker, May 10, 2005

37. Outreach worker, September 28, 2005

38. Outreach worker, May 10, 2005

39. Outreach worker, September 12, 2005

40. Outreach worker, September 12, 2005

41. Freudendal-Pedersen 2005, 30

42. 1957

43. Outreach notes, November 5, 2005

44. Outreach notes, October 4, 2005

45. Outreach worker, May 10, 2005

46. Outreach worker, May 10, 2005

47. Outreach notes, September 20, 2005

48. Outreach worker, May 11, 2005

49. Outreach worker, May 11, 2005

50. Outreach worker, May 6, 2007

51. Outreach worker, May 10, 2005
52. Outreach worker, February 22, 2006
53. Outreach worker, May 10, 2005
54. Outreach worker, August 22, 2009
55. Outreach worker, August 22, 2009
56. Outreach worker, May 2, 2007
57. Outreach worker, September 28, 2005
58. Outreach worker, August 8, 2005
59. Outreach worker, February 22, 2006
60. Outreach worker, May 8, 2007
61. Outreach worker, May 7, 2007

CHAPTER 8

1. Glatzer 1998
2. Dubrovsky 2009
3. The Door 2005
4. Outreach worker, August 22, 2009
5. Outreach worker, August 22, 2009
6. Bolas 2010
7. E-mail correspondence, Reciprocity Foundation, September 14, 2009
8. E-mail correspondence, Reciprocity Foundation, September 14, 2009
9. Kidd 2007

APPENDIX A

1. For a more detail discussion, see Denzin and Lincoln 2003; Naples 2003.
2. For an overview of activist research in critical ethnography, see Thomas 1993; for a detailed discussion of activist research with marginalized populations, see Ferrell and Hamm 1998.
3. Denzin and Lincoln 2003
4. For example, see Aitken 2001; Matthews and Limb 1999; Valentine 2006.
5. A mobile van outreach worker once told me that she felt like an entire outreach could be spent muttering "too old . . . too old . . . too old" or "too clean . . . too clean" as the outreach workers scanned the crowds for visible identifiers of youth homelessness.
6. Jackson 1989
7. Smith 2000, 239
8. Jackson 2000
9. Berry 2001; Park 1926; Sennett 1969a and 1969b
10. Cresswell 2006
11. Harding and Hintikka 1983; Reinharz 1992; Rossman and Rallis 1998; Skeggs 2001; Visweswaran 1994
12. Rossman and Rallis 1998
13. Thomas 1993
14. Thomas 1993, 4
15. Naples 2003; Reinharz 1992; Skeggs 2001

16. Matthews and Limb 1999
17. Aitken 2001
18. van Maanen 1988, 2
19. Emerson, Fretz, and Shaw 1995
20. Naples 2003
21. Naples 2003
22. Thrift 2000
23. Broadhead and Fox 1990
24. Naples 2003, 49
25. May and Pattillo-McCoy 2000
26. Heidegger 1971

APPENDIX B

1. Emerson, Fretz, and Shaw 1995
2. Vissing 2007
3. Kauffman 1992
4. Redwood 1999; Reissman 1993
5. Clandinin and Connelly 2000
6. Cortazzi 1993
7. Childress 2000; Josselson, Lieblich, and McAdams 2003
8. Gubrium and Holstein 2009
9. van Maanen 1988

Bibliography

Abel-Peterson, Trudee, and Richard Hooks-Wayman. 2006. *StreetWorks: Best Practices and Standards in Outreach Methodology to Homeless Youth*. Minneapolis: StreetWorks Collaborative & Freeport.

Adler, Patricia, and Peter Adler. 1998. "Foreword: Moving Backward." In *Ethnography at the Edge: Crime, Deviance, and Field Research*, ed. Jeff Ferrell and Mark S. Hamm, xii–xvi. Boston: Northeastern University Press.

Administration of Children and Family Services. 2007. Available at www.acf.dhhs.gov (accessed January 7, 2007).

Aitken, Stuart. 1998. "Book Review: Young and Homeless in Hollywood by Susan Ruddick." *Annals of the Association of American Geographers* 88, no. 1: 171–74.

———. 2001. *Geographies of Young People: The Morally Contested Spaces of Identity*. London: Routledge.

Ambrosino, Lillian. 1971. *Runaways*. Boston: Beacon Press.

Anbinder, Tyler. 2001. *Five Points: The 19th-Century New York City Neighborhood That Invented Tap Dance, Stole Elections, and Became the World's Most Notorious Slum*. New York: Free Press.

Anderson, Kay. 1987. "The Idea of Chinatown: The Power of Place and Institutional Practice in the Making of a Racial Category." *Annals of the Association of American Geographers* 77: 580–98.

Annie E. Casey Foundation. 2004. Available at www.aecf.org (accessed August 8, 2004).

Artenstein, Jeffrey. 1990. *Runaways: In Their Own Words: Kids Talking about Living on the Streets*. New York: Tor.

Atkinson, Paul, et al., eds. 2001. *Handbook of Ethnography*. London: Sage.

Auge, Marc. 1995. *Non-Places: Introduction to an Anthropology of Supermodernity*. Trans. John Howe. New York: Verso.

Baizerman, Michael. 1999. Foreword to *Caring on the Streets: A Study of Detached Youthworkers*, by Jacquelyn Kay Thompson, xv–xviii. New York: Haworth Press.

Baldwin, Peter C. 2002. "Nocturnal Habits and Dark Wisdom: The American Response to Children in the Streets at Night, 1880–1930." *Journal of Social History* 35, no. 3: 593–611.

Barnes, Trevor. 2000. "Social Construction." In *The Dictionary of Human Geography*, ed. Derek Gregory et al., 747–48. Malden, MA: Blackwell.

Baron, Stephen W. 1999. "Street Youth and Substance Use: The Role of Background, Street Lifestyle, and Economic Factors." *Youth & Society* 31, no. 1: 3–26.

———. 2003. "Street Youth Violence and Victimization." *Trauma, Violence and Abuse* 4, no. 1: 22–44.

Beazely, Harriet. 2000a. "Home Sweet Home? Street Children's Sites of Belonging." In *Children's Geographies: Playing, Living, Learning*, ed. Sarah L. Holloway and Gill Valentine, 194–210. London: Routledge.

———. 2000b. "Street Boys in Yogyakarta: Social and Spatial Exclusion in the Public Spaces of the City." In *A Companion to the City*, ed. Gary Bridge and Sophie Watson, 472–88. Oxford: Blackwell.

Becker, Howard S. 1963. *Outsiders: Studies in the Sociology of Deviance*. New York: Free Press.

Beckett, Katherine, and Stephen Herbert. 2009. *Banished: The New Social Control in Urban America*. Oxford: Oxford University Press.

Bennett, Andy, and Keith Kahn-Harris. 2004. *After Subculture: Critical Studies in Contemporary Youth Culture*. New York: Palgrave Macmillan.

Bernstein, Saul. 1964. *Youth on the Streets: Work with Alienated Youth Groups*. New York: Association Press.

Berry, Brian J. L. 2001. "The Chicago School in Retrospect and Prospect." *Urban Geography* 22: 559–61.

Best, Amy. 2000. *Prom Night: Youth, Schools, and Popular Culture*. New York: Routledge.

———, ed. 2007. *Representing Youth: Methodological Issues in Critical Youth Studies*. New York: New York University Press.

Birch, Maxine, et al. 2002. Introduction to *Ethics in Qualitative Research*, ed. Melanie Mauthner et al., 1–13. London: Sage.

Blustein, Jeffery, et al., eds. 1999. *The Adolescent Alone: Decision Making in Health Care in the United States*. Cambridge: Cambridge University Press.

Bolas, James, ed. 2004. *State of the City's Homeless Youth Report, 2004*. New York City Association of Homeless and Street-Involved Youth Organizations. New York: Empire State Coalition of Youth and Family Services.

———, ed. 2005. *State of the City's Homeless Youth Report, 2005*. New York City Association of Homeless and Street-Involved Youth Organizations. New York: Empire State Coalition of Youth and Family Services.

———, ed. 2006. *State of the City's Homeless Youth Report, 2006*. New York City Association of Homeless and Street-Involved Youth Organizations. New York: Empire State Coalition of Youth and Family Services.

———, ed. 2007. *State of the City's Homeless Youth Report, 2007*. New York City Association of Homeless and Street-Involved Youth Organizations. New York: Empire State Coalition of Youth and Family Services.

———, ed. 2009. *State of the City's Homeless Youth Report, 2009*. New York City Association of Homeless and Street-Involved Youth Organizations. New York: Empire State Coalition of Youth and Family Services.

———, ed. 2010. *State of the City's Homeless Youth Report, 2010*. New York City Association of Homeless and Street-Involved Youth Organizations. New York: Empire State Coalition of Youth and Family Services.

Bondi, Liz. 2005. "The Place of Emotions in Research: From Portioning Emotion and Research to the Emotional Dynamics of Research Relationships." In *Emotional Geographies*, ed. Joyce Davidson, Liz Bondi, and Mick Smith, 231–46. Burlington, VT: Ashgate.

Bosman, Julie. 2010. "Time Square's Homeless Holdout, Not Budging." *New York Times*, available at http://www.nytimes.com/2010/03/30/nyregion/30heavy.html (2010) (accessed April 2, 2010).

Bourdieu, Pierre. 1977 [1972]. *Outline of a Theory of Practice*. Cambridge: Cambridge University Press.

Boys Town. 1938. Norman Taurog, dir. DVD. Metro-Goldwyn-Mayer.

Brace, Charles Loring. 1869. "Little Street Arabs." Letter to the editor, *New York Times*, March 27.

———. 1872. *The Dangerous Classes of New York and Twenty Years' Work among Them*. New York: Wynkoop & Hallenbeck.

Brenner, Neil, and Nik Theodore, eds. 2002. *Spaces of Neoliberalism: Urban Restructuring in North America and Western Europe*. Malden, MA: Blackwell.

Bridge, Gary, and Sophie Watson. 2000. *A Companion to the City*. Oxford: Blackwell.

Broadhead, Robert S., and Kathryn J. Fox. 1990. "'Takin' It to the Streets: AIDS Outreach as Ethnography." *Journal of Contemporary Ethnography* 19, no. 3 (October): 322–48.

Brotherton, David C., and Luis Barrios. 2004. *The Almighty Latin King and Queen Nation*. New York: Columbia University Press.

Bunge, William. 1971. *Fitzgerald: Geography of a Revolution*. Cambridge, MA: Schenkman.

Burgess, Ernest W., ed. 1926. *The Urban Community: Selected Papers from the American Sociological Society*. Chicago: University of Chicago Press.

Burgin, Victor, James MacDonald, and Cora Kaplar, eds. 1986. *Formations of Fantasy*. London: Methuen.

Butler, Judith. 1990. *Gender Trouble: Feminism and the Subversion of Identity*. New York: Routledge.

Carlson, Jen. 2009a. Available at http://gothamist.com/2009/02/18/stoop_drinking_case_closed.php (accessed February 18, 2009.

———. 2009b. Available at http://gothamist.com/2009/07/20/marty_markowitz_caught_stoop_drinki.php (accessed July 20, 2009.

Carter, Chelsea J. 1999. "A Life and Death on NYC Streets." *Associated Press*, August 28.

Center for Constitutional Rights. 2009. "Racial Disparity in NYPD Stop and Frisks." Available at http://ccrjustice.org/ (accessed 6/3/10).

Chapin, Henry Dwight. 1857. "Progress in Child Saving." *New York Times*, September 23.

Chatterton, Paul, and Robert Hollands. 2003. *Urban Nightscapes: Youth Cultures, Pleasure Spaces, and Corporate Power*. London: Routledge.

Chauncey, George. 1994. *Gay New York: Gender, Urban Culture, and the Makings of the Gay Male World, 1890–1940*. New York: Basic Books.

Childress, Herb. 2000. *Landscapes of Betrayal, Landscapes of Joy: Curtisville in the Lives of Its Teenagers*. Albany: State University of New York Press.

Christian, Reed. 2005. "Characteristics of West Village Homeless Youth." Outreach Guidelines, New York City.

Clandinin, D. Jean, and F. Michael Connelly. 2000. *Narrative Inquiry: Experience and Story in Qualitative Research*. San Francisco: Jossey-Bass.

Clatts, Michael C., et al. 1999. "Lives in the Balance: A Profile of Homeless Youth in New York City." In *The Adolescent Alone: Decision Making in Health Care in the United States*, ed. Jeffery Blustein et al., 139–59. Cambridge: Cambridge University Press.

Cloke, Paul, Sarah Johnsen, and Jon May. 2007. "Ethical Citizenship? Volunteers and the Ethics of Providing Services for Homeless People." *Geoforum* 38: 1089–1101.

Cohen, Albert. 1955. *Delinquent Boys: The Culture of the Gang*. Glencoe, IL: Free Press.

Cole, Larry. 1970. *Street Kids*. New York: Grossman.

Collins, Damian C. A., and Nick Blomley. 2003. "Private Needs and Public Space: Politics, Poverty and Anti-panhandling By-laws in Canadian Cities." In *New Perspectives on the Public-Private Divide*, ed. Law Commission of Canada, 40–67. Vancouver: University of British Columbia Press.

Collins, Damian C. A., and Robin A. Kearns. 2001. "Under Curfew and Under Siege? Legal Geographies of Young People." *Geoforum* 32: 389–403.

Conquergood, Dwight. 1985. "Performing as a Moral Act: Ethical Dimensions of the Ethnography of Performance." *Literature in Performance* 5, no. 2: 1–13.

———. 1991. "Rethinking Ethnography: Toward a Critical Cultural Politics." *Communication Monographs* 58: 179–94.

Cook, Robert. 1991. *A National Evaluation of Title IV-E Foster Care Independent Living Programs for Youth*. Rockville, MD: Westat Inc.

Corsaro, William. 2005. *The Sociology of Childhood*. Thousand Oaks, CA: Pine Forge Press.

Cortazzi, Martin. 1993. *Narrative Analysis*. London: Falmer Press.

Cotter, Holland. 2005. "Posing, Speaking, Revealing." *New York Times*, August 24.

Crane, Stephen. 1893. *Maggie: A Girl of the Streets*. New York: D. Appleton.

Cressey, Paul G. 1932. *The Taxi-Dance Hall: A Recreation and City Life*. Chicago: University of Chicago Press.

Cresswell, Tim. 1996. *In Place / Out of Place: Geography, Ideology, and Transgression*. Minneapolis: University of Minnesota Press.

———. 2001. *The Tramp in America*. London: Reaktion.

———. 2002. "Introduction: Theorizing Place." In *Mobilizing Place, Placing Mobility: The Politics of Representation in a Globalized World*, ed. Ginette Verstraete and Tim Cresswell, 11–32. Amsterdam: Rodopi.

———. 2004. *Place: A Short Introduction*. London: Blackwell.

———. 2006. *On the Move: Mobility in the Modern Western World*. New York: Routledge.

Creswell, John W. 1998. *Qualitative Inquiry and Research Design*. Thousand Oaks, CA: Sage.

Crocker, D., and V. M. Johnson, eds. 2010. *Poverty, Regulation, and Social Exclusion: Readings on the Criminalization of Poverty*. Halifax: Fernwood Publications.

Cwayna, Kevin. 1993. *Knowing Where the Fountains Are: Stories and Stark Realities of Homeless Youth*. Minneapolis: Deaconess Press.

Cybriwsky, Roman. 1999. "Changing Patterns of Urban Public Space." *Cities* 16, no. 4: 223–31.

Davidson, Joyce, and Liz Bondi. 2004. "Spatialising Affect; Affecting Space: Introducing Emotional Geographies." *Gender Place and Culture* 11: 373–74.

Davis, Mike. 1990. *City of Quartz: Excavating the Future in Los Angeles*. New York: Verso.

Delaney, David. 2005. *Territory: A Short Introduction*. London: Blackwell.

Deleuze, Giles. 1992. "Postscript on the Societies of Control." *October* 59: 3–7.

Dempsey, Sarah E. 2007. "Negotiating Accountability within International Contexts: The Role of Bounded Voice." *Communication Monographs* 34, no. 3: 311–22.

———. 2009. "NGOs, Communicative Labor, and the Work of Grassroots Representation." *Communication and Critical/CulturalStudies* 6, no. 4: 328–45.

Denzin, Norman, and Yvonna Lincoln, eds. 2003. *The Landscape of Qualitative Research: Theories and Issues*. 2nd ed. London: Sage.

Dickens, Charles. 2003 [1838]. *Oliver Twist*. New York: Penguin Classics.

Donovan, Frances. 1920. *The Woman Who Waits*. Boston: Gorham Press.

The Door, an Alternative Center for Youth. 2005. "Survey of the West Side Piers and Environs." New York City.

Driver, Felix. 1988. "Moral Geographies: Social Science and the Urban Environment in Mid-19th Century England." *Transactions of the Institute of British Geographers* 13: 275–87.

Dubrovsky, Anna. "The Light in All of Us." Available at Reciprocity Foundation, wwww.reciprocityfoundation.org (accessed September 12, 2009).

Early, Justin Reed. 2008. *StreetChild: An Unpaved Passage*. Bloomington, IN: AuthorHouse.

Elliot, Stuart. 2007. "Do You Know Where Your Slogan Is?" *New York Times*, March 16.

Emerson, Robert, Rachel Fretz, and Linda Shaw. 1995. *Writing Ethnographic Fieldnotes*. Chicago: University of Chicago Press.

England, Kim. 1994. "Getting Personal: Reflexivity, Positionality, and Feminist Research." *Professional Geographer* 46, no. 1: 80–89.

Ennew, Judith, and Hill Swart-Kruger. 2003. "Introduction: Homes, Places and Spaces in the Construction of Street Children and Street Youth." *Children, Youth and Environments* 13, no. 1: 1–19.

Erikson, Erik H. 1950. *Childhood and Society*. New York: Norton.

———. 1968. *Identity: Youth and Crisis*. New York: Norton.

Ferrell, Jeff, and Mark S. Hamm, eds. 1998. *Ethnography at the Edge: Crime, Deviance, and Field Research*. Boston: Northeastern University Press.

Fine, Yehudah. 2002. *Times Square Rabbi: Finding Hope in Lost Kids' Lives*. Bloomington, IN: Unlimited.

Finkelstein, Marni. 2005. *With No Direction Home: Homeless Youth on the Road and in the Streets*. Belmont, CA: Wadsworth.

Fitzpatrick, Suzanne. 2000. *Young Homeless People*. New York: St. Martin's Press.

Fleisher, Mark S. 1998. "Ethnographers, Pimps, and the Company Store." In *Ethnography at the Edge: Crime, Deviance, and Field Research*, ed. Jeff Ferrell and Mark S. Hamm, 44–64. Boston: Northeastern University Press.

Flores, J. Robert. 2002. *Runaway/Throwaway Children: National Estimates and Characteristics*. National Incidence Studies of Missing, Abducted, Runaway, and Thrownaway Children. Washington, DC: Office of Juvenile Justice and Delinquency Programs, October.

Flynn, Jim. 2003. *Stranger to the System: Life Portraits of a New York City Homeless Community*. New York: Curbside Press.

Foucault, Michel. 1984. *The Foucault Reader*. Ed. Michel Foucault and Paul Rabinow. New York: Pantheon Books.

Freire, Paulo. 1970. *Pedagogy of the Oppressed*. Trans. M. B. Ramos. New York: Herder & Herder.

Freudendal-Pedersen, Malene. 2005. "Structural Stories, Mobility and (Un)freedom." In *Social Perspectives on Mobility*, ed. Thyra Uth Thomsen, Lise Drewes Nielsen, and Henrik Gudmundsson, 29–46. Burlington, VT: Ashgate.

Glatzer, Randi. 1998. "Nowhere to Go: New York Is Hell If You're 18 and Homeless." *Village Voice*. Available at http://www.villagevoice.com/1998-07-14/news/nowhere-to-go (July 14) (accessed September 27, 2009).

Goffman, Erving. 1959. *The Presentation of Self in Everyday Life*. Garden City, NY: Doubleday.

Goldstein, Joseph. 1960. "Police Discretion Not to Invoke the Criminal Process: Low-Visibility Decisions in the Administration of Justice." *Yale Law Journal* 69, no. 4: 543–94.

Greene, Jody M., Susan T. Ennett, and Christopher L. Ringwalt. 1999. "Prevalence and Correlates of Survival Sex among Runaway and Homeless Youth." *American Journal of Public Health* 89, no. 9: 1406–9.

Gregson, Nicky, and Gillian Rose. 2003. "Taking Butler Elsewhere: Performativities, Spatialities and Subjectivities." *Environment and Planning D: Society and Space* 18, no. 4: 433–52.

Greller, Joyce C. 1975. *Young Hookers: The Truth about the Rising Tide of Child Prostitution in America Today.* New York: Dell.

Gubrium, Jaber. 2007. "Urban Ethnography of the 1920s Working Girl." *Gender, Work and Organization* 14, no. 3 (May): 234–58.

Gubrium, Jaber, and James Holstein. 1997. *The New Language of Qualitative Method.* Oxford: Oxford University Press.

———. 2009. *Analyzing Narrative Reality.* Thousand Oaks, CA: Sage.

Guthrie, Amy. 2003. "When Cops Are Thugs." *Village Voice.* Available at www.villagevoice.com (August 26) (accessed March 7, 2007).

Gwadz, Marya Viorst, et al. 2005. "Work Experiences of Homeless Youth in the Formal and Street Economies: Barriers to and Facilitators of Work Experiences, and Their Relationships to Adverse Outcomes." Manuscript, New York City.

Hagan, John, and Bill McCarthy. 1998. *Mean Streets: Youth Crime and Homelessness.* Cambridge: Cambridge University Press.

Hale, Edward Everett. 1917. *Man without a Country.* Boston: Roberts Bros.

Hall, Stuart, and Tony Jefferson, eds. 1976. *Resistance through Rituals: Youth Subcultures in Post-war Britain.* New York: Routledge.

Harcourt, Bernard. 2001. *Illusion of Order: The False Promise of Broken Windows Policing.* Cambridge, MA: Harvard University Press.

Harding, Sandra, and Merrill B. Hintikka, eds. 1983. *Discovering Reality: Feminist Perspectives on Epistemology, Metaphysics, Methodology, and Philosophy of Science.* Dordrecht: D. Reidel.

Hart, Roger. 1979. *Children's Experience of Place.* New York: Irvington.

Harter, Lynn M., et al. 2005. "The Structuring of Invisibility among the Hidden Homeless: The Politics of Space, Stigma, and Identity Construction." *Journal of Applied Communication Research* 33, no. 4: 305–27.

Haugen, Marty. 1977. "All Are Welcome." *Music Lyrics.*

Hebdige, Dick. 1979. *Subculture, the Meaning of Style.* London: Methuen.

Heidegger, Martin. 1971. "Building Dwelling Thinking." In *Poetry, Language, Thought,* trans. Albert Hofstadter. New York: Harper Colophon.

Herbert, Stephen. 2005. *Policing Space: Territoriality and the Los Angeles Police Department.* Minneapolis: University of Minnesota Press.

———. 2006. *Citizens, Cops, and Power: Recognizing the Limits of Community.* Chicago: University of Chicago Press.

Hickler, Benjamin, and Colette Auerswald. 2009. "The Worlds of Homeless White and African American Youth in San Francisco, California: A Cultural Epidemiological Comparison." *Social Science and Medicine* 68, no. 5: 824–31.

Hinton, S. E. 1967. *The Outsiders.* New York: Puffin Books.

Holloway, Sarah L., and Gill Valentine, eds. 2000. *Children's Geographies: Playing, Living, Learning.* London: Routledge.

Homberger, Eric. 1994. *The Historical Atlas of New York City: A Visual Celebration of Nearly 400 Years of New York City's History.* New York: Holt.

Hopper, Kay. 2003. *Reckoning with Homelessness*. Ithaca, NY: Cornell University Press.

Huff, C. Ronald, ed. 1990. *Gangs in America*. London: Sage.

Hugo, Victor. [1862] 2007. *Les Misérables*. Trans. Julie Rose. New York: Vintage Classics.

Hunter, A. 2003. "A Discussion of Squeegeeing, Panhandling, Youth Homelessness, and Criminalizing the Poor." Halifax, NS: Community Action on Homelessness, ARK Outreach.

Inciardi, James, Ruth Horowitz, and Anne E. Pottieger. 1993. *Street Kids, Street Drugs, Street Crime: An Examination of Drug Use and Serious Delinquency in Miami*. Belmont, CA: Wadsworth.

Irigaray, Luse. 1985. *Speculum of the Other Woman*. Trans. Gillian Gill. Ithaca, NY: Cornell University Press.

Jackson, John B. 1984. *Discovering the Vernacular Landscape*. New Haven, CT: Yale University Press.

———. 1957. "A Stranger's Path." *Landscape* 7: 11–15.

Jackson, Kenneth, and David Dunbar. 2002. *Empire City: New York through the Centuries*. New York: Columbia University Press.

Jackson, Peter. 1989. *Maps of Meaning*. London: Routledge.

———. 2000. "Ethnography." In *The Dictionary of Human Geography*, ed. R. J. Johnston et al., 238–39. Malden, MA: Blackwell.

Jacobs, Jane. 1961. *Death and Life of Great American Cities*. New York: Blackwell.

Jenks, Chris. 2005. *Childhood: Critical Concepts in Sociology*. 2nd ed. London: Routledge.

Joanes, Ana. 2000. "Does the New York City Police Department Deserve Credit for the Decline in New York City's Homicide Rates? A Cross-City Comparison of Policing Strategies and Homicide Rates." *Columbia Journal of Law and Social Problems* 33: 303–4.

Johnson, E. Patrick. 2003. *Appropriating Blackness: Performance and the Politics of Authenticity*. Durham, NC: Duke University Press.

Johnston, Ron J., et al., eds. 2000. *The Dictionary of Human Geography*. Malden, MA: Blackwell.

Josselson, Ruthellen, Amia Lieblich, and Dan P. McAdams. 2003. *Up Close and Personal: The Teaching and Learning of Narrative Research*. Washington, DC: American Psychological Association.

Karabanow, Jeff. 2002. "Open for Business: Exploring the Life Stages of Two Canadian Street Youth Shelters." *Journal of Sociology and Social Welfare* 29, no. 4: 99–116.

———. 2004. *Being Young and Homeless: Understanding How Youth Enter and Exit Street Life*. New York: Peter Lang.

———. 2010. "Street Kids as Delinquents, Menaces and Criminals: Another Example of the Criminalization of Poverty." In *Poverty, Regulation, and Social Exclusion: Readings on the Criminalization of Poverty*, ed. D. Crocker and V. M. Johnson, 140–47. Halifax, NS: Fernwood Publications.

Karmen, Andrew. 2000. *New York Murder Mystery: The True Story behind the Crime Crash of the 1990s*. New York: New York University Press.

Katz, Cindi. 2004. *Growing Up Global: Economic Restructuring and Children's Everyday Lives*. Minneapolis: University of Minnesota Press.

Kauffman, Bette J. 1992. "Feminist Facts: Interview Strategies and Political Subjects in Ethnography." *Communication Theory* 2, no. 3: 187–206.

Kelling, George, and Catherine Coles. 1996. *Fixing Broken Windows*. New York: Free Press.

Kerouac, Jack. 1957. *On the Road*. New York: Viking Press.

Kidd, Sean. 2004. "'The Walls Were Closing In, and We Were Trapped': A Qualitative Analysis of Street Youth Suicide." *Youth & Society* 36, no. 1: 30–55.

———. 2007. "Youth Homelessness and Social Stigma." *Journal of Youth and Adolescence* 36: 291–99.

Kids. 1995. Larry Clark, dir. DVD. New York: Shining Excalibur Pictures.

Kilian, Ted. 1998. "Public and Private, Power and Space." In *The Production of Public Space*, ed. A. Light, and J. Smith, 115–34. Lanham, MD: Rowman & Littlefield.

Kryder-Coe, Julee H., Lester M. Salamon, and Janice M. Molnar. 1991. *Homeless Children and Youth: A New American Dilemma*. New Brunswick, NJ: Transaction.

Langworthy, Robert H., and Lawrence P. Travis. 1999. *Policing in America*. Upper Saddle River, NJ: Prentice Hall.

Lankenau, Stephen E. 1999. "Panhandling Repertoires and Routines for Overcoming the Nonperson Treatment." *Deviant Behavior: An Interdisciplinary Journal* 20: 183–206.

Latham, Alan. 2003. "Research, Performance, and Doing Human Geography: Some Reflections on the Diary-Photograph, Diary-Interview Method." *Environment and Planning A* 35: 1993–2017.

Latham, Alan, and David Conradson. 2003. "Guest Editorial: The Possibilities of Performance." *Environment and Planning A* 35: 1901–6.

Lau, Evelyn. 1995. *Runaway: Diary of a Street Kid*. Toronto: Coach House Press.

Law Commission of Canada, ed. 2003. *New Perspectives on the Public-Private Divide*. Vancouver: University of British Columbia Press.

Lawson, Victoria. 2007. "Geographies of Care and Responsibility." *Annals of the Association of American Geographers* 97, no. 1: 1–11.

Lee, Francis Wing-Lin. 2000. "Teens of the Night: The Young Night Drifters of Hong Kong." *Youth & Society* 31, no. 3: 363–84.

Lefebvre, Henri. 1991. *The Production of Space*. Oxford: Blackwell.

LeGates, Richard, and Frederic Stout, eds. 1982. *The City Reader*. London: Routledge.

Lewnes, Alexia. 2001. *Misplaced: New York City's Street Kids*. New York: Xenium Press.

Light, A., and J. Smith, eds. 1998. *The Production of Public Space*. Lanham, MD: Rowman & Littlefield.

Lister, Ruth, ed. 1996a. *Charles Murray and the Underclass: The Developing Debate*. London: IEA.

———, ed. 1996b. "Introduction: In Search of the 'Underclass.'" In *Charles Murray and the Underclass: The Developing Debate*, ed. Ruth Lister, 1–18. London: IEA.

Lofland, John, and Lyn Lofland. 1995. *Analyzing Social Settings: A Guide to Qualitative Observation and Analysis*. Belmont, CA: Wadsworth.

Low, Setha, and Neil Smith, eds. 2006. *The Politics of Public Space*. New York: Routledge.

Lule, Jack. 1998. "News Values and Social Justice: U.S. News and the Brazilian Street Children." *Howard Journal of Communications* 9: 169–85.

Lundy, Coleman. 1995. *Sidewalks Talk: A Naturalistic Study of Street Kids*. New York: Garland.

Lynch, Kevin. 1977. *Growing Up in Cities*. Cambridge, MA: MIT Press.

Macek, Steve. 2006. *Urban Nightmares: The Media, The Right, and the Moral Panic over the City*. Minneapolis: University of Minnesota Press.

Madison, Arnold. 1979. *Runaway Teens*. New York: Lodestar Books.

Mahtani, Minelle. 2002. "Tricking the Border Guards: Performing Race." *Environment and Planning D: Society and Space* 20: 425–40.

Mallet, Shelly, et al. 2004. "Practicing Homelessness: A Typology Approach to Young People's Daily Routines." *Journal of Adolescence* 27: 337–49.

Mananzala, R., ed. 2005. "FIERCE! Call to Action." Flyer. New York City, 2005.

Massey, Doreen. 1994. *Space, Place, and Gender*. Minneapolis: University of Minnesota Press.

———. 1998. "The Spatial Construction of Youth Cultures." In *Cool Places: Geographies of Youth Cultures*, ed. Tracey Skelton and Gill Valentine, 121–29. London: Routledge.

Matthews, Hugh. 1992. *Making Sense of Place: Children's Understanding of Large-Scale Environments*. Hertfordshire: Harvester Wheatsheaf.

Matthews, Hugh, and Melanie Limb. 1999. "Defining an Agenda for the Geography of Children: Review and Prospect." *Progress in Human Geography* 23, no. 1: 61–90.

Matthews, Hugh, Melanie Limb, and Mark Taylor. 1999. "Reclaiming the Streets: The Discourse of Curfew." *Environment and Planning A* 3, no. 10: 1713–30.

Mauthner, Melanie, et al., eds. 2002. *Ethics in Qualitative Research*. London: Sage.

May, Reuben A. Buford, and Mary Pattillo-McCoy. 2000. "Do You See What I See? Examining a Collaborative Ethnography." *Qualitative Inquiry* 6, no. 65: 65–87.

Mayers, Marjorie. 2001. *Street Kids & Streetscapes: Panhandling, Politics & Prophecies*. New York: Peter Lang.

McArdle, Andrea, and Tanya Erzen. 2001. *Zero Tolerance: Quality of Life and the New Police Brutality in New York City*. New York: New York University Press.

McLaughlin, Eugene, and Karim Murji. 2001. "Lost Connections and New Directions: Neo-liberalism, New Public Managerialism, and the 'Modernization' of the British Police." In *Crime, Risk and Justice: The Politics of Crime Control in Liberal Democracies*, ed. Kevin Stenson and Robert R. Sullivan, 104–21. Portland, OR: Willan Publishing.

McRobbie, Angela. 2000. *Feminism and Youth Culture*. London: Routledge.

Miles, Bart W., and Scott K. Okamoto. 2008. "The Social Construction of Deviant Behavior in Homeless and Runaway Youth: Implications for Practice." *Childhood, Adolescence and Social Work Journal* 25: 425–41.

Miller, Julie. 2008. *Abandoned: Foundlings in Nineteenth-century New York City*. New York: New York University Press.

Miller, Linda, and Karen Hess. 2005. *Community Policing: Partnerships for Problem Solving*. 4th ed. Belmont, CA: Wadsworth.

Mintz, Steven. 2004. *Huck's Raft: A History of American Childhood*. Cambridge, MA: Belknap Press.

Mitchell, Don. 1997. "The Annihilation of Space by Law: The Roots and Implications of Anti-homeless Laws in the United States." *Antipode* 29, no. 3: 303–35.

———. 2003. *The Right to the City: Social Justice and the Fight for Public Space*. New York: Guilford Press.

———. 2005. "Property Rights, the First Amendment, and Judicial Anti-Urbanism: The Strange Case of Virginia V. Hicks." *Urban Geography* 26, no. 7: 565–86.

Mitchell, Don, and Lynn Staeheli. 2006. "Clean and Safe? Property Redevelopment, Public Space, and Homelessness in Downtown San Diego." In *The Politics of Public Space*, ed. Setha Low and Neil Smith, 143–75. New York: Routledge.

Modan, Gabriella Gahlia. 2007. *Turf Wars: Discourse, Diversity, and the Politics of Place*. Malden, MA: Blackwell.

Molnar, Beth E., et al. 1998. "Suicidal Behavior and Sexual/Physical Abuse among Street Youth." *Child Abuse and Neglect* 22, no. 3: 213–22.

Molnar, Janice M. 1991. Introduction to *Homeless Children and Youth: A New American Dilemma*, ed. Julee H. Kryder-Coe, Lester M. Salamon, and Janice M. Molnar, 3–9. New Brunswick, NJ: Transaction.

Moore, Mark Harrison, and D. Stephens. 1991. *Beyond Command and Control: The Strategic Management of Police Departments*. Washington, DC: Police Executive Research Forum.

Murphy, Jarrett. 2006. "Out-Rudying Rudy." *Village Voice*. Available at www.villagevoice. com (2006) (accessed April 26, 2006).

Naples, Nancy. 2003. *Feminism and Method: Ethnography, Discourse Analysis, and Activist Research*. New York: Routledge.

(NAEH) National Alliance to End Homelessness. 2006. *Issue Brief: FY 2006 Appropriations: Runaway and Homeless Youth Program*. Available at http://www.endhomelessness. org/section/policy/focusareas/youth (2006) (accessed April 26, 2007).

National Center on Family Homelessness 2009. Available at http://www.familyhomeless- ness.org/ (2009) (accessed June 2, 2010).

National Coalition for the Homeless. 2009. *Homes Not Handcuffs: The Criminalization of the Homeless in U.S. Cities*. Available at http://www.nationalhomeless.org/publications/ crimereport/index.html (accessed June 2, 2010).

National Law Center on Homelessness and Poverty. 2004. Available at http://www.nlchp. org/ (2004) (accessed August 8, 2004).

New York Times. 1990. "Opinion." Available at http://www.nytimes.com/1990/04/11/opin- ion/for-new-york-more-than-money.html (1990) (accessed November 29, 2006).

———. 2006. "Filmography." Available at http://movies2.nytimes.com/gst/movies/filmog- raphy.html?p_id=177545&inline=nyt-per (2006) (accessed November 29, 2006).

Novak, Kenneth J. 1999. "Assessing Police-Citizen Encounters: Do Community and Beat Officers Differ?" PhD diss., University of Cincinnati.

O'Connor, Stephen. 2001. *Orphan Trains: The Story of Charles Loring Brace and the Children He Saved and Failed*. Chicago: University of Chicago Press.

O'Grady, Bill, and Caroline Greene. 2003. "A Social and Economic Impact Study of the Ontario Safe Street Act on Toronto Squeegee Workers." *Online Journal of Justice Studies* 1, no. 1: 1–11.

Ogden, Philip. 2000. "Mobility." In *The Dictionary of Human Geography*, ed. Ron J. Johnston et al., 507. Malden, MA: Blackwell.

Pain, Rachel, and Peter Francis. 2004. "Living with Crime: Spaces of Risk for Homeless Young People." *Children's Geographies* 2, no. 1: 95–110.

Park, Robert E. 1926. "The Urban Community as a Spatial Pattern and a Moral Order." In *The Urban Community: Selected Papers from the American Sociological Society*, ed. Ernest W. Burgess, 3–18. Chicago: University of Chicago Press.

Park, Robert E., and Ernest W. Burgess 1984 [1925]. *The City*. Heritage Sociology Series. Chicago: University of Chicago Press.

Pfeffer, Rachel. 1997. *Surviving the Streets: Girls Living on Their Own*. New York: Garland.

Platt, Anthony M. 1977. *The Child Savers: The Invention of Delinquency*. Chicago: University of Chicago Press.

Popa, Laura. 2005. "Oversight: Residential and Non-Residential Runaway and Homeless Youth Services Concept Paper." Unpublished report, Committee on Youth Services, New York City.

Redhead, Steve, Derek Wynne, and Justin O'Connor. 1997. *The ClubCultures Reader: Readings in Popular Cultural Studies*. Malden, MA: Blackwell.

Redwood, Rachel. 1999. "Narrative and Narrative Analysis." *Journal of Clinical Nursing* 8: 663–74.

Reinharz, Shulamit. 1992. *Feminist Methods in Social Research*. New York: Oxford University Press.

Reissman, Catherine K. 1993. *Narrative Analysis*. Newbury Park, CA: Sage.

Relph, Edward. 1976. *Place and Placelessness*. London: Pion.

Riis, Jacob. 1971 [1901]. *How the Other Half Lives*. New York: Scribner.

Ringwalt, Christopher L., Jody Greene, and Marjorie Robertson. 1998. "Familial Backgrounds and Risk Behaviors of Youth with Thrownaway Experiences." *Journal of Adolescence* 21: 241–52.

Riviere, Joan. 1986. "Womanliness as Masquerade." In *Formations of Fantasy*, ed. Victor Burgin, James MacDonald, and Cora Kaplar, 35–44. London: Methuen.

Robertson, Marjorie. 1989. *Homeless Youth in Hollywood: Patterns of Alcohol Use*. Bethesda, MD: National Institute on Alcohol Abuse and Alcohol (NIAAA).

———. 1991. "Homeless Youth: An Overview of Recent Literature." In *Homeless Children and Youth: A New American Dilemma*, ed. Julee H. Kryder-Coe, Lester M. Salamon, and Janice M. Molnar, 33–70. New Brunswick, NJ: Transaction.

Robinson, Catherine. 2000. "Creating Space, Creating Self: Street-Frequenting Youth in the City and Suburbs." *Journal of Youth Studies* 3, no. 4: 429–43.

Rosenberg, Tina. 1998. "Helping Them Make It through the Night." *New York Times*, July 12. Available at http://www.aliforneycenter.org/nyt-editorial.html.

Rosenthal, Doreen, and Mary Jane Rotheram-Borus. 2005. "Young People and Homelessness." *Journal of Adolescence* 28: 167–69.

Rossman, Gretchen, and Sharon Rallis. 1998. *Learning in the Field: An Introduction to Qualitative Research*. Thousand Oaks, CA: Sage.

Rotherman-Borus, Mary Jane, et al. 2003. "Reductions in HIV Risk among Runaway Youth." *Prevention Science* 4, no. 3: 173–87.

Rothman, Jack. 1991. *Runaway & Homeless Youth: Strengthening Services to Families and Children*. New York: Longman.

Roy, Elise, et al. 2009. "The Challenge of Understanding Mortality Changes among Street Youth." *Journal of Urban Health* 87, no. 1: 95–101.

Ruddick, Sue. 1996. *Young and Homeless in Hollywood*. New York: Routledge.

Runaway and Homeless Youth Management Information System. 2003. U.S. Department of Health and Human Services (DHHS) / Administration for Children and Families (ACF). Available at http://aspe.hhs.gov/hsp/06/catalog-ai-an-na/RHYMIS.htm (accessed June 2, 2010).

Savage, Jon. 2007. *Teenage: The Creation of Youth Culture*. London: Viking.

Sedlak, Andrea J., David Finkelhor, Heather Hammer, and Dana J. Schultz. 2002. *National Estimates of Missing Children: An Overview*. Washington, DC: U.S. Department of Justice, Office of Justice Programs, Office of Juvenile Justice and Delinquency Prevention.

Sennett, Richard, ed. 1969a. *Classic Essays on the Culture of Cities*. New York: Appleton-Century-Crofts.

———. 1969b. "The Classic Schools of Urban Studies: An Introduction." In *Classic Essays on the Culture of Cities*, ed. Richard Sennett, 3–19. New York: Appleton-Century-Crofts.

Sheller, Mimi, and John Urry. 2006. "The New Mobilities Paradigm." *Environment and Planning A* 38: 207–26.

Sibley, David. 1991. "Children's Geographies: Some Problems of Representation." *Area* 23, no. 3: 269–70.

———. 1995. *Geographies of Exclusion*. London: Routledge.

Silverman, Eli B. 2001. *NYPD Battles Crime: Innovative Strategies in Policing*. Boston: Northeastern University Press.

Skeggs, Beverley. 2001. "Feminist Ethnography." In *Handbook of Ethnography*, ed. Paul Atkinson et al., 426–42. London: Sage.

Skelton, Tracey, and Gill Valentine, eds. 1998. *Cool Places: Geographies of Youth Cultures*. New York: Routledge.

Slater, Tom. 2002. "Looking at the 'North American City' through the Lens of Gentrification Discourse." *Urban Geography* 23, no. 2: 131–53.

Slesnick, Natasha, et al. 2008. "Predictors of Homelessness among Street Living Youth." *Journal of Youth Adolescence* 37: 465–74.

Smith, Neil. 1996. *The New Urban Frontier: Gentrification and the Revanchist City*. New York: Routledge.

Smith, Roger. 2008. *Social Work with Young People*. Cambridge: Polity Press.

Smith, Susan. 2000. "Ethnomethodology." In *The Dictionary of Human Geography*, ed. Ron J. Johnston et al., 239–40. Malden, MA: Blackwell.

Sorkin, Michael, ed. 1992. *Variations on a Theme Park*. New York: Noonday Press.

Spradley, James P. 1970. *You Owe Yourself a Drunk: An Ethnography of Urban Nomads*. Boston: Little, Brown.

Staeheli, Lynn, and Don Mitchell. 2008. *The People's Property? Power, Politics, and the Public*. New York: Routledge.

Staller, Karen. 2003. "Constructing the Runaway Youth Problem: Boy Adventurers and Girl Prostitutes 1960–1978." *Journal of Communication*, June, 330–46.

Stateman, Alison. 2003. "Postcards from the Edge." *New York Times*, June 15.

Stenson, Kevin, and Robert R. Sullivan, eds. 2001. *Crime, Risk and Justice: The Politics of Crime Control in Liberal Democracies*. Portland, OR: Willan Publishing.

Sumption, Jonathan. 1975. *The Age of Pilgrimage: The Medieval Journey to God*. Mahwah, NJ: Hidden Spring.

Swanson, Kate. 2005. "Begging for Dollars in Gringopampa: Geographies of Gender, Race, Ethnicity and Childhood in the Ecuadorian Andes." PhD diss., University of Toronto.

Taylor, Donald M., et al. 2004. "'Street Kids': Towards an Understanding of Their Motivational Context." *Canadian Journal of Behavioral Science* 36, no. 1: 1–16.

Thomas, Jim. 1993. *Doing Critical Ethnography*. Qualitative Research Methods Series 26. London: Sage.

Thompson, Jacquelyn K. 1999. *Caring on the Streets: A Study of Detached Youthworkers*. New York: Haworth Press.

Thomsen, Thyra Uth, Lise Drewes Nielsen, and Henrik Gudmundsson, eds. 2005. *Social Perspectives on Mobility*. Burlington, VT: Ashgate.

Thrasher, Frederic Milton. 1927. *The Gang: A Study of 1313 Gangs in Chicago*. Chicago: University of Chicago Press.

Thrift, Nigel. 2000. "Performance." In *The Dictionary of Human Geography*, ed. Ron J. Johnston et al., 577. Malden, MA: Blackwell.

———. 2003. "Performance and. . . . " *Environment and Planning A* 35: 2019–24.

Tonkiss, Fran. 2005. *Space, the City and Social Theory: Social Relations and Urban Forms*. Oxford: Polity Press.

Travlou, Penny. 2003. *Teenagers and Public Space: Literature Review*. Edinburgh: OPENspace: Research Centre for Inclusive Access to Outdoor Environments.

Tuan, Yi-Fu. 1974. "Space and Place: A Humanistic Perspective." *Progress in Human Geography* 6: 233–46.

Valentine, Gill. 1996. "Children Should Be Seen and Not Heard: The Production and Transgression of Adults' Public Space." *Urban Geography* 17, no. 3: 205–20.

———. 2004. *Public Space and the Culture of Childhood*. London: Ashgate.

———. 2006. "Moral Geographies? Ethical Commitment in Research and Teaching." *Progress in Human Geography* 29: 483–87.

Valentine, Gill, and Tracey Skelton. 1998. "Cool Places: An Introduction to Youth and Youth Cultures." In *Cool Places: Geographies of Youth Cultures*, ed. Tracey Skelton and Gill Valentine, 1–32. London: Routledge.

van Maanen, John. 1988. *Tales of the Field: On Writing Ethnography*. Chicago: University of Chicago Press.

Venkatesh, Sudhir. 2008. *Gang Leader for a Day: A Rogue Sociologist Takes to the Streets*. New York: Penguin.

Verstraete, Ginette, and Tim Cresswell, eds. 2002. *Mobilizing Place, Placing Mobility: The Politics of Representation in a Globalized World*. Amsterdam: Rodopi.

Vissing, Yvonne. 2007. "A Roof over Their Head: Applied Research Issues and Dilemmas in the Investigation of Homeless Children." In *Representing Youth: Methodological Issues in Critical Youth Studies*, ed. Amy Best, 110–32. New York: New York University Press.

Visweswaran, Kamala. 1994. *Fictions of Feminist Ethnography*. Minneapolis: University of Minnesota Press.

Vitale, Alex. 2008. *City of Disorder: How the Quality of Life Campaign Transformed New York Politics*. New York: New York University Press.

Wacquant, Loïc. 2008. *Urban Outcasts: A Comparative Sociology of Advanced Marginality*. New York: Polity Press.

———. 2009. *Punishing the Poor: The Neoliberal Government of Social Insecurity*. Durham, NC: Duke University Press.

Walters, Ronald. 1978. *American Reformers: 1815–1860*. New York: Hill & Wang.

Ward, Colin. 1978. *The Child in the City*. New York: Pantheon Books.

Ward, David. 1971. *Cities and Immigrants: A Geography of Nineteenth Century America*. New York: Oxford University Press.

Wardhagh, Julia. 2000. *Sub City: Young People, Homelessness and Crime*. Brookfield, VT: Ashgate.

Webber, Marlene. 1991. *Street Kids: The Tragedy of Canada's Runaways*. Toronto: University of Toronto Press.

West Side Story. 1957. J. Robbins and R Wise, dirs. DVD. Mirisch Corp.

Westwater, Judy. 2006. *Street Kid*. London: Harper.

Whitbeck, Les, and Dan Hoyt. 1999. *Nowhere to Grow: Homeless and Runaway Adolescents and Their Families*. New York: Aldine de Gruyer.

Whitbeck, Les, et al. 2001. "Deviant Behavior and Victimization among Homeless and Runaway Adolescents." *Journal of Interpersonal Violence* 16, no. 11: 1175–1204.

Wilder Research Center. 2003. "Youth and Young Adults on Their Own." *Homelessness in Minnesota: A Closer Look*. St. Paul: Wilder Research Center.

Wilson, James Q., and George L. Kelling. 1982. "Broken Windows." In *The City Reader*, ed. Richard LeGates and Frederic Stout, 253–63. London: Routledge.

Wilson, William Julius. 1987. *The Truly Disadvantaged*. Chicago: University of Chicago Press.

———. 1993. *The Ghetto Underclass: Social Science Perspectives*. London: Sage.

Willis, Paul. 1977. *Learning to Labor: How Working Class Kids Get Working Class Jobs*. New York: Columbia University Press.

Winchester, Hilary. 1991. "The Geography of Children." *Area* 23, no. 4: 357–60.

Wines, Enoch C. 1880. *The State of Prisons and of Child-Saving Institutions in the Civilized World*. Cambridge, MA: Harvard University Press.

Witkin, Andrea L., et al. 2005. "Finding Homeless Youth: Patterns Based on Geographical Area and Number of Homeless Episodes." *Youth & Society* 37, no. 1: 62–84.

Wojnarowicz, David. 1991. *Close to the Knives: A Memoir of Disintegration*. New York: Vintage Books.

Wosh, Peter. 2005. *Covenant House: Journey of a Faith-Based Charity*. Philadelphia: University of Pennsylvania Press.

Wright, Kai. 2008. *Drifting toward Love: Black, Brown, Gay and Coming of Age on the Streets of New York*. Boston: Beacon Press.

Wyn, Johanna, and Rob White. 1997. *Rethinking Youth*. London: Sage.

Yoder, Kevin A., Les B. Whitbeck, and Dan R. Hoyt. 2001. "Event History Analysis of Antecedents to Running Away from Home and Being on the Street." *American Behavioral Scientist* 45, no. 1: 51–65.

Young, Lorraine, and Hazel R. Barrett. 2001. "Adapting Visual Methods: Action Research with Kampala Street Children." *Area* 33, no. 2: 141–52.

Young, John A., ed. 2005. *Case Studies on Contemporary Social Issues*. Belmont, CA: Wadsworth.

Index

About the Author

KRISTINA E. GIBSON is Assistant Professor in Residence of Geography and Urban and Community Studies at the University of Connecticut, Waterbury.